Beyond Spaceship Earth

Environmental Ethics and the Solar System

Eugene C. Hargrove

EDITOR

Sierra Club Books · San Francisco

The Sierra Club, founded in 1892 by John Muir, has devoted itself to the study and protection of the earth's scenic and ecological resources—mountains, wetlands, woodlands, wild shores and rivers, deserts and plains. The publishing program of the Sierra Club offers books to the public as a nonprofit educational service in the hope that they may enlarge the public's understanding of the Club's basic concerns. The point of view expressed in each book, however, does not necessarily represent that of the Club. The Sierra Club has some sixty chapters coast to coast, in Canada, Hawaii, and Alaska. For information about how you may participate in its programs to preserve wilderness and the quality of life, please address inquiries to Sierra Club, 730 Polk Street, San Francisco, CA 94109.

Copyright © 1986 by Eugene C. Hargrove

All rights reserved under International and Pan-American Copyright Conventions. No part of this book may be reproduced in any form or by any electronic or mechanical means, including information storage and retrieval systems, without permission in writing from the publisher.

LIBRARY OF CONGRESS CATALOGING-IN-PUBLICATION DATA

Beyond spaceship Earth.

1. Solar system—Exploration—Environmental aspects. 2. Environmental impact analysis. 3. Environmental protection—Moral and ethical aspects. I. Hargrove, Eugene C., 1944–
QB501.5.B49   1986   333.9′4   86-3946
ISBN 0-87156-768-7

Cover Jacket design by Paul Gamarello/Eye Tooth Design
Book design by Wolfgang Lederer

Printed in the United States of America

10 9 8 7 6 5 4 3 2 1

*To Eleanor Mae Lade Hargrove
and Oren Keith Hargrove, Sr.*

Contents

Acknowledgments

Most of the papers in this volume were originally written for a conference called "Environmental Ethics and the Solar System," held at the University of Georgia's Georgia Center, June 4 to 6, 1985, with a grant from the Program on Ethics and Values in Science and Technology of the National Science Foundation. As a result of the discussion at that meeting various changes were made to improve the manuscripts of individual authors. In addition, two presentations at the conference were deleted from this book and one was added. Thomas Karas' "Nuclear/Military Uses of Space" was omitted because it significantly overlapped with Dean Rusk's presentation, which also focused on the militarization of space but with more emphasis on the ethical dimension. Lamar Dodd's "The Beauty of Space," although excellent as a conference presentation, did not lend itself to presentation in book form.* The addition, William Hartmann's "Space Exploration and Environmental Issues," was published before the conference took place in *Environmental Ethics* 6 (1984): 227–39. It is included for two reasons: (1) It was used by most of the contributors to this volume as a background document in the writing of their own papers and is occasionally referenced as such; (2) It complements Geoffrey Briggs's discussion of the

*The presentations by Karas and Dodd are included in a video proceedings of the conference available through the Georgia Center for Continuing Education, The University of Georgia, Athens, GA 30602.

future of space exploration and resource exploitation and serves as a transition to the environmental discussions that follow. I wish to thank the Georgia Center, the Planetary Society, and the journal *Environmental Ethics* for their involvement in the conference, Sierra Club Books for publishing this book, and especially the EVIST Program of the National Science Foundation for its support of both the conference and the book, without which neither would have been possible. Any opinions, findings, and conclusions or recommendations expressed in this publication are those of the authors and do not necessarily reflect those of the National Science Foundation.

E.C.H.

Introduction:
Beyond Spaceship Earth

EUGENE C. HARGROVE

---

*A*lthough the Earth has been in the Space Age since 1957 with the launching of Sputnik, very little has been written about the environmental implications of the exploration of our Solar System. Indeed, most people have acted as if there are no environmental implications at all. Curiously, science-fiction writers, with only a few exceptions, have ignored the very possibility of an environmental dimension in their short stories and novels. Comments in professional philosophy papers on environmental ethics have made only passing remarks about space, the stars, and the Solar System, and these have generally suggested that extraterrestrial natural objects are safe from human interference and exploitation and thus not proper objects of environmental concern. Even among environmentalists, concern about off-planet environmental issues has been slow in developing. The concept of "Spaceship Earth," for example, although inspired by space exploration, remains steadfastly focused on earthbound environmental issues.

Since the mid-1960s, nevertheless, scientists have been concerned about the biological contamination of other planets—and this has led to disputes between the United States and Russia—but this concern is not really an environmental one. The sterilization procedures used by space scientists in preparing space probes for landings on other planets are not employed for the purpose of protecting non-Earth environments for the long term, but rather only until all appropriate scientific experiments have been conducted.

Despite the lack of attention that the Solar System has received so far from philosophers, scientists, engineers, and environmentalists, the time for careful reflection on ethical issues concerning the space program and on environmental issues related to the Solar System as a whole is now long overdue. We human beings not only have the ability to reach the Moon, but most other planetary bodies in the Solar System as well. Russia has already landed unmanned spacecraft on Venus, and the United States has landed them on Mars. Many of the planets are partially or completely mapped and photographed, and only the most distant planets remain completely unvisited. It is really only because of reduced spending levels after the success of the Apollo missions that the United States does not have a space station in orbit and men living on the Moon and Mars.

While it may be tempting to say that we do not need to face the environmental issues involved in our exploration of the Solar System for many decades to come, such an attitude overlooks the fact that planning for space missions also begins decades in advance so that the technology needed for the missions can be developed. If serious planning begins without adequate ethical and environmental input, then future NASA and associated industrial/commercial projects in the Solar System may simply produce a new environmental crisis that dwarfs our current one. To avoid such a crisis scientists, engineers, environmentalists, and philosophers must get together, clarify the issues involved, and begin solving them. This book is intended as a first step toward the accomplishment of these goals.

In applying environmental ethics to the Solar System, two conceptual hurdles need to be overcome. First of all, environmental ethics is a relatively new field in philosophy and its theoretical foundations are still very much up in the air. From the standpoint of traditional ethics, ethics applies only to human beings and not to animals, plants, ecosystems, or natural objects. Environmental intuitions, nevertheless, seem to demand some kind of moral considerability for these kinds of entities, and environmental ethics is in large measure a search for the proper foundations for these intuitions. If this search is successful, then ethics will be transformed into something that transcends the human moral communities of the past. Although many of the issues discussed in this book can be dealt with in terms of a traditional conception of ethics—specifically, the social-political and scientific-technical issues—the attempts to apply environmental concepts to the Solar System represent a significant challenge for environmental ethics, since so far as we know at present the Solar System, except for Earth, is a collection of nonliving natural objects, the kind of entity that offers the greatest conceptual difficulties for environmental ethics.

Second, it is not unlikely that the environmental movement in the United States will split into warring camps over the issue of resource exploitation of the Solar System. As William Hartmann points out in his paper "Space Exploration and Environmental Issues," some environmentalists will decide that we should exploit the resources of the Solar System to the full in order to bring resource exploitation on Earth as close to an end as is reasonably possible; others will conclude that such resource exploitation is simply a continuation of improper environmental policies long pursued on this planet. The split is likely to be comparable to the breakup of the environmental movement into two irreconcilable factions at the beginning of the twentieth century: the conservationists, primarily concerned with the proper use of nature, and the preservationists, primarily concerned with the protection of nature from use.

Although it is difficult to sort out all the issues covered in this book and place each paper under one and only one label, there are a number of conceptual frameworks that may be helpful for readers to keep in mind. One way to distinguish the papers is to divide them into social and political concerns, scientific and technological policy concerns, and environmental and ethical concerns. Seen in this way, the book may be divided into three parts. The first two papers and the last four are concerned with social and political issues: the social costs of the exploration of the Solar System, the health costs to those who live and work in space, the theological or religious dimension, and the problem of international or solar politics. The central portion may be divided into two parts: a set of papers dealing with various scientific-technical issues followed by more general discussions of the application of environmental and ethical concepts to the Solar System. These technical papers, moreover, can be divided into those concerned primarily with problems in Earth orbit and those concerned with planetary bodies.

To divide the book up in this way, however, diminishes the ethical and environmental dimension so that it appears to be an important consideration in only a few of the papers in the later part of the volume. There are two slightly different ways in which the term *environmental ethics* is routinely used: (1) in a general sense in which any ethical issues dealing with the environment are part of environmental ethics, and (2) in a narrower sense in which environmental ethics is an ethical position that goes beyond traditional ethical limits to include questions about the moral considerability of nonhuman living and nonliving entities (and in this sense is considered in opposition to traditional ethical limits). All of the papers in this book deal with environmental ethics in the first sense, and it is in this sense that the book achieves its overall unity.

On theoretical grounds, nevertheless, it is also useful to divide the papers into those that are focused primarily on anthropocentric issues, the interests and welfare of human beings, and those that also have a nonanthropocentric dimension, that is, try to deal with value considerations that are independent of human interests and welfare and may occasionally even be opposed to them. For example, should strip mining be permitted on the Moon? Should discharges from factories in space be permitted if they will have no harmful effects, other than perhaps changing the color of the sky to yellow or brown and making it impossible for us to see the stars from the surface of this planet? If we colonize Mars, is there anything wrong with mining the moons of Mars to the degree that they cease to be planetary bodies? Is there anything wrong with terraforming Mars and Venus and perhaps other planetary bodies in order that they may someday have Earth-like biospheres? Should we ban nuclear testing in space or welcome it? Is there anything wrong with simulating nuclear disasters, for example, a meltdown on the Moon, or blowing a small planetary body to pieces to test our latest weapons or to study the interior of a planet? If we find life somewhere in the Solar System, should we preserve it or destroy it? If we decide to preserve it and it will cost money, what should our spending limit be before we write those life forms off? In these cases, what we think we *ought* to do and what is in the best interest of some or all human beings may be in conflict. We will not have an adequate understanding of ethical and environmental issues raised by our exploration and exploitation of the Solar System until we have begun not only asking but also answering questions like these with some certainty.

We should not, nonetheless, let these strange new nonanthropocentric issues prevent us from paying proper attention to the traditional anthropocentric ones. When we contemplate human life in a future dominated by space exploration, it is easy and very tempting to think of sparkling and pristine extraterrestrial human environments like those depicted in the film *2001* and to fantasize about exciting and romantic adventure in terms of such films as the *Star Wars* trilogy. These, however, are not the only, and certainly not even the most likely, visions of human life in the Space Age. Some filmmakers have provided us with darker visions. Consider, for example, the deplorable social and environmental conditions of a very polluted Earth as depicted in *Blade Runner,* the unhappy crew of the ore-processing ship Nostromo in *Alien,* and the inhuman working conditions of miners on the moons of Jupiter in *Outland.* For these visions to become reality we do not need a nuclear war or the violent overthrow of our democratic institutions, only the continuation of current trends and practices in government and business.

To address these issues, whether anthropocentric or nonanthropocentric, I have brought together here a collection of papers by experts from government, the aerospace industry, and academia who were likely to have the best grasp of the issues as they relate to their particular fields and occupations. As a result most of the discussions are reflective more than speculative—that is, they reflect the current state of thinking in each area, or in some cases what current thinking might be if such thinking were to occur. Put another way, the collection of papers as a whole documents where we stand today in dealing with the ethical and environmental dimensions of space. As such, I believe, it should be the starting point for any serious study or discussion in the future.

The Social Dimension

The Arguments
against Space Exploration

DAVID BRIN

A special exhibit recently toured cities across the country under the auspices of the Smithsonian Institution. It was a unique collection of colorful imaginings of the future, drawn by artists who lived in the decades between Edison and Sputnik. In these renderings one glimpsed extravagant tomorrows—gilded, faery towers linked by spiderweb bridges, palatial liners cruising the sky, clanking robots, and ornithopters in every garage.

We moderns chuckle at these images, for in the true-to-life eighties our cities are not made of stainless steel or shimmering adamantine. Although New York and Atlanta do shine prettily, at night, they nevertheless seem mundane, unmysterious when compared to the *futuristic* pictures in the pulps of the twenties.

And yet, perhaps the most amusing thing is that we feel this way about the time in which we live, for in fact it is an era far more extraordinary than all but the most daring of yesterday's fantasies.

This is a theme that will run through my critique of

the arguments for and against space exploration—that it is our fundamental attitude toward the future that determines whether this effort to move upward into the skies will prove worthy or merely worthless.

In preparing this introduction, I find myself drawing on somewhat conflicting roles. As a professional in space science, I interact frequently with NASA and other agencies carrying our nation step by gradual step into the new frontier. As a writer of science-fiction novels, I am paid to be a professional spinner of dreams. My remarks here are largely in the latter capacity.

Philip José Farmer, another science-fiction writer, has entertained millions and, moreover, introduced many to concepts they might not have encountered in any other way. In the afterword to his famous novelette, *Riders of the Purple Wage,* Farmer expressed the concern of many—during the late sixties and early seventies—that too much attention was being paid to flashy, physical endeavors . . . that we should be investing our research energies instead in the exploration of the human spirit, in discovering ways to tame the savage within us, before the power of our tools outgrows our ability to control them.

Farmer has since returned to enthusiasm for space exploration, but the questions he asked earlier remain valid. They demonstrate that the community of science-fiction authors has shared the angst of society as a whole —wondering "Whither goest mankind?" during a time of furious change.

Another author, John Brunner, in his stunning novels *Stand on Zanzibar* and *The Sheep Look Up,* raised issues of environmental conscience with startling clarity, long before they were widely discussed in the popular media. Ursula K. LeGuin was another of the many writers who turned to ecological and ethical matters during the sixties, and one collection by Isaac Asimov was tellingly entitled *Earth Is Room Enough.*

I find that my own fiction is colored by a sensitivity to these issues, generated, perhaps, by having been a member of the Sierra Club generation. One of my novels in progress—a collaboration with Gregory Benford—superficially deals with Halley's Comet, but reduces, in the end, to considering the basic question of how life arose and maintains its precarious tenancy on Earth.

In creating frightening images of potential ecological chaos, or in focusing on the possible desperation of fictional scenarios on Earth, science-fiction writers have not declared an end to their long-standing love affair with space exploration. Instead they see themselves as asking hard *questions* —a major objective of any crafter of good literature. Contrary to popular belief, a science-fiction author is generally not interested in *predicting* the future. Real life is infinitely more surprising than even the most colorful extrapolations.

No story prepared us for the sulfur volcanoes of Io, or the iceberg oceans of Europa, or the daunting mystery of extragalactic jets. No daring writer predicted that, within our own lifetimes, women police officers and female astronauts and Black mayors would become so routine that they would drop from our awareness into the background of everyday life.

Science-fiction stories of the 1970s projected a time when people would have computing power in their homes, and yet every one of those tales extrapolated along the trends of those days, and predicted remote, slave links to huge time-sharing centers . . . exactly the sort of arrangement that would be prey to sabotage or abuse . . . and incidentally make for good drama.

Not one story proposed that by 1990 the majority of American homes would have independent and *autono-*

mous computing power matching the average Russian *city*. And while a few stories (very few) predicted we would be on the Moon before 1970, none projected that it would happen the way it did. To paraphrase Norman Mailer, NASA's engineers accomplished *two* bona fide miracles in 1969. First, they actually *landed men on the Moon*. Second, they *somehow managed to make it boring!*

This is my first crucial observation, in critiquing space exploration from the point of view of an author. People everywhere agree about one fact concerning the space program, that it is usually about as romantic as a stone.

While perhaps the greatest adventure in human history is taking place in the heavens, we have become the first culture since ancient Ireland whose principal heroes are *entertainers*. We spend far more on cosmetics, or movies, or record albums than we do on space, clearly showing where our priorities lie. Children dream of becoming rock stars more often than astronauts.

Of course there are important reasons for this dichotomy between science-fictional dreams of space and the dull reality. Adventure fiction involves putting interesting characters into dangerous settings, usually brought about by some terrible *mistake*. Perhaps the blunder was made by unseen bureaucrats. Perhaps the situation looks hopeless as the hero arrives on the scene. All the better for the story. The novelist or screenwriter knows that his or her audience wants to see brave and resourceful *individuals* overcome potential disaster.

A good science-fiction story is built around correcting terrible errors. But if this defines "drama," then drama is exactly what NASA cannot afford. Early in 1986 we saw why, when the loss of a space shuttle crew threw the nation's space effort into total suspension for a year or more.

What other enterprise so large and ambitious must be so cautious? In war—or in maintaining preparedness against war—errors, overruns, and deaths in training are expected. In the semi-Darwinistic environment of big business, mistakes are the way inefficient participants are supposed to be culled, making way for better competitors. (At least that is the way it is supposed to work, and the way it does for small concerns.) Even in academia there is allowance for error. In fact, experiments with surprising results often have led to famous scientific papers.

But NASA finds itself in an unusual quandary. From one side, the agency is criticized for lack of boldness. From other directions it faces constant demands for explicit justification, as if it were expected to turn a profit, quarterly. The situation is even worse now. There are those who say that the space agency cannot afford even one more mistake.

The traveling Smithsonian Exhibition on images of the future is a demonstration of our people's long-standing romance with the future. Few would disagree that the United States is the most tomorrow-oriented culture in history. It is no accident that such a people have sent representatives to the Moon and robot messengers to the farthest reaches of the Solar System.

So why does NASA find itself forced to justify everything in terms of cost-benefit ratios and quadruple safety factors? One possibility is because our national passion for the future is carried to excess by many who seem to have more enthusiasm than common sense, whose passion rings alarm bells in others and gives futurism a bad name. What engineer or official involved in space has not cringed in dismay as an irate "space-fan" berates our failure already to have colonies on Mars, or hyperdrive, or giant solar collectors that—*of course*—would solve the energy crunch overnight?

Is it any wonder that a "rock and a hard place" mentality develops when the same official must then proceed to testify before a skeptical Congress, and try to present economic justifications for an essentially exploratory endeavor?—he must supply lists of services barely yet conceived and customers for products still in their infancy.

NASA is under assault for *both* timidity and wasteful adventuring. Some of these criticisms of the U.S. space program—many laughable and others much more difficult to dismiss—are discussed later. But at this point it should be emphasized that many of NASA's problems are caused by this enforced schizophrenia toward the future—that it is charged with leading the way but dares not lead from too far ahead.

The Environment for Change

Is part of the problem that America is *too* future-oriented? So flexible is this society that we seem barely to notice any longer changes that thirty years ago would have been rejected as too weird for even the pulp magazines—from test-tube babies to husbands assisting their wives in delivery rooms to weather satellite photos on the evening news.

Some world leaders, with command over nuclear missiles, can recall being excused from one-room schoolhouses to run outside and stare at a primitive biplane, or even an automobile.

The very words we use in our daily lives show how much alters without notice. But to read a newspaper from the sixties is to find one's self immersed in what seems almost an archaic dialect. For instance, until not long ago the use of the word world was discouraged in official United States Government documents. Believe it or not, it was suspect as somehow subversive. Instead, everything was "international."

In the last eight years, however, the word *planet* has crept into widespread use, along with its deep-seated semantic implication—once considered dangerous—that we are all in it together, and must somehow learn to manage a "Spaceship Earth," drifting lonely and vulnerable through a harsh universe.

In these emotional and linguistic changes, the space program has played a major role. Arguably, the photos brought back by Apollos Eight and Ten—showing our frail, cloud-shrouded blue globe against the stark galactic night—were perhaps the most important and influential visual works ever produced, and the most widely seen.

When viewed as a planet—with a complex, interlaced ecosphere hard-pressed by five (and soon six to eight) billion human beings, the *world* becomes the central criteria against which images of the future are measured. Leaders and social planners cannot rationally contemplate perpetuating *status quo* anymore, but must think in terms of *goals* for a future planetary design.

In the end, political decisions must be measured against questions as simple as these. Will those six to eight billion people live prosperous lives of diversity, accomplishment, and freedom? Can the United States maintain a position of leadership, generating much of the wealth and innovation to make such a world possible?

There are those who believe that investment in space exploration hinders us from accomplishing goals such as these. Others say that the program is the very essence of tomorrow's hope. This is the true debate, the criterion against which the arguments for and against space must be measured.

Limits to Growth?

How can we find a perspective from which to measure the value of endeavors in space? Let us start by calling up a few facts.

First, it is clear that humanity has developed a great facility for seeking out and moving and using matter and energy. In recent years we have become aware of the distinction between those resources that are renewable (if we are careful with them) and those that are intrinsically limited. The former include air, water, animals, and vegetation—all more or less renewed by interacting with each other and with solar energy.

There are also those resources that are extracted out of the Earth itself, by copious use of power. Careful tending may slow their depletion[1] but cannot create a never-ending, renewable supply.

This latter type of material has sometimes been called demandite.[2] By mass it consists of approximately 45 percent fossil fuels, 46 percent construction materials, 2 percent process chemicals, 1 percent agricultural chemicals, and 6 percent metals. Americans use roughly 17 tons of demandite per year, per person, a great deal of material to be ripped out of the ground and converted for use.

The figures are also impressive in energy use. Per capita gross American power consumption is about 11 kilowatts, of which about 2.2 kilowatts go into producing and processing demandite. More than six-sevenths of this energy comes from carbon fuels.

During the mid-seventies, many awakened to the fact that this rate of use—of both demandite and energy—was a considerable fraction of worldwide consumption, and that if it continued growing at an exponential rate, as it then appeared to be doing, the carrying capacity of the Earth would soon be exceeded.

This was the era during which it was stylish to speak of limits to growth. That phrase still calls forth strong emotions, and in itself often stands in the way of understanding, but clearly, in at least some sense, it was a necessary realization. For instance, the rate of demandite processing now already exceeds the formation of new Earth crust at ocean-rift boundaries.

If the rate of growth of consumption really had been exponential, the situation would, indeed, have been hopeless. But there is another curve being discussed these days, the so-called S-curve, demonstrating that human affairs often pass through long initial phases during which growth is slow. Then once initial infrastructure is formed, abilities at last match ambitions, and expansion is rapid, apparently exponential.

But this second phase is followed by a third—a turnover, a self-correction or damping of growth to far lower levels again. Long ago Malthus perceived the S-curve, and his contention was that expanding populations inevitably smash into the limits of the capability of their environment and technology to support them. The damping mechanism is death—a fearsome controller.

To our relief, today we seem to be seeing another group of self-limiters coming into play. Mercifully, our species seems to be satiable, if greedy, a trait that did not have to be in our repertoire, and for which either Heaven or Evolution or both are to be praised.

Technologically advanced states have experienced plummeting birthrates and—under moderate economic pressure—have throttled back their appetites for energy and mineral consumption. Perhaps more importantly, they have begun altering their basic myths, for example by including wild animals in their definition of tribesmen, worthy of being defended. In this way our very ethics have been changing, and within fractions of a generation.

Seventeen tons of demandite and eleven kilowatts of power now seem to satisfy American appetites. The rate at which species are going extinct, in North America and Europe, appears to be at its lowest level in two hundred years. The threats of poisoned aquifers and eroded farmland are still chilling, but on those two continents, at least, a nascent caretaker attitude is growing, one whose view encompasses centuries, and entire ecospheres.

This has been accomplished by approximately a fifth of the people on the globe. True, in Africa and Latin America the outlook still appears bleak, but the success story of Asia seems to promise that another two-fifths will enter the third phase of the S-curve, the phase of stability, of low birth rates, and of having a vested interest in a serene world.

All very promising. But is it really necessary, in order to live a third-phase life, for each human being to use seventeen tons of demandite and eleven kilowatts of power? Alas, even with space-borne cameras helping us search, it is clearly impossible to provide that much material and energy without both population limitation *and* major advances in technology.

Take just one example. Carbon-based fuels are presently being consumed at about a million times the rate at which they were laid down. Eleven kilowatts over a year is equivalent to about ten tons of coal. Six billion "Americans" would consume the world's much-vaunted coal reserve in only 150 years. A quandary, indeed. But what is the relevance of all this to the space program? All the relevance in the world, in fact, for it explains a fundamental conflict in public attitudes toward space exploration.

A strange polarization has occurred, in which those who most believe in the limits-to-growth thesis—often bundled together and called Old Liberals—are among those most suspicious of space exploration. To a motley alliance of interests, money spent on space is being wasted on technological toys while the ship we are all riding is sinking. Some even declaim that we are only exporting our problems, and filth, to a pristine Universe. It doesn't help ease this knee-jerk antagonism that many of the individuals and companies involved in space programs are also involved in programs to develop weapons of mass destruction.

At the other extreme, one sees many in popular societies for the promotion of space who loudly proclaim that limits to growth is nothing more than a red herring, a catch phrase of effete left-wingers. Because of their contempt for so-called liberals, everything their opponents say is denigrated, dismissed. Often these "technoconservatives" deny that there is any ecological or resource problem at all.

In the process, space is dragged into political quagmires completely unrelated to its own merit. Space advocacy groups, in becoming more and more stridently right wing, have driven out those who might be called "technoliberals," Democrats and environmentalists who nevertheless believe in technology, and in the promise of space as one of many potential paths toward salvation of humanity and the planet. What might have been a powerful alliance across party lines instead has become a reflex polarization that can only hurt the prospects of space exploration.

There is an important point to be made here, a reduction to simplest terms. Where we are discussing long-term acquisition of demandite and power from the Earth, limits to growth is proven. Period. But those limits do not have to apply to our exploitation of resources outside of our home world.

The best ore bodies on the planet are being depleted. By one estimate, humans have moved seven times ten to the eleventh tons of demandite during the last four hundred years, creating immense valleys and inundating canyons in their excavations. And yet, that is less mass than is contained in *one* asteroid only eight kilometers across, or the matter expelled from one lunar crater of equivalent size.

There are millions of asteroids, and studies have shown that their resources, and those of the Moon, are accessible, no farther beyond our grasp than the oil beneath the Beaufort Sea was thirty years ago. And in space there are no natives to fear exploiting. It will be a long, long time before our activities out there begin to threaten the pristine natural beauty of the Solar System.

Certainly much too much enthusiasm was given to solar-power satellites, a decade ago, when back-of-the-envelope calculations should have shown that lifting such masses from the Earth would be prohibitive. But a related idea, lunar-based power stations using material found on-site, is now receiving serious, if cautious, consideration.

George Von Thiesenhausen of NASA has even proposed that a version of Turing's idealized self-replicating machines may become real someday—may, in fact, be "grazing" the lunar surface within a generation or two, using sunlight and bare regolith to multiply into thousands and millions, and be "harvested" the way sheep are now on Earth. The image is mind boggling, since it suggests a rate of demandite production as much exceeding our own as ours goes beyond the material use of Plato or Socrates. For a stabilized population, such wealth would mean not just an end to poverty, but the opportunity to ban all industry from the face of the Earth, allowing our shaky ecosphere to settle down to what it does best, the nurturing of diversity.

The opportunities, the promises, are all there on paper. Many have seen the studies, which seem to offer ways to leverage a better life for all.

If this is so, then there are two basic questions we must ask: "Why aren't we bending all our efforts to this goal?" and "What are the hidden costs?"

I have touched lightly upon some of the social and psychological reasons for timidity in the nation's space effort. But, in truth, the first question is really one to be wrestled with in other places. The question concerning hidden costs is of greatest concern. And it strikes me that, perhaps, the most important fact is that we are asking it at all.

Are we growing up at last, when we start asking about hidden costs *before* embarking on a great venture? Although I am very much pro space, I find it encouraging that serious thinkers are being asked to explore the ramifications, especially the environmental ones, before we roar off to melt asteroids or to mine the Moon.

Famed scientist and artist William Hartmann asks if the aesthetic and historic value of the Moon deserves protection in advance. Certainly many scientists, including myself, will scream if near-Earth-crossing asteroids are exploited before these ancient relics of Creation are fully investigated.

If most of the lunar material we mine goes into propellant for military rockets and armor plate, will much of this activity ever trickle down to help the common man?

If water is the most valuable commodity to be found in near-Earth space (so valuable that robot asteroid miners would be programmed to spurn platinum in favor of ice), what are the chances of finding ice in permanently shaded caves on the lunar poles? (This might be one of the most important scientific questions in human history.) Is it true that only one H-bomb, exploded anywhere near the Moon's surface, would devastate our chances of finding such ice with gamma-ray spectrometers?

What about the problem of orbital debris? Along just the orbital inclinations between 81 and 83 degrees, there are more than 500 tracked objects, comprising 39 percent of the 13,000 square meters of known hazardous debris out there. Is it possible we might be able to clean up the worst-polluted orbits? By using "tether" lassoes, perhaps?

Consider the problems we have with "GEO Transfer Stages." These are rocket upper stages that carry cargoes to *geosynchronous* orbit, 40,000 kilometers overhead, where communications satellites remain fixed over a specific longitude. Most of the propellant burned by these stages is hurled back into the atmosphere (to what long-term effect?). But one malfunctioning stage in 1982 spewed exhaust in all directions resulting in anomalous performance loss by the solar cells of satellites orbiting far away, only days later.

In the short term, how will the space station separate the three intrinsically different environmental conditions and requirements presented by fuels transfer and industry, by manned laboratories, and by sensitive optics?

Back in the seventies, the Skylab astronauts spoke glowingly of the convenience of having a capacious "trash can" in the former Saturn stage's old oxygen tank. Will the space station have such a facility? Can one decade's accumulated garbage be recycled as the next decade's valued resource?

Can we learn, in developing self-contained life-support systems for spaceflight, information that will be valuable in becoming wise managers of our own planet?

These are all questions of concern to scientists and, ultimately, to the citizens of the United States and of the Earth.

The Emergence

In olden days, shamans and mystics sought magical knowledge. Today we seek science. What is the difference? Don't let anyone tell you that it has to do with verifiability, predictability, or any of the other catchphrases philosophers of science use. The difference is simpler than that.

All human beings want miracles—ways to wrest power and the wherewithal of life out of nature. The practitioners of *magic* believe that this is something best done by an *individual.* The knowledge of how to work miracles is therefore private, *secret,* for if it is shared it is squandered and lost. Take my word for it, as a writer who also dabbles in fantasy tales. Magic is a zero-sum game.

Ah, but *science* is another matter. Science, along with its child, technology, is a *cooperative* endeavor. Knowledge is useless unless it is shared. A practitioner achieves glory by *giving away* more truths than his peers, for the common enlightenment of all.

Of the two, science has proven to be vastly more powerful. In fact, magic appears to possess only one property science lacks, and that is *romance.* The soulstirring beauty of the Jovian storms, the haunting desolation of the Chrysium plains, the godlike power of being able to send the equivalent of the entire Library at Alexandria, at the speed of light, from one coast to another bounced off a patient robot servant hovering twenty-thousand miles high upon nothingness—these are *miracles.* No cost-benefit analysis is necessary to demonstrate their utility to me. They are too beautiful to require justification—and yet a substantial portion of the citizenry of the nation that *did* these things does not see this glory, does not share in the pride, or in the dream of things to come.

They *want* to see it. As we saw earlier, Americans are friendly to the future. They will believe in it, given a chance. But science feels cold and unromantic to many.

Perhaps many of the arguments against space exploration are based on something as straightforward as this —that, deep in their hearts, people would rather it were more magical, that the first man on the Moon had built his craft with his own two hands and perhaps had to punch out a few bug-eyed monsters on the way back as well. Simply put, this vast enterprise, engaging hundreds of thousands of skilled professionals, involving great complexity and grit—and the occasional deaths of real fathers, mothers, schoolteachers—may seem, at times, too daunting.

Still, it is my personal belief that the prospects are good. After all, what can we expect from a species only now emerging from six thousand years of darkness and fear? Our people can be forgiven if they rub their shoulders and peer suspiciously at the horizon where a gray glow is spreading. We sniff the air suspiciously, and inspect carefully the ground upon which we are about to tread.

But step by step, we *are* going forward. And I have every confidence that that glow on the horizon is the dawn.

Notes

1. H.E. Goeller and A. Zucker, "Infinite Resources: The Ultimate Strategy," *Science* 223 (1984): 456–62.
2. David R. Criswell, "CES-Lunar Industrialization and Higher Human Options," presented at the 35th Congress of the International Astronomical Federation, 7–13 October 1984, Lausanne, Switzerland (IAF-84-313).

Space and Society

T. STEPHEN CHESTON

Introduction

*O*ne of the intriguing aspects of space is its evocative
quality. Its seemingly unlimited size, extreme temperatures and gravitations, strange chemistries, and exotic
visual images excite the intellect and emotions with end-
less energy. Humans have projected upon space their
hopes, fears, analytic abilities, and other paraphernalia
of their psyche with unending vigor. Be it the Inca rite
of "tying down" the Sun during the winter solstice or the
cool hum of computers calculating the trajectories of
distant planetary probes, we see the human mind and
spirit trying to react, learn, control, and, finally, recon-
figure itself with nature and its own essence through the
medium of space. Human interactions with space draw
upon culture's entire baggage of myths, science, accom-
plishments, and destructions. To view space from other

than this fuller context can be intellectually and ethically misleading.

Prior to the twentieth century space was wonderfully inaccessible and therefore a vent for the brimming exuberance of the human imagination. The gods and their heavens were located there and exerted beneficent or malevolent control over human affairs. Divination of the night sky guided the affairs of the state and the individual. The inventions of astrology and primitive cosmology in ancient Mesopotamia and Egypt were wellsprings for their articulations in Greek, Roman, and Judeo-Christian cultures.[1] To venture into the heavens held the specter of violating the domain of the divine or the eating of the forbidden fruit of knowledge by the unclean, imperfect human. This subconscious imagery still haunts our reactions to the achievements of the space-flight revolution of the twentieth century.

The space-flight revolution has made it imperative, however, that we come to grips with the fundamental phenomenon of the physical marriage of human culture with space. Not to do so would condemn us to be prisoners of our unconscious predispositions, misdirecting our energies or, in the extreme case, laying the seedbed for the extinction of civilization. To do so can enrich the entire fabric of human knowledge, shine fresh light on old questions, and generally elevate the human condition. The work is just beginning and, no doubt, much of what we do now will someday be seen as alchemy, as further manifestation of the ability of humans to delude themselves in the face of obvious reality. But the first childlike steps are being taken. We should hope that we gain a slightly broader perspective, a deeper capacity for analysis, and a greater sense for the interrelationship between man and the environment.

Space Social Science

The systematic study of space from a social science or humanities perspective is an emerging intellectual invention.[2] Work in this area is done by individuals who are trained in particular disciplines, such as history, philosophy, or political science, and so on, but who live in a professional no-man's land. Those who venture into the area of space run great risks, especially if they are not tenured. Their work is often seen as exotic side trails with little or no relevance to the central commerce of their disciplines. Social scientists and humanities scholars who focus on space become intellectual, stateless persons who are not fully intelligible in the disciplines of their training but who have no recognized community to go where they are understood.

The first contours of space social science as a separate entity are only now issuing from the jumble of other disciplines, although it still lacks a coherent identity and integrity of its own. Space social science, or spaceology, if we are to coin a word for economy of language, will become first a recognized area of study that integrates the methodologies and insights of mainline disciplines. An analogous social science area, albeit a very mature one, is international relations.

In the natural sciences, space science is a counterpart. Although it is not a single discipline in itself, the natural science study of space does have a coherent identity sufficient to serve as a powerful cohesive force to merge the resources of traditional disciplines. Geology and gravitational physics converge in the space science explanation of the volcanism on Io, one of the moons of Jupiter.[3] Climatology, biology, and geology together can address the space science subject of the impact of a large meteor on Earth.[4] Departments of space science do, in fact, exist on university campuses and unite personnel from many physical science disciplines, training a new generation of space scientists who will move with ease through a variety of natural sciences in their focus on space. A unit of NASA exists solely to support the development of space science, and there are a number of organizations that focus on specific space science topics, such as the Lunar and Planetary Institute near Houston, Texas.[5] Moreover, there is a consortium of 52 universities, known as the Universities Space Research Association, that has functioned since 1969 to stimulate and coordinate space sciences.[6]

We might define spaceology as that branch of knowledge that treats the origin, development, and varieties of the interaction between human culture and the extraterrestrial environment. Spaceology would draw upon the humanities, social sciences, and natural sciences with equal facility.

Further delineation can be wrought by looking at fundamental human dispositions: intellectual (abstract rational), emotional, and practical. Humans engage space, so to speak, through these dispositions. Space phenomena have traditionally stimulated the human capacity for the rational: to think logically and quantitatively, inductively and deductively, to predict accurately and undertake other activities that relate to the left side of the brain. Space has been the seeding ground for much physics and mathematics since civilization's early days.[7] From Aristotle and Pythagoras to Newton and Einstein, our basic knowledge of the physical universe has been advanced by seminal minds focusing, frequently, on the extraterrestrial environment. Prior to the twentieth century space was, with the exception of the Sun and Moon, essentially a very large and complex pattern of points of light in the sky. The repetitive nature and precision of the symmetrical interrelationship of these points of light offered a kind of stimulus not found anywhere else in the perceived environment. The history of much of philosophy, especially of the more ancient variety, is that of trying to make sense of these light patterns. In attempting to do so, mental tools, such as algebra and geometry, were advanced and made more abstract and, in turn, were applicable to other areas of human endeavor.[8]

From the point of human emotions, space indeed has been a godsend. Its vastness, inaccessibility, and seemingly silent imperviousness to human affairs made it an absolute playground for the human capacity for awe, hope, fear, and the like. The right side of the brain was able to "do its thing" without restraint. Utilization of space for religious and mythological purposes ripples throughout history. The ancient art of predicting the future has resorted to the alignment of star patterns (astrology) as a fundamental tool since the early Mesopotamians.[9] The writing of fantasy from Plutarch and Lucian in the Roman era, to Ludovico Ariosto and Johannes Kepler in the sixteenth and seventeenth centuries, to Jules Verne and H. G. Wells in the nineteenth century, to the explosive growth of the space-fantasy genre in the twentieth century has nurtured itself on the exotic attributes of the extraterrestrial environment as a bigger-than-life arena to play out human drama.[10] Very often this drama takes place on a grand scale, such as the rise and fall of empires, to utilize the vast stage that space offers.[11]

Mankind's practical side also has been well served by the extraterrestrial environment, even before the age of communications and earth-sensing satellites. One of civilization's primal concerns has been the organization of time with increasing precision. The planting of crops, predicting of floods, and reckoning of festival dates required having an environmental measuring stick that was reliable and exact. Seasonal changes in the weather offered only vague reference points, and there was nothing in the realm of human perception that provided a level of punctuality as did the annual rotation of the stars. For instance, the priests of ancient Egypt used the rising of the star Sirius in July to predict the annual flooding of the Nile with an accuracy within a few days, a feat that greatly impressed the peasantry.[12] Navigation of the seas outside of sight of land would have been impossible without the aid of the stars. The voyages of Columbus, Magellan, Cook, and others would have been out of the question if they had had to deal with permanently clouded skies. The history of the rise of ocean navigation is a fascinating study of ever-increasing human capacity for exactitude in observation, time measurement, and recordkeeping.[13]

The Twentieth Century

The twentieth century provides a very useful framework for analyzing the human engagement of space. It is the first century in which humans and their machines have actually entered the extraterrestrial environment and thereby greatly broadened and intensified the entire portfolio of interactions looked for in spaceology. From the point of view of the intellectual engagement of space, it is almost banal to call the era revolutionary; the changes have been so great that they challenge the adequacy of the adjective. Theoretical constructs of the universe have moved from Newton's eternal, predictable machine housed in a backdrop of time and space to Einstein's space/time continuum in which the universe as a whole begins and ends much the way the components within it do.[14] Space, instead of being an area where discrete elements of matter and light energy interact with a serene stability, is now seen as a continuous and violent interchanging of matter and energy, which transact their business in radio, micro, infrared, ultraviolet, x, and gamma rays as much as in standard light.[15] Matter is now viewed as having an infinite number of densities, sometimes with bizarre effects. What young mind has not been fascinated by the fantastic nature of black holes?[16] The Earth once viewed as the large and permanent "world" is now seen as a transient, fragile island floating in cold, unforgiving vastness.[17]

The development of machines that help mankind think—computers—has been stimulated by men and instruments in space as well as advances in mathematics, physics, geology, and climatology. The new broader conceptual frameworks established by the space-flight revolution have provided the imaginative freedom to develop theories that integrate "galactic weather" into the evolution of life on this planet, as exemplified by the recent dinosaur and Nemesis theories.[18] To measure the changes in the assumption base and capabilities of the human intellect between the years 1900 and 2000 may be better handled by the discipline of anthropology than by history.

Human emotions have not been left out. They have benefited from the new detailed knowledge about the physical nature of the universe in its various forms and the reality of people actually operating in space. A genre of literature, whose embryos are found in late nineteenth-century science fiction, took concrete form and blossomed in the twentieth century with a gusto and vitality not often seen in other literary forms.[19] With science fiction, a new twilight zone of the mind was established in which the facts of science intertwined with human imagination to form vicarious experiences that both prepared people for future realities and stimulated young minds to create those realities. The novels of Jules Verne and H. G. Wells helped incite Konstantin Tsiolkovsky, Robert Goddard, and Herman Oberth to design, and in the cases of Goddard and Oberth to build, prototypes of the kinds of machines necessary for going into space.[20] Their work, in turn, was exploited by international military competition—first between Nazi Germany and the Allies and later between the Soviet Union and the United States—to build the actual hardware that ignited the space-flight revolution.[21] That then gave fresh impetus to the science-fiction art form. It provided an ocean of new information to be played with by writers. Quasars, neutron stars, and other space exotica that would have been unknown if it had not been for x-ray and gamma-ray orbiting observatories are showing up in science-fiction stories. The knowledge provided by Pioneer and Voyager spacecraft about Jupiter's moons and that planet's gaseous physics set the stage for Arthur Clarke to shape his *2010.*[22] In some ways the advances made by science satellites chastised science fiction to move on, as the old realms of fiction fell to reality. The demise of Mars as a fictional base for intelligent life, as exemplified by H. G. Wells's *War of the Worlds* and Ray Bradbury's *Martian Chronicles,* was caused by the Mariner and Viking probes that revealed the reality of the Martian environment. The myths about a canal-building civilization spawned by the work of Schiaparelli and Lowell in the nineteenth century fell to the scientifically exciting but fictionally disappointing photographs of craters,

dust storms, and rarified atmosphere.[23] For the future it will be curious to see what space-propulsion systems will be developed by young minds who have never genuinely understood that going into "warp drive" or "hyperspace" violates current laws of physics.

Recently the emotional engagement of space has taken a new, somewhat odd twist. Newspapers carried the account of funeral homes offering patrons the option to rocket one's ashes into the Van Allen Belt in orbiting mausoleums that would remain in place for 63 million years. These orbits would be unusable for other purposes because of their high radiation. Public response to this opportunity has been strong despite derisive references to "ash-tronauts" and the "right stiffs." The appeal of depositing one's remains in such a place apparently relates to memories of our religiously defined location for heaven and a permanence unachievable in our geologically active planet.[24] In the future will cathedrals built in space be somehow nearer to God than their planet-bound ancestors or will orbiting monasteries provide a more appropriate environment to contemplate the divine than the Mount Athoses of Earth?

The practical engagement of space has bifurcated into the normal channels of many major new technologies—civilian and military. Communications satellites led off the utilization of space for civilian purposes. Initially suggested by science-fiction writer Arthur Clarke in a May 1945 memorandum to the British Interplanetary Society, the concept of three geostationary satellites providing a global, wireless communications system was well in place by the time of the launch of Sputnik.[25] The first communications satellite, Telstar 1, was launched in July 1962 with the capacity to handle 240 transatlantic phone calls that were routed to ground stations costing two to three million dollars each. Since that time there has been a continuous succession of ever larger and more powerful satellites, such as the Intelsat 5 series, transmitting video and digital data as well as voice communications to ever smaller and less expensive ground equipment.[26] There are now well over 20,000 satellite circuits utilizing, in some cases, receiver equipment costing a few thousand dollars. And the process of smaller and cheaper ground equipment continues. One organization, Geostar Corporation of Princeton, New Jersey, plans to build a satellite system in the next few years that will permit digital communications and navigation through hand-held devices costing eventually only $450.[27] Overall, communications has been a dramatic success spawning a bevy of companies in an essentially new industry.

Though not a commercial success as yet, Earth-sensing satellites have played an important role in a variety of fields. Names like Tiros and GOES are associated with satellites providing weather-forecasting photographs. The Landsat satellite series concentrates on visible light and infrared images of the Earth's surface and oceans to assist in agriculture, forestry and rangeland management, mapmaking, detecting fish and ice movements in the oceans, the assessing of oil and air pollution, and the discovery of oil and mineral deposits.[28] The recent experimental introduction of orbiting radar probing the immediate substructures of the Earth's surface is offering such intriguing possibilities as the discovery of ancient Mayan irrigation systems and riverbeds undergirding parts of the Sahara Desert. The science of navigation, dependent upon stars since ancient times, now uses various orbits around Earth to do its business. Transit and Navstar are two satellite-based navigation systems providing ever-increasing precise and timely navigational and positioning information to ships and airplanes on a global basis.[29] Soon land transportation will also enjoy satellite services in the tracking of trucks and railroad cars.

Expectations for the practical engagement of space in the future focus on utilizing the zero gravity, hard vacuum, and cryogenic temperatures naturally available in space for a variety of industrial-related activities. Operating under the generic name of "materials processing," Space Shuttle and Salyut experiments are now being undertaken and aimed toward the eventual production of pharmaceuticals, electronic crystals, high-temperature alloys, fiber optics, and other products during the 1990s.[30] A recent study by the Center for Space Policy in Cambridge, Massachusetts, estimates that materials processing will be a $40-billion business by the year 2000.[31] The U.S. Space Station to be completed in the mid-1990s is seen as a prototype in the evolution of space factories for the late 1990s and the early decades of the next century. These, in turn, will be stepping stones to the eventual mining of the Moon and Earth-passing asteroids and the building of large-scale metal-processing factories in Lagrangian, geosynchronous, and other high orbits in a kind of Masabi Range-Pittsburgh in the sky.[32] This Earth/Moon industrial infrastructure would be expected to extend to Mars and the other planets as the twenty-first century progresses. Some futurists see this type of large-scale industrial development in space as being a turning point in the economic, social, and political development of civilization.[33]

As the very birth of space technology is owed to man's primal fear of and combat with his brothers, it is not surprising that military needs have continued to animate its further development. The initial post-Sputnik generation of space technology ironically enhanced the maintenance of peace. Discoverer, Big Bird, Key Hole-

11, Cosmos 4, 208, and 758, and Salyut 3 and 5 were code names for increasingly sophisticated U.S. and Soviet photoreconnaissance satellites that tracked ground activities with exquisite precision, making nonadherence to arms agreements a very difficult art. These eyes of the superpowers were matched by ears that monitored the competitor's radio traffic. The "ferret" satellites that went by such code names as Rhyolite, Aquacade, and Cosmos 189 and 389 made it all the more difficult to have military shenanigans.[34]

While explicit and tacit international agreements of the 1950s and 1960s kept space virgin of permanent weaponry, arms experts were not to be denied their ingenuity. The Fractional Orbital Bombardment System (FOBS), Dyna-Soar, and Manned Orbital Laboratory (MOL) were but a few of the many Soviet and American projects that aimed to use the new "high ground" of space.[35] Even though the proposed military projects of the late 1950s, 1960s, and early 1970s were not actualized, they were symbolic seeds of the incipient predatory instincts that lay in the womb of future space development.

These seeds began to blossom in February 1976 when the Soviets began a new series of tests for their antisatellite (ASAT) program that had been quiescent since 1971. There are various reasons offered for this Soviet action, but whatever the case it began a process of American response and Soviet counterresponse that had its crescendo in President Reagan's "Star Wars" speech of March 1983. This, in turn, has accelerated the development of a portfolio of weaponry that, according to proponents, promises to technologically neutralize the current system of "mutually assured destruction" that emerged in the early 1960s as the principal deterrent to war between the superpowers. The promise of shifting the psychological base of international security away from fear of mutually suicidal offensive warfare to a fear of the enemy having an effective defense against nuclear weapons has energized many to support the development of space technologies that up to now have been housed mainly in our science fiction. Visible light and x-ray lasers, particle beams and kinetic energy guns have entered the popular consciousness and national policy dialogue as possible options for the not too distant future.[36]

Space Technology and Spaceology

With all this thumping technological progress, we should take a fresh look at our original categories in spaceology, the intellectual, emotional, and practical engagements of space, and see if further refinement is in order. Indeed the pivoting of the Industrial Revolution process begun in the eighteenth century from its exclusive focus on Earth to the extraterrestrial environment and the translation of battlegrounds from the Earth's surface to space represents sufficient breaks with the past to deserve further delineation of the categories of the human dance with space.

Be it in space or on the ground, technology is still technology and is a product of human culture. It is created in response to particular human needs, and once created it in turn affects culture. Peculiar to space technology, however, it also places people for the first time in physical environments radically different from those found on Earth. We might, therefore, establish three categories of spaceology that are focused on the twentieth century: (1) Developmental Factors, (2) Impact Analysis, and (3) Orbital Human Factors.[37]

Developmental Factors may be defined as those factors in the social environment that give birth and form to space technology. Humans entered into the extraterrestrial environment more than a quarter of a century ago as the result of a long and intricate set of technological, military, geographical, and political factors. The subsequent exploration, utilization, and development of space have resulted from the interplay of economics and politics with science and technology. Future development of space technology will probably evolve from the interaction of an increasingly complex set of factors. To properly understand them, resources of a large number of social science disciplines will be needed. Anthropology, architecture, business administration, communications, economics, education, geography, history, international relations, law, literature, philosophy, political science, psychology, public administration, social psychology, and sociology can all contribute to our understanding of the social context of space technology in its past, present, and future forms.

The social context of space technology development possesses two levels or tiers. The first is the fundamental one of emotional impulses that form the substrata of our attitudes toward space and space ventures. Drives, hopes, dreams, and fears are the wellsprings of human behavior, the often vaguely articulated deeper feelings that tap ancient memories, myths, and images, seek moral improvement, and touch humankind's unending need to learn its full identity. Some of the drives important to space include the drives to explore, to achieve, to improve society, and to search for our relationship to the universe. But space development also triggers negative emotions: the perennial fears of change, the unknown, the untried, the unattainable, of stepping into unauthorized territory, of polluting virgin lands, and of acquiring prohibited knowledge. Suggested space projects, whether positive or negative, activate ancient symbols that override the pragmatic justifications such as "near-term, cost-benefit" analysis. One prime example was the Apollo project to the Moon that tapped images, mythologies, and folklore that spanned millennia: Men traveling to the moon has been a recurring theme in literature since the Roman author Lucian wrote *Vera Historia* in the second century A.D.[38]

The second tier of the social context of space technology development comprises the immediate issues, processes, and institutions that cause the precise form of space technology at a given time. For instance, in the 1970s, why did United States public investment in the application of space technology increase dramatically while the proportion of the gross national product invested in overall space technology declined? Questions such as this require analyzing the way a space technology is economically institutionalized (e.g., exclusively government, mixed public/private, multinational cooperation); the interplay between the civilian and the military aspects of space; the basic political culture; the climate of public opinion of a given period; and the relationship of space technology to other concerns of a society.

Impact Analysis is the study of the consequences to society of the introduction of new technology. This type of study arose in the 1960s to a large extent because of the stimulation of NASA. At that time the Apollo project was having considerable effect on certain local economies, some areas of higher education, and various sectors of industry, such as semiconductors. In addition, the endeavor of going to new territory, the Moon, was unique for the twentieth century. It was the fifteenth through the nineteenth centuries that saw new lands opened up for exploration, economic development, and colonization. The question arose, what was going to be the overall impact on society of Apollo and space exploration in general? MIT Professor Raymond Bauer began to study the question and was struck by the absence of available methodologies. He responded by devising a comprehensive system of measurement that was published in the book *Social Indicators* (Cambridge, Mass.: MIT Press, 1966). The work trail blazed the rise of a number of works that attempted to develop methodologies to quantify, as well as possible, the impact of a new technology on political, legal, and social institutions, the family, international relations, land use, population distributions, and, very importantly, the environment. Technology assessment became the generic name for this kind of study and was used to entitle an office established by Congress in the early 1970s to help policymakers decide which technology development programs should receive federal support.[39]

Technology assessment had a heyday in the 1970s with its presence vigorously felt throughout federal and state governmental establishments and seems to have left a permanent mark on American political culture. The Environmental Protection Agency, the Department of Energy, and other arms of the federal government incorporated studies using various technology assessment methodologies as part and parcel of their decision-making process. A dramatic example of technology assessment's involvement with space technology occurred in 1978 when the Department of Energy (DOE) undertook a $20-million study of the satellite power-system (SPS) concept.[40] SPS was a controversial proposal to build gigantic satellites with solar collectors that were miles in length on each side. These would be able to collect solar electrical energy 24 hours a day to be beamed to Earth either by microwave or laser for input into the nation's power grid.[41] Given the conflicting interests that were at play the study was a broadly gauged technology assessment, examining the international, environmental, economic, and social issues as well as engineering aspects. Completed in 1980 the DOE study concluded that there were no fundamental show-stoppers to SPS and had its results turned over to the National Academy of Sciences, which undertook its own independent study.[42] The National Academy drew more questioning conclusions of SPS, which, given its already controversial status, forced the audacious energy concept into a period of quietude that has lasted to the present.

Some aspects of space technology are more accessible to impact analysis than others. Applications of specific commercial technologies can be quantified, at least to a degree. For instance, the upcoming Geostar satellite system mentioned earlier is a case in point. Here impact analysis begins with market studies on who would most likely be the first buyers of a technology that provided navigational and digital, not voice, communications from hand-held devices that operated nearly anywhere without resort to telephone lines. How would these first users apply the technology, and what prices would they be willing to pay? In this case, organizations that manage trucking and railroad fleets and need to locate and communicate with their rolling stock and forestry managers who need to communicate with individual field staff on foot are the first users. They help create greater economic efficiency and environmental quality and set the stage for this space technology to be used by the broader public for intrafamily coordination and safety, such as in pleasure boating. Internationally, the impact of these devices on eastern-block and some third-world societies that try to control the information flow of their citizens would be looked at in a study. A checklist of these and other impacts could be fairly well organized to predict the effect of the technology, at least for the near future.

On the other hand, the impact of deep-space probes is more difficult to assess, except for the generation of scientific information. A probe's effect on society's more practical concerns is generally secondary or tertiary and, therefore, considerably more elusive. The precise nature of the application of knowledge about the weather structures of Venus and Mars to our understanding of long-term climatic change on Earth could not be predicted through an Impact Analysis of the Pioneer and Viking probes prior to their construction and launch.[43] Whereas impact analysis can make only limited contributions to space exploration in other than drawing broad-brush pictures, it does have a productive role to play in assessing the increasing number of space technologies that are designed for commercial use.

Orbital Human Factors (OHF) is the study of human behavior and needs of people operating in the extraterrestrial environment.[44] There is almost an intoxicating quality about this category of spaceology. People traveling, working, and living in space have been a key part of science-fiction folklore and a central element of the emotional engagement of space in the twentieth century. Humans have never before been exposed to different gravities, atmospheres, and having a location relative to the Sun different from that of Earth. In addition, people in space operate in encapsulated environments that amplify many aspects of social relations and create, in effect, a laboratory for studying the human animal.[45]

As of 1985 well over one hundred men and women have gone into space for stays of fifteen minutes to over seven months. Programs such as Mercury, Gemini,

Apollo, Skylab, Shuttle, Spacelab, Vostok, Voskhod, Soyuz, and Salyut have populated our minds with images of people floating about in and out of spacecraft or bouncing on the Moon's surface in scientific research, launching and rescuing satellites, and doing repair work. As time has passed space missions have tended to involve greater numbers of people, with increasingly diverse backgrounds, and, in the case of the Soviets, with much greater time in orbit. The future promises a continuation of these trends until going into space will begin to take on characteristics of some of the more ordinary work and play activities of Earth.

There are earthbound analogies to our more immediate future in space useful to the social scientist. Antarctica, undersea labs, submarines, and certain offshore oil rigs have groups of people operating in encased facilities in physically hostile environments.[46] The space stations of the 1990s will be similar. People will be there for months on end with little ability to take unscheduled leave, sometimes even in dire emergency. All work and leisure will be in one location, in generally densely populated living quarters. Human error or aberrant behavior may be lethal to the community as a whole. Questions such as selection, training, and on-board procedures challenge the behaviorist, psychologist, and social psychologist to push their disciplines to new levels of competency in application. Being able to predict human behavior in emergencies and to maintain high productivity in monotonous work for extended periods of time assign the social sciences very demanding tasks. NASA has long recognized this and is involving sociologists and psychologists in the space-station development, even in its fundamental planning stage. The architecture of the space station is taking into account human psychological needs. The layout, traffic flow, compartment design, windows, furnishings, and lighting are aimed to enhance human alertness, attentiveness, motivation, and flexibility, while reducing stress.

The data collected during the 1990s will be of immense value in preparing for the long-duration, interplanetary, manned missions of the next century. It is far easier to redress a human-relations problem only 100 miles overhead than when it is 100 million miles away in deep space. Just as important, it can be expected that in the twenty-first century we will scale up the size of operational units in space from space stations and bases to space towns. Whether on the surface of the Moon or Mars, or floating in open space as envisioned by Konstantin Tsiolkovsky or Gerard K. O'Neill, these relatively large aggregations of population will repeat in some ways Earth-based experience and, in other ways, represent something totally new. Their social mores will be determined in large degree by their sponsoring entity. It is one thing to be in a Moon base controlled by the Soviet military and another to be in a floating space colony founded by the Quakers. Whatever the sponsoring organization, all space-borne towns will have to have procedures for the citizenry to respond to a sudden "leakdown" in the air supply due to meteor impact, or to punish certain criminal behavior on location, or any number of situations special to large groupings of people living in isolated extraterrestrial environments.[47] The social sciences will be very active here in developing procedures and possibly in establishing mores. Each relevant social-science discipline, however, should be pushed to new, higher levels of performance, and it is this challenge that students of "Orbital Human Factors" will have to meet.

Developmental factors, impact analysis, and orbital human factors are elements of our intellectual, emotional, and practical engagements of space in the twentieth and twenty-first centuries. As we plow forward in the new field of spaceology, we should not forget to mine the rich store of knowledge and wisdom that lies within the humanities. There, knowledge is rooted in experience speaking directly and in emphasizing human individuality, not through the artificial constructs of disciplines that have pretense of reducing humans to scientific specimens. Ethics as the study of morality and the delineation of the complex choices between good and evil needs to be ever present, for spaceology will forever seek to reduce the individual to a data point of scientific study and thereby build knowledge of use to those who would invade the autonomy and freedom of the individual. This is the basis for tyranny unless men and women of good will and intelligence forever recognize that eating the magic fruit of knowledge does not make one a god with prerogatives and privileges over one's fellow man.

Notes

1. Benjamin Farrington, *Science in Antiquity* (London: Oxford University Press, 1969), pp. 16–36; Colin Ronan, *Changing Views of the Universe* (New York: Macmillan, 1961), pp. 13–36; Colin Ronan, *The Astronomers* (New York: Hill and Wang, 1964), pp. 31–95; Alastair C. Crombie, *Augustine to Galileo—The History of Science, A.D. 400–1650* (Cambridge, Mass.: Harvard University Press, 1953), pp. 1–69.

2. T. Stephen Cheston, "Space and Society: Suggested Paths to an Emerging Discipline," *The Space Humanization Series* Vol. 1, ed. T. Stephen Cheston and David C. Webb (Washington, D.C.: Institute for the Social Science Study of Space, 1979), pp. 1–14;

T. Stephen Cheston, Charles M. Chafer, and S. Birket Chafer, eds., *Social Sciences and Space Exploration,* NASA EP-192 (Washington, D.C.: U.S. Government Printing Office, 1984), pp. xiii–xvii.

3. David Morrison and Jane Samz, eds., *Voyage to Jupiter,* NASA SP-439 (Washington, D.C.: U.S. Government Printing Office, 1980), pp. 152–67; L.A. Soderblom, "The Galilean Moons of Jupiter," *Scientific American* 242, no. 1 (1980): 88–100.

4. Richard A. Muller, "An Adventure in Science," *New York Times Magazine,* 24 March 1985; "Did Comets Kill the Dinosaurs?" *Time Magazine,* 6 May 1985.

5. Lunar and Planetary Institute, 3303 NASA Road #1, Houston, Texas 77058.

6. University Space Research Association, Suite 311, American City Building, Columbia, Maryland 21044.

7. Farrington, *Science in Antiquity,* pp. 16–36.

8. Ibid., pp. 27–36; Ronan, *Changing Views of the Universe,* pp. 24–31.

9. Ibid., pp. 24–31.

10. Robert Scholes and Eric S. Rabin, *Science Fiction: History, Science and Vision* (New York: Oxford University Press, 1977), pp. 3–25 and 113–21; Lester del Rey, *The World of Science Fiction: 1926–1976* (New York: Ballantine Books, 1979), pp. 12–21; H.G. Wells, *The Time Machine/The War of the Worlds: A Critical Edition,* Frank B. McConnell, ed. (New York: Oxford University Press, 1977); Robert Holdstock, ed., *Encyclopedia of Science Fiction* (London: Octopus Books, 1978), pp. 144–45, 154–55.

11. For example see Isaac Asimov's *Foundation* trilogy (New York: Doubleday & Co., 1951–1953) or George Lucas' *Star Wars* movie trilogy (1977–1983).

12. Ronan, *Changing Views of the Universe,* p. 32.

13. Boies Penrose, *Travel and Discovery in the Renaissance* (Cambridge, Mass.: Harvard University Press, 1952).

14. A. Rupert Hall, *From Galileo to Newton* (New York: Dover Publications, 1981), pp. 276–328; Lincoln Barnett, *The Universe and Dr. Einstein* (New York: Bantam Books, 1957); Nigel Calder, *Einstein's Universe* (New York: Greenwich House, 1979).

15. Homer E. Newell, "Continuing Harvest: The Broadening Field of Space Science," *Space Science Comes of Age: Perspectives in the History of Space Sciences,* Paul A. Hanle and Von Del Chamberlain, eds. (Washington, D.C.: Smithsonian Institution Press, 1981), pp. 149–92.

16. Walter Sullivan, *Black Holes: The Edge of Space, the End of Time* (New York: Doubleday, 1979); Paul Davies, *Other Worlds: A Portrait of Nature in Rebellion, Space, Superspace and the Quantum Universe* (New York: Simon and Schuster, 1980), pp. 164–69.

17. Apollo astronaut photographs of Earth from more than 100,000 miles in space have been credited as making a major contribution to the environmental movement's development.

18. See Footnote 4.

19. Del Rey, *The World of Science Fiction,* pp. 12–157.

20. A. Kosmodemyansky, *Konstantin Tsiolkovsky: His Life and Work* (Moscow: Foreign Languages Publishing, 1956); Robert H. Goddard, *Autobiography* (Worcester, Mass.: St. Onge, 1966); Helen Walters, *Hermann Oberth: Father of Space Travel* (New York: Macmillan, 1962).

21. Walter A. McDougall, . . . *The Heavens and the Earth: A Political History of the Space Age* (New York: Basic Books, 1985), pp. 20–134.

22. Arthur C. Clarke, *2010* (New York: Ballantine Books, 1982).

23. William G. Hoyt, *Lowell and Mars* (Tucson: University of Arizona Press, 1976); Henry S.F. Cooper, *The Search for Life on Mars* (New York: Holt, Rinehart, and Winston, 1980).

24. "Orbit the Departed," *New York Times,* 25 January 1985; "SSI Finds First Launch Customer," *Space Business News,* 21 January 1985.

25. Arthur C. Clarke, "Can Rocket Stations Give Worldwide Radio Coverage?" *Wireless World,* October 1945.

26. Kenneth Gatland, *Space Technology: A Comprehensive History of Space Exploration* (New York: Harmony Books, 1981), pp. 86–95.

27. "You Will Never Walk Alone," *London Times,* 27 May 1984.

28. Gatland, *Space Technology,* pp. 106–15.

29. Ibid., pp. 79, 82.

30. Ibid., pp. 218–25.

31. *Space,* a publication of Shearson Lehman/American Express, Inc., January 1985. The results of the Center for Space Policy Study have been challenged for excessive optimism in projection of space processing revenues.

32. Brian O'Leary, ed., *Space Industrialization,* 2 vols. (Boca Raton, Fla.: CRC Press, 1982).

33. Gerard K. O'Neill, *The High Frontier* (New York: William Morrow and Company, 1977); G. Harry Stine, *The Third Industrial Revolution* (New York: G. P. Putnam's Sons, 1975).

34. Gatland, *Space Technology*, pp. 78–85; Philip Klass, *Secret Sentries in Space* (New York: Random House, 1971).

35. Gatland, *Space Technology*, pp. 72, 204, and 206; Michael A.G. Michaud, "The Anti-Satellite Program: A Threat to Space Humanization?" *The Space Humanization Series*, pp. 81–84.

36. In recent years there have been numerous newspaper and magazine articles on antisatellite activities, the evolution of space weaponry in general, and the international conditions that stimulate such development. For an overview of these subjects see Paul B. Stares, *The Militarization of Space: U.S. Policy, 1945–1984* (Ithaca, N.Y.: Cornell University Press, 1985).

37. This subject was first explored in "Space Social Science: Suggested Paths to an Emerging Discipline," *The Space Humanization Series*, pp. 1–14.

38. Ralph B. Baldwin, *The Face of the Moon* (Chicago: University of Chicago Press, 1949); Henry C. King, *The World of the Moon* (New York: Thomas Y. Crowell Co., 1967); *Encyclopedia of Science Fiction*, p. 144.

39. Cheston, *The Space Humanization Series*, pp. 7–9.

40. U.S. Department of Energy, Office of Energy Research, Solar Power Satellite Project Division, *A Bibliography for the Satellite Power System (SPS) Concept Development and Evaluation Program*, DOE/ER-0098 (April 1981).

41. Peter E. Glaser, "Power from the Sun: Its Future," *Science*, 22 November 1968.

42. National Research Council, *Electric Power from Orbit: A Critique of a Satellite Power System* (Washington, D.C.: National Academy Press, 1981).

43. Newell, *Space Science Comes of Age*, pp. 157–58.

44. Cheston, *The Space Humanization Series*, pp. 7, 9–11.

45. Cheston, *Social Sciences and Space Exploration*, pp. 65–71.

46. E.K. Gunderson, ed., *Human Adaptability to Antarctic Conditions* (Washington, D.C.: American Geophysical Union, 1974); Roland Radloff and Robert Helmreich, *Groups Under Stress: Psychological Research in Sealab II* (New York: Appleton-Century-Crofts, 1968);

J.H. Earls, "Human Adjustment to an Exotic Environment: The Nuclear Submarine," *Archives of General Psychiatry* 20 (1969), pp. 117–23.

47. Richard D. Johnson and Charles Holbrow, eds., *Space Settlements: A Design Study,* NASA SP-413 (Washington, D.C.: National Aeronautics and Space Administration, 1977), pp. 21–35.

Scientific and Technological Issues

Earth Orbital
Pollution

DONALD J. KESSLER

Introduction

O rbital debris was first studied in the early 1970s by NASA's Johnson Space Center and Marshall Space Flight Center. These early studies concentrated only on the less than 2,000 objects that were cataloged by North American Aerospace Defense Command (NORAD) at that time. The major conclusion of these studies was that the collision probabilities, although of some concern, were not significant except for large structures (greater than 100 m in diameter). In the mid-1970s NASA's Langley Research Center expanded the level of concern by predicting that, as a consequence of explosions in space, the real orbiting population was 2.5 times the cataloged population.[1] In the late 1970s studies at the Johnson Space Center concluded that fragments resulting from collision between artificial satellites would be a major source of debris, possibly as early as the 1990s.[2] Later studies[3] identified explosions of the U.S. Delta rocket second stage and U.S.S.R. satellite tests as major contributors to debris in space. As a result, the United States changed the Delta rocket operational procedures to minimize the possibility of future explosions. In 1981 the American Institute of Aeronautics and Astronautics (AIAA) issued a position paper on space debris, concluding that the space debris issue is real and that action must begin now to forestall a serious problem in the future.[4]

In 1982 the Johnson Space Center sponsored a workshop on orbital debris.[5] Solid rocket motors fired in space were presented as a potential source of very small orbital debris. Data were presented which concluded that some experiments flown in Earth orbit to detect meteoroids actually detected mostly aluminum oxide particulates from these rockets. Therefore, in the two debris size ranges that were measured (the micrometer size detected by meteoroid sensors and the greater than 10-cm size detected by ground radar), the orbital debris flux in certain regions of Earth orbit was either comparable to or greatly exceeded the interplanetary meteoroid flux. The workshop concluded that orbital debris is a potential problem for future space operations. However, before initiating major efforts to control the environment, new data should be obtained on the population smaller than 10 cm. Consequently, since this workshop the major emphasis has been upon obtaining such data. Most of this work was summarized by Kessler[6] and will be updated in this paper to include later results.

Fundamentals of Orbital Debris Issues

Orbital debris is becoming a concern due to a combination of fundamental issues. First, the volume for Earth-orbiting objects is much smaller than that occupied by interplanetary meteoroids. Consequently, practically since the beginning of the space program, collision probabilities from payloads and rocket bodies alone have been orders of magnitude higher than collision probabilities from meteoroids of the same size. Second, just as in the case of interplanetary meteoroids, large objects act as a source of smaller objects by fragmenting. Fragmentation of man-made satellites occurs either by accidental explosion of rocket bodies, by intentional explosion or breakup of an object, or by collision between two objects. To date, 80 satellites are known to have broken up in Earth orbit. Depending on the size distribution of fragments, the mass in a *single,* average man-made satellite is sufficient to cause the flux from these fragments to exceed the interplanetary meteoroid flux over the entire size spectrum of fragments and over several hundred kilometers of altitude. Finally, the large orbital inclinations coupled with the rapid precession of the ascending node produce high collision velocities in low Earth orbit. The average collision velocity between two objects in low Earth orbit is 10 km/sec, compared to an impact velocity of 15 to 20 km/sec for interplanetary meteoroids. Consequently, the damage caused by an orbital debris impact is not very different from that caused by meteoroids.

Sources of Orbital Debris

Cataloged Population

Currently, only five countries and the European Space Agency (ESA) are capable of launching objects into Earth orbit. Over the last five years, as seen in

TABLE 1   Launch Operations

Country or Organization	Number of Launches in Given Year				
	1980	1981	1982	1983	1984
• U.S.S.R.	89	98	101	95	97
• United States . .	13	17	17	23	22
• Japan	2	3	1	4	3
• India	1	2	1	2	0
• China	0	1	1	1	3
• European Space Agency . .	0	2	0	2	4
Totals	105	123	121	127	129

Table 1, the U.S.S.R. has the largest launch rate, representing about 80 percent of the launch schedule. However, since most of the U.S.S.R. satellites have very short orbital lifetimes, their contribution to debris is less than that suggested by Table 1. Both the United States and the U.S.S.R. roughly share equal responsibility for the current orbital debris environment.

Figure 1 shows how the cataloged population has increased over the past 15 years, leading to an official "box score" of 5,403 objects in orbit as of 31 December 1984.[7] The reduction in the rate of increase of objects in space between 1978 and 1983 is the result of two factors: (1) This period corresponds to the second highest solar activity since records have been kept. High solar activity heats the upper atmosphere and increases the atmospheric density by more than an order of magnitude at

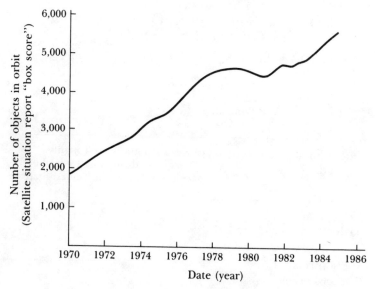

Fig. 1. Historical record of objects in space

most satellite altitudes. This causes an above-average number of objects to reenter the atmosphere. (2) Between 1978 and 1981 there happen to have been no major explosions. However, in January 1981 a Delta second stage exploded, and in July 1981 COSMOS 1275 broke up. These two events account for the temporary increase in number during 1981. Both of these events are meaningful. Since 1981 all Delta stages perform a depletion burn to eliminate excess fuel after placing their payloads in orbit. Consequently, none of the rockets have since exploded, and future explosions are highly improbable. The COSMOS 1275 breakup is unexplained. It may be significant that this payload was in an orbit that had a relatively high probability of collision

TABLE 2 Source of In-Orbit Population
Cataloged by NORAD

[31 December 1984 Population of 5,403 Objects]

Space Object	Percentage of Tracked Population in Orbit	Notes		
Operational payloads	5	Distributions are roughly equally divided between the U.S.S.R. and the United States.		
Nonoperational payloads	21			
Mission related (rocket bodies, shrouds, etc.)	25			
Satellite breakups •Explosions •Unexplained	49	7 Delta stages 4 U.S. other 8 U.S.S.R. satellite tests 4 U.S.S.R. other	These 23 breakups account for 93% of the tracked fragments resulting from the 74 known explosions to date.	

with other objects orbiting at an altitude between 900
and 1,000 km.

The importance of satellite breakups is shown in
Table 2, where nearly one-half of the cataloged population is shown to result from satellite breakups. All but a
few of these breakups were explosions—most were accidental, but some were intentional. With only five percent
of the catalog consisting of operational payloads, it is

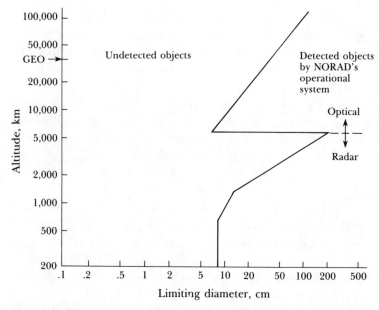

Fig. 2. NORAD's operational capability to detect objects

obvious that debris control has little to do with limiting the number of operational payloads in orbit.

Uncataloged Population

The first suggestion of a significant un-cataloged population is found by comparing the fragment distribution from ground explosions with that detected by NORAD radars.[8] Based on these types of considerations, it is estimated that between 10,000 and 15,000 objects larger than 4 cm are in Earth orbit. Figure 2 is an estimate of NORAD's capability to detect objects in Earth orbit. However, an object, although detectable, may not appear in the catalog, either because of a low probability of detection or because of an administrative decision to ignore the object. As is reported by Johnson,[9] special tests conducted by NORAD radars confirm the existence of a significant uncataloged population.

However, explosions have the potential of producing a much larger number of smaller objects. This is especially true in high-intensity explosions, or in explosions where the payload is designed to break up into some particular size. It is possible for a single 100-kg payload to break up into 10^5 1-cm objects or into 10^8 1-mm objects.

The major source of very small particles is solid rocket motors fired in space. A single rocket can be responsible for placing 10^{20} particles in space, ranging in size from 1×10^{-4} mm to 1×10^{-2} mm. Fortunately, most of these particles reenter quickly. However, the small fraction that remains in orbit is still capable of producing a flux that exceeds the meteoroid flux, as shown by Mueller.[10]

Unmodeled sources of small debris surely exist. The most likely sources include the material that may be released as a by-product of separation techniques used in orbit. Another possibility is shedding of spacecraft surfaces resulting from fatigue in space. For example, the thermal expansions and contractions of spacecraft surfaces may cause painted surfaces to flake off slowly. Currently, insufficient data exist to model these potential sources adequately, but new data from recovered spacecraft, as discussed later, are becoming available.

However, even if all of these sources were removed, a significant source would remain that is essentially a by-product of having objects in orbit. This source is collisional fragmentation. As shown in Figure 3, if past growth rates continue, collisions between objects larger

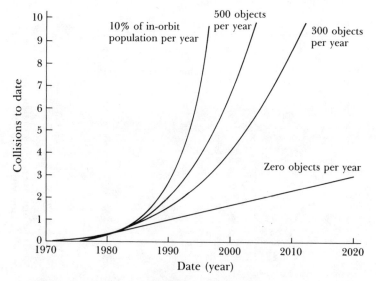

Fig. 3. Number of collisions expected by given date
assuming various population growths from the 1978
corrected to 4-cm population

than 4 cm can be expected within the next few years. A
typical collision would be between an old rocket body or
payload and an explosion fragment larger than 4 cm and
untracked by NORAD. The collision would produce 10^4
particles larger than 1 cm and more than 10^6 particles
larger than 1 mm. Figure 4 compares the predicted 1995
environment for these two sizes resulting from collisional fragmentation with the current environment. This
figure presents the environment expected in 1995, assuming that the major source of smaller particles at
lower altitudes is from collisions at higher altitudes,
where the fragments either drift down because of atmospheric drag or eject into lower orbits as a result of the
change in velocity of collision fragments.[11] Monte Carlo

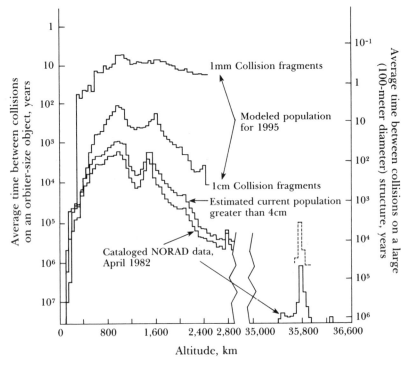

Fig. 4. Average time between collisions, modeled
population for 1995 compared to current population

modeling presented by Su[12] shows the results of using
lower change in velocities for smaller fragments.

Measurements

Measurements of orbital debris at sizes
smaller than those cataloged by NORAD were nonexist-
ent until a few years ago. The first measurements of
orbital debris were apparently taken in 1973–74 during

the Skylab program. The Skylab Cosmic Dust Experiment S149 was returned to Earth for analysis. Chemical analysis of residues in individual craters showed a high incidence of aluminum.[13] The windows on the returned Skylab IV Apollo Command Module were also examined for meteoroid impacts using the scanning electron microscope. It was discovered that about one-half of the hypervelocity pits were aluminum lined.[14] The size distribution and frequency of these pits were about what one would expect as a result of solid rocket motors fired in space.

With the beginning of the Orbiter launches, windows were again examined for hypervelocity impacts. However, because these windows are reused, the windows could not be used in destructive testing, unless they contained a pit too large for safe reuse. On the morning of the third day of the seventh Shuttle flight (STS-7), the crew detected a pit on the outside window that was about 5 mm in diameter. They were reasonably sure the pit had not been there before. This pit caused the window to be replaced, hence the pit could be examined. The pit contained titanium oxide with traces of carbon, aluminum, potassium, and zinc. These elements are consistent with those found in thermal paints using an organic binder. It was concluded that the particle had a diameter of about 0.2 mm and an impact velocity between 3 and 6 km/sec.

The Explorer 46 Meteoroid Bumper Experiment was flown in 1972 to test the effectiveness of bumpers against meteoroids. The very strong directional flux measured by this experiment can only be explained by impacts from an Earth-orbiting population.[15] The experiment was sensitive to impacts by particles larger than about 0.1 mm. The orbital debris flux determined by the 43 highly directional impacts is 1.9 impacts/m²/year. This is about a factor of 3 below the flux derived from Orbiter window examination, assuming one impact every 50 days in space. The Orbiter window flux is about the same as the meteoroid flux.

The Solar Maximum Mission (SMM) satellite was launched on 14 February 1980 into a near circular orbit at 570 km altitude. By 10 April 1984, the orbit had decayed to 500 km and SMM was captured for repair in the Shuttle payload bay, after nearly 50 months of exposure to space. The returned surfaces included about 1.5 m² of thermal insulation material and 1.0 m² of aluminum thermal control louvers. The thermal insulation consisted of 17 layers of aluminized kapton or mylar, each separated by a dacron net, and the louvers consisted of two layers of heavy aluminum foil separated by about 3 mm. These types of surfaces offered an excellent opportunity to obtain the chemistry of impacting particles. Analysis of these surfaces is continuing, but three different types of hypervelocity impacts have been found: meteoritic material, paint particles (consisting both of titanium and zinc pigments with potassium silicate binders and of an unknown chlorine source), and particles of an unknown origin (aluminum droplets were detected, but these may have originated from the aluminized surfaces).[16] Future analyses of these surfaces are expected to provide a more definitive definition of the debris environment for sizes smaller than about 0.2 mm.

Early studies within NASA determined that ground-based telescopes could be used to detect 1-cm orbiting debris. NASA contracted Lincoln Laboratories to use their two 31-inch telescopes to search for this debris. The two telescopes, located 60 m apart, were pointed near the zenith just after sunset and just before sunrise.

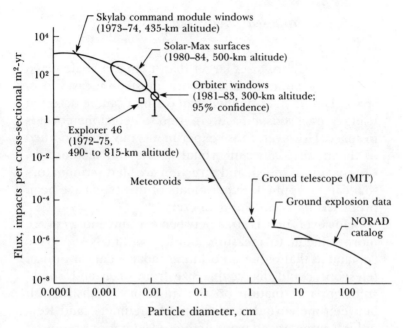

Fig. 5. Existing orbital debris measurements compared to
meteoroid flux

Orbiting objects were then detected by reflected sunlight transiting the field of view. The data were recorded
on videotape. The data-reduction technique included
applying the parallax observed between the two telescopes to discriminate against meteors that were detected near 100 km altitude. The results of this search
revealed a population eight times the cataloged population, or about 40,000 objects that are 1 cm or larger.[17]
These measurements are summarized in Figure 5 and
compared with the meteoroid environment.[18] Note that
in all cases the measured debris environment is comparable to, or exceeds, the meteoroid environment.

Proposed Measurements

Debris sizes larger than 1 cm can be detected from the ground. Smaller debris must be measured in space. Debris sizes smaller than 0.1 mm can be detected using impact sensors, as were used to detect meteoroids in space. However, those experiments must be modified to distinguish between orbital debris and meteoroids. Composition, speed, and direction are all discriminators that can be applied. Experiments of this type have been proposed by Grün[19] and Kuczera.[20]

However, debris sizes between 0.1 mm and 1 cm are more difficult to measure. Studies within NASA have concluded that either an orbiting radar, lidar, or optical telescope could detect this size from orbit and obtain sufficient information on the trajectory to distinguish between meteoroids and debris. Sanguinet[21] and Reynolds[22] summarized many of the considerations required for such a detector. Meteoroid experiments on the Long-Duration Exposure Facility (LDEF) should also provide data.

Space Debris Assessment Program

NASA has prepared a Space Debris Assessment Program Plan. The objective of this plan is to define the activities and resources required over the next ten years to develop the necessary understanding of the man-made orbital debris environment, its effects upon future mission operations, and the related requirements for appropriate policy and policy implementation. The major elements of the plan are environment definition, hazard assessment, space object management, and policy. The most immediate requirement of the plan is to define the environment, with primary emphasis on collecting data on debris sizes smaller than 4 cm.

Environment definition combines data from modeling, ground tests, ground data collection, and flight data collection to define the debris environment in terms of flux and velocity as a function of altitude, orbit, debris size, and future population growth. Most of the current data have been compiled and modeled. Some of this data indicates that there are sources of orbital debris that are not understood. Consequently, more data are required.

Hazard assessment combines the environment with systems-damage criteria and hypervelocity impact theory to determine the hazard to any particular spacecraft. A significant amount of hypervelocity testing was conducted during the Apollo program. This was testing of aluminum and glass structures at sizes and velocities that are directly applicable to orbital debris issues. Currently, additional testing is being conducted into composite materials.

Space object management consists of identifying and assessing the effectiveness of various control techniques. These techniques include removal from orbit by retrieval or planned reentry, placing a payload in a "disposal orbit," and minimizing the possibility of explosions in orbit. These last two techniques have already been used. That is, several payloads have been placed just outside geosynchronous orbit before the end of their operational life. Also, new operational procedures have minimized the possibility of new Delta second-stage rocket explosions. Other control techniques may prove to be expensive; consequently, it is important to understand the effectiveness of them before they become required policy. In view of what is known today, the following policies would be prudent:

1. Satellites should remain "intact" until reentry. This would require that both payloads and rockets be designed to minimize the possibility of on-orbit explosions and that their structural integrity and thermal surfaces remain intact.

2. The population growth of debris sizes smaller than those currently detected from the ground should be monitored. This would not only provide a check for model predictions but would also detect any unmodeled sources and provide sufficient data either to eliminate the sources or to design shields to protect spacecraft from the measured environment.

3. Rocket stages used to transfer payloads from low Earth orbit to geosynchronous orbit should be reentered within a year. If planned, these stages could easily be reentered. However, if not planned, they could remain in orbit for a very long time and pose a hazard to satellites in both low Earth orbit and geosynchronous orbit.

4. Any program that plans to place either large structures or a large number of objects in Earth orbit should be carefully examined for orbital debris implications. Such programs, if not carefully conceived, could initiate a collisional fragmentation process that could cascade to other satellites.

Any other policy concerning orbital debris must await further evaluation. Although it is clear that certain future space activities may be jeopardized by orbital debris, it is not clear what limits are required to minimize the increase in debris while maintaining a growing space program. Policy to deal with these issues will require a complete understanding of debris, its propagation, and its effect on future space activities.

References

1. D.R. Brooks, G.G. Gibson, and T.D. Bess, "Predicting the Probability that Earth-orbiting Spacecraft Will Collide with Man-made Objects in Space," in *Space Safety and Rescue* (Tarzana, Calif.: American Astronautical Society, 1975), pp. 79–139.

2. D.J. Kessler and B.G. Cour-Palais, "Collision Frequency of Artificial Satellites: The Creation of a Debris Belt, *Journal of Geophysical Research* 83, no. A6 (1978): 2637–46.

3. D.J. Kessler, "Sources of Orbital Debris and the Projected Environment for Future Spacecraft," *Journal of Spacecraft and Rockets* 18, no. 4 (1981): 357–60.

4. AIAA Technical Committee on Space Systems, Space Debris, *An AIAA Position Paper* (New York: American Institute of Aeronautics and Astronautics, 1981).

5. D.J. Kessler, "Summary of Orbital Debris Workshop," in *Space Safety and Rescue 1982–1983*, ed. G.W. Heath (San Diego: American Astronautical Society, 1984), pp. 3–10.

6. D.J. Kessler, "Orbital Debris Issues," in *Space Debris, Asteroids and Satellite Orbits*, D.J. Kessler, E. Grün, and L. Sehnal, eds., *Advances in Space Research*, vol. 5, no. 2 (Oxford, England: Pergamon Press, 1985), pp. 3–10.

7. NASA Office of Public Affairs, "Satellite Situation Report, vol. 24, no. 5 (Greenbelt, Md., Goddard Space Flight Center, 1984).

8. See notes 1 and 3 above.

9. N.L. Johnson, "History and Consequences of On-orbit Break-ups," in *Space Debris, Asteroids and Satellite Orbits*, D.J. Kessler, E. Grün, and L. Sehnal, eds., *Advances in Space Research*, vol. 5, no. 2 (Oxford, England: Pergamon Press, 1985), pp. 11–19.

10. A.C. Mueller and D.J. Kessler, "Effects of Particulates from Solid Rocket Motors Fired in Space," in *Space Debris, Asteroids and Satellite Orbits*, D.J. Kessler, E. Grün, and L. Sehnal, eds., *Advances in Space Research*, vol. 5, no. 2 (Oxford, England: Pergamon Press, 1985), pp. 77–86.

11. See note 9 above.

12. S.Y. Su and D.J. Kessler, "Contribution of Explosion and Future Collision Fragments to the Orbital Debris Environment, in *Space Debris, Asteroids and Satellite Orbits*, D.J. Kessler, E. Grün, and L. Sehnal, eds., *Advances in Space Research*, vol. 5, no. 2 (Oxford, England: Pergamon Press, 1985), pp. 25–34.

13. D.S. Hallgren and C.L. Hemenway, "Analysis of Impact Craters from the S-149 Skylab Experiment," in *Lecture Notes in Physics* (Berlin, Heidelberg, New York: Springer-Verlag, 1976), pp. 270–74; also, K. Nagel, H. Fechtig, E. Schneider, G. Neukum, "Micrometeorite Impact Craters on Skylab Experiment S-149," in *Lecture Notes in Physics* (Berlin, Heidelberg, New York: Springer-Verlag, 1976), pp. 275–78.

14. U.S. Clanton, H.A. Zook, and R.A. Schultz, "Hypervelocity Impacts on Skylab IV/Apollo Windows," *Proceedings of the 11th Lunar and Planetary Science Conference,* 1980, pp. 2261–73.

15. D.J. Kessler, "Explorer 46 Meteoroid Bumper Experiment: Earth Orbital Debris Interpretation," presented at the IAU Colloquium on Properties and Interactions of Interplanetary Dust, Marseilles, France, 9–12 July 1984.

16. D.J. Kessler, H.A. Zook, A.E. Potter, D.S. McKay, U.S. Clanton, J.L. Warren, L.A. Watts, R.A. Schultz, L.S. Schramm, S.J. Wentworth, and G.A. Robinson, "Examination of Returned Solar-Max Surfaces for Impacting Orbital Debris and Meteoroids," *Proceedings of the 16th Lunar and Planetary Science Conference,* 1985, pp. 434–35.

17. L.G. Taff, P.E. Betty, A.J. Yakutis, and P.M.S. Randall, "Low Altitude, One Centimeter, Space Debris Search at Lincoln Laboratory's (M.I.T.) Experimental Test System," in *Space Debris, Asteroids and Satellite Orbits,* D.J. Kessler, E. Grün, and L. Sehnal, eds., *Advances in Space Research,* vol. 5, no. 2 (Oxford, England: Pergamon Press, 1985), pp. 35–45.

18. H.A. Zook, R.E. Flaherty, and D.J. Kessler, "Meteoroid Impacts on the Gemini Windows," *Planetary and Space Sciences* 18 (1970): 953–64.

19. See note 5 above.

20. H. Kuczera, H. Iglseder, V. Weishaupt, and E. Igenbergs, "Acoustic Penetration and Impact Detector," in *Space Debris, Asteroids and Satellite Orbits,* D.J. Kessler, E. Grün, and L. Sehnal, eds., *Advances in Space Research,* vol. 5, no. 2 (Oxford, England: Pergamon Press, 1985), pp. 91–94.

21. J.A. Sanguinet, "Satellite-Based Instrument Concepts for the Measurement of Orbital Debris, in *Space Debris, Asteroids and Satellite Orbits,* D.J. Kessler, E. Grün, and L. Sehnal, eds., *Advances in Space Research,* vol. 5, no. 2 (Oxford, England: Pergamon Press, 1985), pp. 59–62.

22. R.C. Reynolds, "Design Considerations for Orbiting Detectors

for the Large Low-Earth Orbit Debris Population," in *Space Debris, Asteroids and Satellite Orbits,* D.J. Kessler, E. Grün, and L. Sehnal, eds., *Advances in Space Research,* vol. 5, no. 2 (Oxford, England: Pergamon Press, 1985), pp. 63–75.

The Commercial/Industrial Uses of Space*

RADFORD BYERLY, JR.

I. Introduction

The first and longer part of this paper discusses several commercial or industrial space activities that might show ethical or at least equity considerations. The second part very haltingly discusses questions about an environmental ethic for the use of outer space.

There have been commercial operations in space for more than twenty years, yet today's newspaper stories about "space commercialization" hardly recognize them. This refers, of course, to the communications satellites that have become a part of our everyday life. We seem to be getting along fine with little environmental concern. Some other commercial uses, such as commer-

---

*These are personal views and not the views of the Committee on Science and Technology or of any member of Congress. On most issues the Congress or an individual member by voting takes a definite position that can be clearly stated. However, in this particular area there is virtually no relevant legislation, and therefore most of what I have to say cannot be validated by specific legislative action.

cial remote sensing, would presumably be very similar to existing NASA research programs in that they would have very little environmental impact. What is new now —and what the popular press senses—is that we seem to be entering an era in which there will be commercial manufacturing (or "material processing") in space. In other words, we may have smokestack industries in space.

It may be helpful to divide commercial space activities into two broad classes. The first class includes the provision by a private company of those infrastructure elements or services that have previously been provided by NASA. Most of these services support payloads. For example, commercial communications satellites traditionally have been launched into orbit by NASA using government facilities and rockets. These satellites now could be placed into orbit by private rocket operators. One would expect commercial performance of this service to be very similar to the current NASA activity. After all, the performance required is exactly the same, and one would expect that both the means and the results would be virtually identical whether a launch were carried out by NASA or by a private operator.

Some of this type of commercial activity is already underway. Consider a simple example: Fully loaded the Shuttle can only go up to about 250 miles altitude, and yet communications satellites must be put into geostationary orbit at about 23,000 miles altitude. Therefore a second rocket—called an upper stage—is needed to take such a satellite from the maximum Shuttle altitude up to geostationary altitude. The McDonnell-Douglas Corporation, a major aerospace firm, makes such an upper-stage rocket, which they call a Payload Assist Module (PAM). PAMs have been used a number of times, and their manufacture and sale is a commercial operation.

That is, this rocket was developed by McDonnell-Douglas and is sold to satellite operators who need to go higher than the Shuttle can take them. One reads more about such small, start-up companies as Orbital Systems Corporation, which wants to make and sell a similar but more capable upper stage, and Transpace Carriers, Inc., which wants to operate commercially the old NASA Delta rocket system. In any case it is clear that if a commercial activity is only doing privately what has been done for years by NASA, then no significantly different environmental impact would be expected. Further, for purposes of this paper we will not consider the impact on Earth of launch activities as they have been dealt with (at least in principle).[1]

The second broad class of commercial activity in space includes the generation of services in space. Most of these activities are carried out by the payloads delivered to space. For example, the communications satellites can be thought of as providing a switching service in space: A message comes up from the Earth and is turned around and sent back down to the correct destination on Earth.

The second class of commercial activity would, of course, also include the processing of materials in space to acquire specific properties that cannot be acquired on Earth. This is probably the area with most potential for new commercial development in the immediate future. In the long term there is the possibility of mining the planets, the Moon, or asteroids, and this could be a major activity if economically successful. These are the kinds of new commercial activities that could have significant impact on at least their local environment.

Many observers of space commercialization believe that there has been at least a degree of overoptimism in this area. For example, *Atlantic* in May 1985 referred to "the opening of a new economic frontier" in space.[2] A counterexample is in the use of satellites to broadcast directly from orbit to individual home-receiving stations on Earth. This was predicted several years ago to be a booming new market but now seems to be at best a very limited market with several companies ceasing or scaling back plans and operations.[3]

Another cautionary example is in the commercial use of observations of the Earth's surface from space, that is, "aerial photography" from space. This area, generically referred to as land remote sensing, has been advertised as a great boon to mineral prospecting, crop forecasting, and land-use planning.[4] For various reasons, this application of space technology has not achieved its potential.[5]

A problem faced particularly by start-up companies offering commercial launch services is the high cost of launching the payloads and the consequent demand for very high launch reliability. There is simply no way that a new company can demonstrate the same kind of reliability as an ongoing government launching operation, which makes it difficult for such new companies to obtain business.

Despite all this, some of the new space commercial ventures may become roaring successes. It seems that the best chance for success is in those cases where the space technology can, in effect, replace a weak link in a system that is already a commercial success on Earth. The best example of this is communications satellites, where there was an existing system with a large cash flow and the development and use of satellites enabled the industry to offer more services at a lower price to the same customers.[6] Once existing customers were being more economically served, industry could search for additional customers for new services, and of course this was done and a large market developed. However, as the experience in direct-broadcast satellites indicates, not every new technology will be successful. And if no market exists, growth may be slow.

United States civilian space activities have been carried out largely under the National Aeronautics and Space Act of 1958, which provided in Section 102(a) that such activities be carried out "for the benefit of all mankind."[7] This act has been amended to give NASA the duty of commercializing space activities wherever possible.[8] A second amendment passed at the same time[9] added gaining knowledge and understanding of the Earth to NASA's mission. This is worth mentioning for two reasons—first, because the idea that we can study the Earth as a system was made believable by our space programs, especially the Apollo views of Earth, and will be realized largely through observation from space; and second, because it illustrates how Congress often balances one act (encouraging commercialization) with another (studying the Earth as a system).

II. Breadth of Interest in the Use of Space

A recent report by the Congressional Research Service shows that there are some 160 countries involved in space-related activities that do not have their own independent launch capability. In other words, these are countries that, in one way or another, and in some cases rather indirectly, gain benefits from space programs even though they are not able to put their own satellites into orbit.[10] Most of these countries make use of weather satellites or communications satellites. It should be pointed out that weather services are governmental and that in most countries the use of communications satellites is organized through that country's national government and so would not be called "commercial" in the United States. Nevertheless, the point is that there is a very broad beneficial use of space by the various nations of the Earth. This precedent represents a loss of innocence that probably cannot be recovered.

The Outer Space Treaty has been agreed to by 104 nations.[11] The wording of this treaty makes it clear that the signatories intend to use if not exploit outer space and its resources. For example, the very beginning of the treaty characterizes the signatories as "inspired by the great prospect opening up before mankind as a result of man's entry into outer space." At several places in the treaty, reference is made to the "exploration and use of outer space." Article I of the treaty states that outer space "shall be free for exploration and use by all states . . . in accordance with international law. . . ." On the other hand, Article II states that outer space "is not subject to national appropriation by claim of sovereignty by means of use or occupation, or by any other means." This provision might seem to allow commercial operations as long as there was no claim of sovereignty.

The only environmental reference is in Article IX of the treaty, which states that signatories shall "conduct exploration of [outer space including the Moon, etc.] so as to avoid their harmful contamination and also adverse changes in the environment of the Earth resulting from the introduction of extraterrestrial matter and, where necessary, shall adopt appropriate measures for this purpose." The phrase "harmful contamination" is surely vague enough to cause significant legal mischief if any enforcement actions were ever attempted under its authority.[12] Nevertheless, there seems to be general agreement that space will be used and that there should be some vague, minimal protection for celestial bodies.

A United Nations conference on the peaceful uses of outer space, Unispace 82, was held in Vienna in August 1982. Ninety-four nations sent delegations to the conference. The report of the conference describes great benefits from the use of space, but also mentions ethical and environmental concerns.[13] The report mentions "our common ancestry and innate unity, not only with each other, but with all things in the Universe." The report goes on to say that "apart from the philosophical and ethical implications of the view from space, there are also immense immediate and future benefits." This is followed by a list that includes communications satellites, remote sensing, and position location and navigation. However, the report recognizes that as of now only the developed countries with advanced technology can fully exploit the benefits of space, and it states that the international community, and in particular the developed countries, should intensify their efforts to promote the wider exploitation of space technology by developing countries. As to present space activities, the principal ethical consideration in this report seems to be to ensure equitable sharing among the nations of the Earth of the benefits of space technology with relatively little worry over environmental concerns.

The report does note that future advances in space technology may make new applications feasible, including manufacturing or processing in space: "The operational applications of these are probably many years away, but it is already time to examine their relevance and their implications. Their possible biological, ecological, and radio frequency interference impacts must therefore be studied. . . ." Even for these future activities that could be more disruptive, the principal thrust of the report is that more widely shared benefits on Earth should be a major goal and "even if this is not completely possible, an understanding of the technical, economic, social, environmental, and legal implications of likely future developments could help in achieving this desired goal."

In October of 1984, the Pontifical Academy of Sciences held a study week in the Vatican on "the impact of space exploration on mankind"[14] with participation from several nations. In discussing telecommunications satellites, the participants noted that the future evolution of those systems would inevitably raise nontechnical issues. That is, although technology will continue to evolve (and indeed because its evolution will offer more and more choices), the types of services provided will certainly be more a function of what sponsors and users want rather than what is technically achievable. Therefore, the "political, economic, technical, cultural and last, ethical factors involved" must be adequately understood and discussed.

Further discussion in the report makes it clear that the ethical factors have to do mainly with distribution of benefits on Earth. For example, there is concern that millions of people would become dependent upon satellite communications services, which would then confer a certain social responsibility on the providers of those services to make them continuously available. There is also discussion of such problems as hunger and lack of facilities for basic education and health care, which "cannot be solved through space technology alone and certainly not through the use of a uniform version of the technological configurations evolved to meet the needs of affluent developed societies." Further, a discussion of the benefits from space explorations states that "spectacular achievements of space exploration have not as yet fully contributed their potential to the reduction of poverty, of illiteracy, or to the improvement of public health among the poorer nations of the world, or to improving food production and food security."

In other words, there is in the Vatican report a strong echo of the report of the Unispace 82 conference, stating that the use of space should be for the equal benefit of all mankind. Nevertheless, as we have seen before, there is demonstrated a great faith in the potential of space utilization, and this faith is the relevant factor.

In summary, many nations around the globe have a deep faith that there are great benefits to be achieved from the exploration and use of space, and their main concern seems to be that these benefits be equitably shared here on Earth with little thought that these benefits should be delayed or differently distributed because of environmental concerns.

III. Examples of Commercial or Industrial Use of Space

The following paragraphs discuss several examples of the utilization of space for commercial or industrial purposes. Some of these examples are in operation now, some are in development, and some are only dimly visible as future possibilities. No distinction is made here between activities that might be carried out by the private sector or by government, as long as they are industrial. For example, U.S. satellite communications is a private-sector activity, but in most other countries it is an activity of the national government.

Before listing the various activities it might be help-

ful to give a scale to the economic values being discussed. A recent study of future growth prospects for
major space-related industries estimates total annual
commercial revenues to be between $16.8 and $51.3
billion by the turn of the century.[15] Although this study
is characterized by its principal author as "a realistic and
conservative assessment," the reader is advised to note
that the range of the estimate is very large.

Communications satellites, as mentioned above, are
now big business. Their use began with NASA experiments using the satellite Echo I in 1960. NASA conducted ten successful development flights between then
and 1974. NASA's latest research program, the Advanced Communications Technology Satellite, known as
ACTS, is being developed for launch in 1989. In addition, NASA has its own operational Tracking and Data
Relay Satellite System (TDRSS), which provides communications for NASA scientific satellites and the Space
Shuttle and is planned to be able to serve commercial
operations in space as well. During the time that satellite
communications have been in operation, the capacity of
a single satellite has gone up more than 50 times, while
the annual cost of operating a standard communications
circuit has been reduced by a factor of 50.[16]

This is a healthy industry. For example, the most
recent figures show that about $2 billion worth of U.S.-
produced satellite-communications ground systems
were shipped in 1984, and service revenues for the seven
U.S. common carriers were $555 million in 1984. In
addition, the Communications Satellite Corporation
(COMSAT) earned about $291 million in operating
revenues in 1983 from communications to and from the
United States.[17] Currently, COMSAT has a monopoly on
this international service, but there are efforts by other
companies to enter this field. Some 109 nations are

members of the International Telecommunications Satellite Organization and seven nations have their own domestic communications satellites.[18]

A significant issue facing the communications-satellite industry is the emerging congestion of the geostationary arc. The geostationary arc is an imaginary circle in space above the Earth's equator. A satellite placed in orbit along this arc will appear to remain motionless above a given point on the Earth (actually a point on the Equator) because in such an orbit the satellite goes around the Earth in exactly 24 hours, that is, it rotates with the Earth. This arc is becoming crowded, not because the satellites are near to bumping into one another but because of radio interference between adjacent satellites. There needs to be about a 2-degree angular spacing between satellites in order to avoid such radio interference.[19] Closer spacing could be achieved, but this would necessitate the use of larger antennas and make costs significantly higher.

At this point, it is also appropriate to mention the crowding of the radio-frequency spectrum. Each communications channel operating in a given region must use a different radio frequency to avoid interference. If large amounts of information are to be transmitted, the transmitting channel must actually use a significant range of frequencies—called a band width—which range is determined ultimately by basic laws of physics. Because of the demand for more and more information-transmission capacity, both the radio-frequency spectrum and the geostationary arc are filling up, and therefore there is some contention about the assignment of slots in this arc and in the frequency spectrum.[20]

Damage to solar photovoltaic cells by natural radiation sets an upper limit to the lifetimes of communications satellites using today's technologies. Since space debris is addressed in another paper, it is only noted here that there are provisions for pushing failed satellites out of this orbit to make room for replacements.

Governance of satellite communications occurs through the International Telecommunications Union, a United Nations agency with 157 members.[21] Periodic meetings, called World Administrative Radio Conferences (WARC), make the operating rules on the basis of one nation, one vote and consensus. That is, although each nation is allowed one vote when issues must be resolved by vote, whenever possible positions are reached by a general consensus of all nations. As long as the principle of consensus prevails, this allows one nation to have a virtual veto. In early 1986 there will be a "Space WARC" to consider satellite-communications issues, particularly congestion of the geostationary arc.

The question of how to deal with congestion of the geostationary arc has for the most part polarized around two positions that are referred to as rational planning versus first come, first served. The latter process is the one in operation now, and as the phrase suggests, the nation first able to put a satellite into a slot is given that slot for the lifetime of that satellite. There is no guarantee that that slot will be again available to that nation when the satellite originally occupying it fails. Rational planning refers to methods that would guarantee all countries access to the geostationary arc, even if they do not have a satellite to launch. The general position taken by the United States and other advanced nations is that the first come, first serve principle has been adequate in the past and that technological development will solve any problems arising in the future. Up to now there have always been enough slots for everyone, but extrapolation of trends indicates that all slots will soon be filled unless new technology is developed.

The principal federal responsibility for developing satellite technology lies with NASA. At present, NASA has one satellite-communications flight program in development: the Advanced Communications Technology Satellite (ACTS) mentioned above. NASA also conducts some research on components for space-communications systems, for example, antennas and high-reliability amplifiers. The new technologies on the ACTS satellite will, if successful, help relieve some of the pressure on the frequency spectrum. However, these technologies are probably too advanced to be of much use in developing countries. Such technology will therefore help the United States, Europe, and Japan. However, it should be noted that just the portions of the geostationary arc that serve the United States and Europe are the most congested at present.

Other issues in the international governance of satellite communications have to do with prior consent and sovereignty over the geostationary arc. Prior consent refers to the desire of countries on Earth to be able to control signals broadcast into their territory from space. Many countries are worried about the cultural shock that could occur if programs intended for the United States were received in their areas. The sovereignty issue arises because several equatorial countries have claimed that their territory (or air space) extends into space to include the geostationary arc. It should be pointed out that these claims appear contrary to the Outer Space Treaty.

In summary, communications satellites represent large investments and cash flows even if not always commercial operations. There is a quasi-legal system, the International Telecommunications Union, for resolving conflicts and achieving a balance of interests. So far, no country has been denied access to space communications because of orbital crowding.

Two additional large operational activities in space are represented by weather satellites and navigation satellites. Weather satellites—called metsats—have been operational since 1964. The United States normally has two of these in polar orbit and two in geostationary orbit. Those in polar orbit are timed so that they always cross over a given point on the equator at the same time of day, giving consistency to the data. These satellites look down at the Earth to generate data on cloud cover, temperature, and water-vapor density and make a significant contribution to our ability to forecast the weather. The data that U.S. satellites generate is broadcast directly from the satellites to the ground and anyone with the proper equipment can receive it. In fact, it is received by a great many nations. This forms the basis for a system of free international exchange of weather data in which other countries get U.S. satellite data and the United States gets the ground-observation data that it needs for its various worldwide operations. There is, therefore, mutual benefit.

Navigation satellites can be used with relatively simple equipment to find one's position on the Earth to within about 100 meters horizontally and about 1,000 meters vertically (that is, in altitude). The first Navstar satellite—the name of the U.S. satellites—was launched in 1978, and several more will be launched until the government constellation is complete in 1988. The total system of all the satellites is called the Global Positioning System. Such a system obviously has great military utility but is also very useful in the civilian sphere. Benefits to maritime navigation are obvious, but there are many other potential uses, such as keeping track of railroad cars. A previous paper has described efforts to launch a system that would provide similar services on a commercial basis.

Both the metsats and the Global Positioning System are run by the government, but they could in principle be private and commercial. Congress has passed legislation prohibiting commercialization of U.S. metsats.[22]

A use of space that has not really become fully operational is civilian remote sensing of the surface of the Earth. This technology can be used to generate data about the Earth's surface, which in turn is used for mineral prospecting, for agricultural surveys and crop monitoring, for planning major construction projects such as pipelines, and for environmental monitoring and research. This technology has not yet been significantly used for human or animal disease control, although it has been used for surveying plant diseases. It has recently been used for fire-fighting purposes: the infrared sensors on a U.S. satellite were used to locate hot-spots despite a very thick blanket of smoke that was preventing firefighters from knowing where to attack the fire. There is currently in planning a large research program called the International Geosphere/Biosphere Program, which will attempt to study the Earth as a system in order to understand how our fundamental life-support system changes due both to natural and man-made causes. This program, when it gets underway, will undoubtedly use much data generated by remote sensing of the Earth from space.[23]

In the United States, land remote sensing is in the process of becoming a commercial operation. Presently, as in the past, all the operations are conducted by the government, but under legislation passed on July 17, 1984, the government systems, called Landsat, can be transferred to the private sector for commercial operation.[24] Congress acted after the administration decided to end federal support for the Landsat program and either let the system die or commercialize it. Given the stringent budget situation in which the United States now finds itself, the Congress thought it wiser to see if the system could be supported by commercial sales of data rather than to attempt to appropriate funds for its operation over the opposition of the administration. The new legislation provides a framework for the transfer, provides a certain amount of financial aid in the early period of private operation, and provides for regulation of private operators. Another important aspect of this legislation is that it directs the Secretary of Commerce (who has overall responsibility) to maintain an archival set of data for use in environmental monitoring. Finally, this legislation covers remote sensing of the oceans as well as of the land surfaces of the Earth.

This legislation was drafted with certain fairness principles in mind. First, the legislation would attempt to protect existing users of Landsat data—who have made an investment in systems for analyzing the data—by providing for data continuity under commercialization. Second, it would protect foreign users of Landsat data during a transition period so that they could work out a viable arrangement with the new commercial operators. Third, it would allow competition between operators of commercial remote-sensing systems; that is, there would be no permanent monopoly.[25] Finally, the legislation for the first time put into statute the principle of nondiscriminatory data access under which the United States has always operated its own federal land remote-sensing systems. Under this principle, data must be made available to all potential buyers on the same terms. Nondiscriminatory data access strikes a balance between those who would not allow their territory to be sensed by any satellite without their prior consent and those individuals who believe that anyone with the funds to build and launch a satellite should be able to take data anywhere on Earth and do anything with it. In other words, nondiscriminatory data access mediates between those who would severely restrict remote sensing and those who would prefer no restrictions.

As embodied in P.L. 98–365 this is a very important principle and therefore should be discussed at some length. Section 601 of the bill provides that the remote-sensing data "shall be made available to users on a nondiscriminatory basis. . . ." What does "on a nondiscriminatory basis" mean with respect to commercial data sales? Very simply, it means that any operator of a land remote-sensing system must make data available to everyone on the same public terms. The operator cannot choose customers or favor one over another. Why was this nondiscriminatory policy written into the legislation?

First, nondiscriminatory data access (NDA) maintains many of the "public good" aspects of remote sensing. It could be argued that a space remote-sensing system should not be commercialized because it represents a public good. Indeed, this was part of the reason that commercialization of weather satellites was prohibited in Title VII of the same legislation.[26] Having system operators make all data available on a nondiscriminatory basis restricts them to operating something like a common carrier in transportation.

NDA tends to promote the broadest use of the data. If NDA were not mandated the system operator would be able to auction the data to the highest bidder for exclusive use, which of course would amount to very discriminatory selling. In other words exclusivity might command a high price. If the operator is not allowed to do this—that is, sell the data to just one person—then market considerations would tend to encourage the operator both to sell broadly and to structure marketing efforts to reach as many customers as possible.[27] That is, in order to maximize profits, operators would have to generate new markets, new applications, and new customers. NDA would also conform remote-sensing policy to the basic policy in the National Aeronautics and Space Act of 1958, which says that activities in space should be devoted to peaceful purposes for the benefit of mankind.

NDA puts the United States in a favorable position *vis à vis* the many countries who argue that no remote sensing should take place without the prior consent of the sensed country. At the Unispace 82 conference in Vienna discussed above, the United States was one of a very small number of countries wishing to maintain the "open skies" policy[28] that allows one nation's satellite to sense any other nation without prior consent. A corollary of the open skies policy that has been followed by the United States is that the data taken by such a satellite are made available to everyone on a nondiscriminatory basis. It seems clear that it is not in the interest of the United States to agree to a prior-consent regime, and therefore it would seem prudent to maintain the nondiscriminatory access aspect of the open skies policy as a balancing consideration. Indeed, the head of the United States delegation at the Unispace conference made a particular point of the broad availability of Landsat data —the fact that these data are "accessible to every country."[29] The formal National Paper of the United States filed at Unispace 82 made the same point:

> The U.S. supports public nondiscriminatory dissemination of remote sensing data from Landsat and U.S. meteorological satellites. In addition, the U.S. has encouraged open availability of such data through its international cooperative programs. These policies

have already led to innumerable beneficial applications of remote sensing worldwide. Open availability
of these basic data has fostered effective application of
remote sensing to such important problems as deser-
tification, food and fiber production, and flooding and
water pollution, all of which transcend national
boundaries.[30]

The same point was made in the 1982 report on
Science, Technology and American Diplomacy in which
the following appears:

> In remote sensing, the readily available products of
> the United States meteorological and land satellites
> are used routinely by the world community. The result
> has been a large measure of goodwill in support of our
> position in the U.N. and other international fora.[31]

NDA conforms with the international commitments
of the United States. For example, Article I of the Outer
Space Treaty states: ". . . the . . . use of outer space
. . . shall be carried out for the benefit and in the interests
of all countries irrespective of their degree of economic
or scientific development and shall be the province of all
mankind." Similarly, at the conclusion of the 1983 Wil-
liamsburg economic summit, a statement was issued
which said that "economic summit members support the
need to assure timely public non-discriminatory data dis-
semination and seek continued availability of satellite
data."[32] NDA apparently does not foreclose significant
commercial opportunities. Only one firm interested in
operating a commercial land remote-sensing system has
maintained that there is a commercial need for exclusive
data rights,[33] while other interested parties have testified
that they could operate successfully under a policy of
nondiscriminatory data access.[34] Indeed there is the pos-

sibility that were the United States to adopt a policy of data exclusivity, negative foreign reactions could close off some foreign markets, not only for data sales, but for other space-related activities.

NDA protects "value-added" firms, the real developers of the market, from the threat of unfair data-marketing practices by a system operator. Data generated from satellites becomes truly valuable only when it is operated on by trained analysts using computers and scientific knowledge. In doing this the value-added industry turns a mass of raw data into information products that are useful, valuable, and highly proprietary. These are the industries that will develop new markets for Landsat data, by seeking potential users and tailoring information products for their use. Clearly, one should not allow a system operator to discourage this industry. A particular danger would arise if a system operator set up a value-adding activity and discriminated against other competing independent firms.

The point of this rather extended discussion is that consideration went into writing legislation that balances conflicting interests and ensures that a commercial remote-sensing operation will be fair.

While land remote sensing has been in an operational status for several years and is only haltingly moving toward commercial operation, the manufacturing or processing of materials in space is moving rapidly toward both commercialization and operational status at the same pace.

At least into the immediate future, space operations will be expensive, and, therefore, any processing in space will have to contribute greatly to the value of the material being processed. For this reason only materials that are badly needed or commercially very useful on Earth will be considered. Two classes of materials immediately come to mind—pharmaceuticals and semi-conductor crystals used for electronics products, proba-bly for use in the defense industry. Because of the high cost of space transportation, only rather small amounts of material can be processed economically, and there-fore it is unlikely that a semiconductor material would be processed in space for consumer electronics. Phar-maceuticals, on the other hand, are sometimes effective in microgram quantities, and therefore relatively small amounts of material could be commercially useful. It should be noted that in the case of both pharmaceuticals and semiconductors a market already exists, and proc-essing in space would introduce an improved or cheaper product into that market.

The two aspects of the space environment often mentioned as relevant to commercial use are the effec-tive absence of weight, that is, weightlessness, and the high vacuum[35] available in space. Processes that involve heating but that are degraded by the thermal convec-tion resulting from gravitational forces often can be improved in space because the weightless state leads to an absence of convection. In other words, the con-vective mixing that can degrade a separation process or induce inhomogeneities in a crystal is absent in space processing.

The process moving most rapidly toward commer-cialization is continuous-flow electrophoresis, which is being developed by the McDonnell-Douglas Aircraft Corporation. Very simply, this process uses an electric field to separate various molecules according to their response to this field. The separatory forces become stronger as the electric field is increased. Unfortunately, a large electric field induces heating in the material, and this causes convection that tends to remix it, that is, to undo or limit the separation. Therefore, on Earth, in the presence of gravity, there is a limit to the efficacy of this separation method. In space, much better separation can be achieved, perhaps 500 or even 1,000 times better. This kind of ratio is needed to make the high cost of space processing commercially worthwhile.

Using the weightlessness of orbital flight would seem to have no direct environmental impact, but use of the vacuum of space could have an impact. On the one hand, one might use the high vacuum of space merely to achieve ultraclean conditions, for example, to be able to clean a substrate in order to deposit a very pure thin film on it. This type of use might have no significant environmental impact because only small amounts of material would be involved. Another use of the high vacuum of space might be to evaporate solvents used in processing. Such a use could cause problems if large volumes of solvent were routinely evaporated in the same orbit. Clouds of such solvents as acetone or methyl alcohol could be generated that might lead to problems for others hoping to use the same region of space as a very clean place. The photochemical possibilities are also very interesting because there are more high-energy photons in space than on Earth, although of course the densities of the chemicals present would be very low.

Even if large amounts of organic solvents were evaporated, the low densities would probably preclude the formation of significant photochemical space smog by reaction among effluents, but the presence of such industrial effluents, especially after their irradiation by sunlight not filtered by the atmosphere, might present a problem to astronomers who count on the high vacuum of space to keep optical components clean.

Another commercial use of space already underway —but on such a small scale that it is probably just a hint of what we will see in the future—is the conducting of experimental research in space—that is, using weight-lessness to conduct experiments impossible on Earth, with the intent of using on Earth the understanding gained thereby. Certainly, the United States is planning for the space station to be used for this purpose. Many experiments in outer space probably will take advantage of the weightless conditions, but there might also be a number of experiments in Earth observation.

An interesting question not yet totally resolved is how one would assign patents for inventions made in outer space. NASA has submitted legislation that would provide that any invention made in outer space on a space vehicle under the jurisdiction or control of the United States would be considered as made in the United States for purposes of patent-law jurisdiction. The House Committee on Science and Technology gave its approval to this legislation,[36] but the House Judiciary Committee, which has jurisdiction in the House of Representatives over certain aspects of patent law, raised questions on exactly how this provision would interact with other parts of the patent legislation. Because of this, the proposal was not enacted, but it may be taken up again after the problems are worked out. Therefore, legislation having this effect is likely to become United States law, in which case it would seem that any invention made on the U.S. space station would be subject to U.S. patent law.

Further into the future, perhaps the very distant future, is commercial utilization of extraterrestrial resources, which means mining the Moon, asteroids, and other planets. In 1983, a subgroup of the NASA Advisory Council—the Solar System Exploration Committee (SSEC)—reported on goals for planetary exploration through the year 2000.[37] The SSEC identified as a new goal for the planetary programs "the survey of resources available in near-Earth space." They went on to say "it is essential that the relevant research be done before actual use of such resources can be contemplated." The SSEC has continued its work to give more specificity to its long-range recommendations. Thus, it has recently stated that research on the availability of near-Earth resources offers the following potential benefits: "determination of the nature and availability of near-Earth resources for major future space activities"; "test of feasible extraction and processing techniques"; and "realistic data for economic and planning models." The SSEC has also recommended "bench test studies of extraction processing."[38]

The SSEC is a very responsible part of NASA's scientific advisory system, and therefore one must consider the possibility of NASA proceeding matter of factly to the realization of these recommendations—that is, the opening of mines on the Moon and the asteroids.

A more detailed but perhaps also more uncertain look at commercial use of space involving exploitation of extraterrestrial resources is contained in the proceedings of a NASA conference on advanced automation for space missions.[39] The conference discussed two activities of interest here. The first one is a space manufacturing facility, which would be in low Earth orbit, would be largely automated, and would use nonterrestrial materials to a greater and greater extent until it was essentially independent of Earth resources. "Given a supply of sufficiently inexpensive nonterrestrial materials, SMF [space manufacturing facility] output could be returned to Earth directly in the form of useful commercial products or indirectly in the form of solar power generation or satellite servicing." The SMF could use "processes unsuitable, unsafe, or otherwise undesirable for application on Earth." The NASA report states that "the implications of a growing SMF are unquestionably complex and, to some degree, unforeseeable." Nevertheless some rather straightforward statements are made, including the following: "The direct environmental impact of the SMF will be significant and positive, mostly because of the relief it will provide from the twin pressures of resource exhaustion and industrial pollution. Many processes now conducted in Earth-based laboratories and factories which pose health hazards could be transferred to the SMF." Again, "environmental benefits of placing the energy plant in space are manifold: There would be no danger from natural disaster such as earthquakes, no thermal or particulate pollution, and no risk of explosions or other failures which might conceivably cause harm to human populations . . . on the negative side must be weighed the possibility of leakage of microwave transmissions . . . still, it is clear that SPS technology has the potential to relieve much of the current global energy shortage."

Finally, the NASA report suggests that a space manufacturing facility would have major social and philosophical benefits. The report states that "the spirit of the American people has taken an introspective turn. Many are no longer convinced that unexplored horizons still exist. Predictions of global calamity are commonplace . . . however, establishing an SMF opens new horizons with the recognition that planet Earth is just one potential source of matter and energy. Recognition of the availability of lunar and asteroidal materials and the abundant energy of the Sun can revitalize the traditional American belief in growth as a positive good and can generate a new spirit of adventure and optimism. It is unnecessary to speculate on the directions of growth and its various dimensions because it is clear that American society would continue its historic tradition of exploring new horizons and avoiding stagnation in an ever-changing Universe." In other words, manifest destiny can be resurrected. Let me quote a little more on the putative social benefits of a space manufacturing facility: "On a more fundamental level, the proposed mission is species-survival oriented. Earth might at any time become suddenly uninhabitable through global war, disease, pollution or other man-made or natural catastrophies. A recent study has shown that an asteroid collision with Earth could virtually turn off photosynthesis for up to five years . . . the proposed mission assures the continued survival of the human species by providing an extraterrestrial refuge for mankind. An SMF would stand as constant proof that the fate of all humanity is not inextricably tied to the ultimate fate of Earth."

These words generate several reactions. On the one hand, their naïveté is charming. They recall the *New Yorker* cartoon by James Thurber in which a host—one who today would be called an arrived "yuppie"—is serving wine to his dinner guests. He says, "It's a naïve little wine, but I think you'll be amused by its impertinence." Optimism is good; if we don't have some optimism we will spiral downward in negativism. On the other hand, the report is striking in its naïveté. Its authors seem totally oblivious of the fact that we already have a perfectly good space manufacturing facility, one to which we are well adapted. It is called Earth, and we could, if we chose, take care of it. Thus, the authors completely ignore the basic question: If we can't learn how to take care of Earth, then how can we learn how to take care of a space manufacturing facility in orbit around Earth?

The second activity that the NASA conference considered was a "self-replicating lunar factory." The argument is that as terrestrial resources are consumed, the development of an industrial capacity on the Moon becomes increasingly desirable. "Given the expense and danger associated with the use of human workers in such a remote location, the production environment of a lunar manufacturing facility (LMF) should be automated to the highest degree feasible." The conference, however, saw a problem in that such facilities would wear out and become obsolete. Therefore, it was proposed that these facilities would be self-replicating. That is, the LMF would be "capable of constructing duplicates of itself, which would themselves be capable of further replication." According to the NASA report, this opens great possibilities. They see that "the initial LMF may be viewed as the first step in a demonstration-development scenario leading to an indefinite process of automated exploration and utilization of nonterrestrial resources." These replicating factories would be able to make "space probes, planetary landers, and transportable 'seed' factories for siting on the surfaces of other worlds." There is more than a suggestion that interstellar exploration could be carried out on a grand scale by these automatons. This leads one to question whether such activities would qualify as space exploration. From the point of view that "the most fundamental role for human beings in space is, simply, to be there,"[40] the answer would be negative. One could ask whether or not turning such automatons loose into space would not amount to the most pungent example of mindless progress ever envisioned. To the credit of writers of this report, they do acknowledge that the use of such self-replicating systems *on Earth* would pose "many problems." They say "a compact, freely replicating system released on the surface of the Earth potentially could compete with humans for resources such as living space and energy. It could also smother us in its waste products." However, we are assured that there is nothing to worry about, because when these machines usher in the age of plenty, "human society will be sufficiently wealthy to regard environmental integrity and beauty as indispensable outputs of any manufacturing system. These functions may be designed into machines as a matter of course." If this means that the use of such SRS will be postponed until we fully understand how the Earth functions as a living system, then by that time humans also should have made a great deal of social progress and may even be able to deal with the more difficult problems of how humans will interact with such machines and with each other. In other words, the problem is not achieving sufficient wealth, rather sufficient wisdom.

The main point of discussing the SMF and LMF at such length is to illustrate how easy it is to get carried away with technology and to forget to ask such basic questions as these: Why are we doing this? What is the purpose of sending robots churning through the solar system? How is this related to human values?

In the nearer term there is the space station that NASA is about to begin constructing. This will be a general-purpose facility in near-Earth orbit, and one of its major functions will be to service satellites. For example, a communications satellite with a failed component could be brought to the station and that component replaced or repaired, which might be considerably less expensive than repairing the satellite on Earth and returning it to space or replacing it. At first, one would not expect this facility to generate large additional amounts of space activity, but merely to support activities and equipment already planned. However, if the ability to service satellites in space proves to be a large economic benefit, then there might be positive feedback leading to greater and greater space activity. In any event, operation of the space station should provide useful experience and perhaps some of the wisdom we will need for future activities.

There has already been a proposal that the Space Shuttle external tanks be put into orbit by the federal government and treated as federal land.[41] These external tanks would be modified to be habitable, and some would be preserved by the federal government as national parks. Some of the external tanks might be used as vacation lodges.[42] Others might be made available to individuals or organizations proposing beneficial uses of them. For example, a consortium of universities might propose to develop an external tank as an orbiting laboratory and receive the grant of a tank from the federal government for this purpose. In other words, the concept of a space station must be considered very broadly and could lead to commercial and other uses that we do not presently foresee.

There is one more NASA activity that is not at all commercial but may be very important in the long run. That is the program called Search For Extraterrestrial Intelligence (SETI). In NASA's visits to the planets, no life has been found. Similarly, its SETI radio survey so far has found no life elsewhere in the universe. However, the human aspiration driving this search for intelligence and indeed for life on other worlds is relevant to our consideration of an environmental ethic. That is, we seem to want to find life elsewhere in the universe.

IV. An Environmental Ethic for Space?

Let me now comment on the problem of developing an environmental ethic for space exploration and exploitation. In *A Sand County Almanac*, Aldo Leopold develops a very persuasive argument for a land ethic as a product of social evolution. He argues that when we have a working land ethic, we will no longer be man the conqueror of our world, but man "the biotic citizen." We will not use science as the sharpener of our sword but science as "the searchlight on [our] universe." We will no longer see land as "the slave and servant" but land as "the collective organism."[43] It seems to me that two things are necessary for this particular land ethic: first, life, and second, interaction or interdependence. In other words, it is the interaction or interdependence of all life on Earth that leads us to our environmental ethic, that is, to a way of deciding between right and wrong. Leopold says, "A thing is right when it tends to preserve the integrity, stability, and beauty of the biotic community. It is wrong when it tends otherwise." A living planet like Earth can adjust to man's interferences; a new stability and even beauty may be achieved after a disturbance. One wonders whether the same type of recovery can occur on lifeless planets or asteroids?

Writings on space law have dealt with the space environment, but typically these writings are legalistic in nature and devoid of ethical considerations. The type of legalisms that occur are exemplified by the following statement: "A working group of experts was established with the resulting report concluding that nuclear power could be used safely in outer space, providing that all the necessary safety requirements were met."[44] The same paper indicates a typical lack of consideration of ethical values in the following sentence: "The determination of 'harmful contamination' or the potential of same should be a matter of fact, not law or political philosophy." Of course, the determination of "harmful contamination" has to be first a matter of values—the opposite of facts.

Liability is treated in the literature of space law because the Outer Space Treaty states that nations will be liable for damage caused by activities they conduct in space.[45] Environmental damage could perhaps lead to some kind of liability if there were agreement as to what constitutes environmental damage. Menter[46] in a discussion of the legal implications of commercial utilization of space raises an interesting point, especially in light of our earlier discussion of the self-replicating facilities which contained a suggestion that robots could be designed with an environmental conscience. Menter states, "Automation is expected to be pushed to the extremes of liability. . . ." Presumably, this would be done in order to limit liability claims against the robots.

From a brief survey of the legal literature, it is clear that while there has been some legal thought about environmental problems in space, there seems to be virtually no ethical framework.

Leonard David has made several assertions about environmental ethics. Referring to the preservation of wilderness areas on Earth, he states that "the environmental protection of certain areas of Earth represents an attitude that should be reflected in space exploration."[47] It seems that at the present time this position can be morally maintained, even though some might see it as mindless opposition to progress. Indeed, in contrast to the sort of progress represented if not advocated by the NASA report on self-replicating facilities, David's position seems quite reasonable. Nevertheless, without life in space, it is not clear how the "certain areas" would be determined, unless the criteria were based purely on human aesthetics.

Another approach is taken by David Thompson, who suggests that "the immediate goal of additional research should be formulation of concepts about what resources in Outer Space need conservation and how best to proceed."[48] Thompson seems to be hoping for ethical guidance based on scientific research, although a literal reading of the quoted statement does not yield that interpretation. But scientific research can only answer scientific questions. The point is that research can show us how to implement an ethic but cannot make the fundamental decisions necessary to establish an ethic.

A most cynical approach to an ethical basis for space exploration and utilization is presented by Oberg who says, "Now what right does humanity have to take possession of other worlds? . . . Human history demonstrates that people do what suits them and seek rationalization afterwards. There is no reason to suspect that terraforming will be any different, or that the lack of a good answer to this question will have the slightest impact on what people choose to do on other planets. If terraforming becomes part of our future, justifications will be found."[49] While Oberg may be right, there remains a need to derive an environmental ethic from basic human values.

At this point, it is worth mentioning that many have maintained that resources in outer space should be considered part of "the common heritage of mankind," just as resources on the seabed are now thought to be.[50] One must question the fate of this position should NASA's search for extraterrestrial intelligence uncover other intelligence, presumably not "mankind."[51]

V. Conclusions

I must confess that I had not given serious thought to this subject until asked to write this paper. Nevertheless, I believe that we need a way to structure right and wrong outside of and beyond Earth. Of course, this structure will ultimately be based on human values that are not necessarily logically derived, but I believe that we cannot simply extrapolate concepts derived from the specific conditions of Earth. For example, in my opinion, the concept of wilderness implies something wild, and therefore something alive. I suggest that we now do not have a good ethical basis for space exploration and that the creation of one will be a major step forward for our species because it will be based on widely shared human values, not mere assumptions. We need an ethic that will have the political toughness to convince all the nations of the Earth of its correctness. It will define right and wrong for activities outside Earth. This will be very difficult because we currently agree on very few things here on Earth, and most nations are worried only about getting their share of the benefits of space, not about costs. But we have to begin. As Leopold has suggested, development and acceptance of such an ethic will be further human evolution.

Goedel's Proof seems always to arise when the human condition is considered. Goedel, a mathematician, proved an astounding mathematical theorem. He proved that if one takes a set of mathematical axioms, within that set of axioms there are theorems that are true but cannot be rigorously, logically proved starting only with the given axioms. In order to prove these theorems, one must add another axiom to the original set. What you find then is that this new, enlarged set of axioms will contain new theorems that again are true but cannot be proven. Perhaps we are in a situation like that right now. Perhaps we perceive environmental truths beyond Earth that cannot be proved. Perhaps when we add another axiom, an environmental ethic for extraterrestrial space, we will have taken an evolutionary step and will then be able to go on to an even higher level of truth.

Notes

1. For example, the environmental impact of rocket exhaust gases could be regulated under the Clean Air Act.

2. David Osborne, "Business in Space," *Atlantic* 255, no. 5 (May 1985): 45ff.

3. See, for example, "Western Union Drops Out of DBS," *Satellite News* 7, no. 29 (16 July 1984): 3; and also "British Broadcasters Bail Out of DBS: Plan Independent Study Alternative," *Satellite Week* 7, no. 25 (24 June 1985): 2.

4. See, for example, the testimony of Norman H. Macleod (p. 123) and Michel T. Halbouty (p. 206) in "Civil Land Remote Sensing Systems," Joint Hearings, Committee on Science and Technology, U.S. House of Representatives, and Committee on Commerce, Science and Transportation, United States Senate, 97th Congress, 22–23 July 1981, serial no. 40, U.S. Government Printing Office, Washington, D.C.

5. See, for example, the testimony of Malcolm Baldridge, Secretary of Commerce (p. 14), Richard A. Frank (p. 468), and Dr. Thomas Lillesand (p. 496) in "The Commercialization of Meteorological and Land Remote-Sensing Satellites," Hearing, Committee on Science and Technology, U.S. House of Representatives, 98th Congress, 14 April; 21, 28 June; 14, 21 July; 8–9 November 1983, serial no. 53, U.S. Government Printing Office, Washington, D.C. Hereafter referred to as "Landsat Hearing."

6. See, for example, Delbert D. Smith, *Communication via Satellite: A Vision in Retrospect* (Boston: A.S. Sijthoff, 1976).

7. Public Law 85–568, 42 U.S.C. 2451 et seq.

8. The amendment is in section 109 (a) of Public Law 98–361, the National Aeronautics and Space Administration Authorization Act, 1985, 98 STAT. 422.

9. Ibid., section 109 (b).

10. Patricia E. Humphlett, "Space Activities of the Non-Launching Countries," Congressional Research Service, Report No. 85–72, SPR, March 1985.

11. This treaty, whose full name is the "Treaty on Principles Governing the Activities of States in the Exploration and Use of Outer Space, Including the Moon and Other Celestial Bodies," is reprinted with a discussion in *United States Civilian Space Programs, 1958–1978*, Report for the Committee on Science and Technology, U.S. House of Representatives, 97th Congress, serial D, vol. 1, January 1981.

12. In fact it would seem to allow contamination as long as it is not "harmful," and harmful is not defined.

13. The report of the conference is printed in "Unispace 82," Report and Hearing, Committee on Science and Technology, U.S. House of Representatives, 97th Congress, no. 160, July 1982. Hereafter referred to as "Unispace Hearing."

14. "Study Week: The Impact of Space Exploration on Mankind," October 1–5, 1984, Pontifical Academy of Science, Vatican City, 1985.

15. See the testimony of Mark R. Oderman, Center for Space Policy, Inc., Cambridge, Mass., at Hearings on Space Commercialization, Subcommittee on Space Science and Applications, Committee on Science and Technology, U.S. House of Representatives, 18 June 1985, in press.

16. United States Civilian Space Programs, vol. 2, Applications Satellites, Congressional Research Service Report prepared for the Committee on Science and Technology, U.S. House of Representatives, 98th Congress, serial M, May 1983, U.S. Government Printing Office, Washington, D.C.

17. Private communication, P.E. Humphlett.

18. See note 11.

19. This would leave the satellites about 1,000 miles apart along the orbital arc.

20. A discussion of the use and governance of the geostationary orbit can be found in Patricia E. Humphlett, "Use of Geostationary Satellite Orbit," *Congressional Research Service Review* 6, no. 6 (June 1985).

21. P.E. Humphlett, "Uses of the Geostationary Orbit and U.S. Participation in the 1985 World Administrative Radio Conference," Report no. 85–105 SPR, Congressional Research Service, 1 May 1985.

22. Title VII of Public Law 98–365, "The Land Remote-Sensing Commercialization Act of 1984."

23. See testimony of Dr. John A. Eddy in "1985 NASA Authorization," Hearings, Subcommittee on Space Science and Applications, U.S. House of Representatives, February and March 1984, serial no. 84, vol. 2, U.S. Government Printing Office, Washington, D.C.

24. Public Law 98–365, "The Land Remote-Sensing Commercialization Act of 1984."

25. During a six-year transition period, there is provision for limited federal aid to one commercial operator, which probably would create a monopoly *de facto*, but this aid would end, leaving opportunity for other firms to operate on an equal basis.

26. See p. 29 of "Land Remote-Sensing Commercialization Act of 1984," U.S. House of Representatives Report 98–647, 3 April 1984.

27. That is, if system operators cannot sell data on an exclusive basis to one buyer, then they will probably not be able to command high prices and will therefore go to a high-volume, low-price strategy. NDA does not necessarily preclude exclusive data sales, but makes them difficult. It might be possible to achieve NDA and exclusivity by means of a prospective offering of future data in which nondiscrimination is achieved by advertising and offering the data prior to their generation. In any case, exclusivity may be relatively unimportant with regard to raw data, because most value is added, and the results become proprietary, when the raw data are analyzed and turned into targeted information products. In addition, most systems pass again and again over the same part of Earth, so any area would be sensed many times.

28. Unispace hearing, p. xlv, 346ff., 363ff., 380ff.

29. Unispace hearing, p. lxxvii.

30. Unispace hearings, p. 691.

31. "Science, Technology, and American Diplomacy 1983," Joint Committee Print, Committee on Science and Technology, U.S. House of Representatives, 98th Congress, serial no. W, U.S. Government Printing Office, Washington, D.C.

32. As reported in *New York Times*, 31 May 1983.

33. See the testimony of Klaus P. Heiss, p. 121, in "The Land Remote-Sensing Commercialization Act of 1984—H.R. 4836 and H.R. 5155," Hearings, Committee on Science and Technology, U.S. House of Representatives, 98th Congress, 6 March 1984, no. 74, U.S. Government Printing Office, Washington,

D.C. Hereafter referred to as "Landsat Hearings." See also *Science* 227, 8 February 1985, p. 617.

34. See testimony of D.K. Slayton, p. 650ff., C.A. Schmidt, p. 692ff. in the "Landsat Hearings."

35. The term *high vacuum* refers to a very low density of atmosphere. At a reasonable low-Earth orbit altitude of 500 kilometers, the molecular atmospheric density is roughly 0.0000001 of that at the surface of the Earth.

36. House Report 99–32, "Authorizing Appropriations to the National Aeronautics and Space Administration for Fiscal Year 1986," 99th Congress, 1st Session, 28 March 1985, p. 4.

37. *Planetary Exploration Through Year 2000: A Core Program,* NASA Advisory Council, Solar System Exploration Committee (Washington, D.C.: NASA, 1983).

38. Briefing to the NASA Advisory Council by the SSEC, 30 April 1985.

39. *Advanced Automation for Space Missions,* NASA Conference Publication 2255 (Washington, D.C.: NASA Scientific and Technical Information Branch, 1982). Proceedings of a conference held at the University of Santa Clara, Santa Clara, California, 23 June–29 August 1980. See also James E. Long and Timothy J. Healy, "Advanced Automation for Space Missions, Technical Summary," University of Santa Clara, Santa Clara, California, 15 September 1980.

40. T.F. Rogers, "The Near-Term Role of Human Beings in Space Exploration," preprint of paper offered at the 25 May 1982 meeting of the American Institute of Aeronautics and Astronautics in Baltimore, Md.

41. T.F. Rogers, A "Space Phoenix Program," paper delivered at the 1985 annual meeting of the American Institute of Aeronautics and Astronautics, Washington, D.C., 11 April 1985. Subsequently the same concept was published in "Housesteading the New Frontier," T.F. Rogers, *Space World,* June 1985, p. 4.

42. T.F. Rogers, "Short Visits to Space by the General Public," paper presented at the Fourth Annual Space Development Conference, Washington, D.C., 28 April 1985.

43. Reprinted in *Wilderness,* Spring 1985, p. 14.

44. A.L. Moore and J.B. Lephart, "Manipulation and Modification of the Outer Space Environment: International and Legal Considerations," *Proceedings of the 25th Colloquium on the Law of Outer Space,*

International Institute of Space Law of the International Astronautical Federation, 1982, Paris, France, 82–IISL–06.

45. K.H. Bockstiegel, "Legal Aspects of Space Activities by Private Enterprises," *Proceedings of the 19th Colloquium on the Law of Outer Space,* International Institute of Space Law of the International Astronomical Federation, 1976.

46. M. Menter, "Legal Implications of Commercial Utilization of Space," *Proceedings of the 20th Colloquium on the Law of Outer Space,* International Institute of Space Law of the International Astronomical Federation, 1977.

47. Leonard W. David, "Space Exploration: Prospects and Problems for Today and the Future," in *Life in the Universe: The Ultimate Limits to Growth,* ed. William A. Gale, AAAS Selected Symposium no. 31 (Boulder, Co.: Westview Press, 1979).

48. David Thompson, "Astropollution," *Co-Evolution Quarterly,* Summer 1978, p. 35.

49. James E. Oberg, *New Earths: Restructuring Earth and Other Planets* (New York: New American Library, 1983), p. 265. *Terraforming* refers to making a planet habitable, like Earth.

50. See David, "Space Exploration," p. 55.

51. Allan E. Goodman, Georgetown University, has explored the diplomatic implications of discovering extraterrestrial intelligence. Private communication. See also C. Campbell, "Protocol of Calls From Distant Space," *New York Times,* 10 June 1985, p. A16.

The Exploration
and Utilization
of the Planets

GEOFFREY A. BRIGGS

---

*I*n this essay I describe the current direction of the U.S. program of unmanned planetary exploration along with some possibilities for the renewal of a manned exploration program—one that, in time, could lead also to the exploitation of resources in near-Earth space. In the context of this book, resource exploitation seems likely to pose the greatest number of environmental issues and, therefore, even though the era of such resource exploitation does not seem close at hand, I attempt to focus on this eventuality. My comments are entirely personal and should not be construed as an agency position (NASA has not yet examined in detail such long-range issues to my knowledge).

First, where is our present program headed? The program has been underway for less than a quarter century, and one might, therefore, expect that history would provide a good guide to the future. The early history —one of explosive growth—does not, however, now seem likely to repeat itself. The manned element came to an abrupt end in the early 1970s after the Apollo and Apollo-Soyuz programs and even the unmanned program almost disappeared a decade later—with Voyager as its last hurrah. Since the scientific exploration of the solar system has barely scratched the surface of the subject and since all U.S. planetary exploration projects to date have been spectacularly successful at all levels, one may ask, in the interest of predicting the future, why the U.S. love affair with deep-space exploration so rapidly cooled off. There appears to be no single answer to the lethargy of the last decade, but rather a number of relevant factors, some of which are listed here in no particular order of importance:

1. Our competitor in the dramatic space race of the sixties, the U.S.S.R., had fallen well behind and had given the appearance of dropping out of the race.

2. Other federal spending priorities had created pressures that did not allow for the continued expansion that would have been needed to undertake a manned exploration follow-on to the Apollo program.

3. Delays in the development of the Space Shuttle and a Shuttle-compatible upper stage for unmanned deep-space use had the effect of substantially stretching out the one big new planetary mission—the Galileo Jupiter Orbiter/Probe mission that was started in the late 1970s—and thereby increasing its cost. This situation was exacerbated by the termination of the expendable launch-vehicle program.

4. By the mid-1970s other areas of the space sciences had reached a stage of maturity that demanded larger-scale missions to exploit exciting science opportunities, and these astronomy and space physics disciplines thus justified a larger share of the roughly constant budget made available by NASA for space science and exploration.

5. The lack of evidence from the Viking landers for any extant life on Mars ended an exciting science dream that had in many ways driven the direction of the planetary program from the beginning and inspired enthusiasm in the public in general.

The growing pains for the planetary exploration budget brought on a crisis in 1982 when, in the interest of modestly scaling back the NASA budget, serious thought was given to the termination of the entire planetary program and the closure of the Jet Propulsion Laboratory (JPL), which has the principal responsibility for implementing the program of unmanned exploration. Happily these eventualities were avoided by NASA's adoption of a new strategy for planetary exploration based on the recommendations of a distinguished advisory body, the Solar System Exploration Committee.[1] The strategy, whose earliest steps have been implemented in recent NASA budget plans, has two main elements—a core program of missions that use existing spacecraft capability and an augmented program of missions that will require the development of expensive enabling technologies. These augmentation missions, it is hoped, will be implemented in the 1990s.

The Core Program

The goals of the core program of the Solar System Exploration Committee (SSEC) are the same ones that had inspired the program from the beginning: to understand the origin and evolution of the solar system; to better understand the history and behavior of the solar system; and to determine how this history is related to the appearance of life on Earth.

A new secondary goal was recommended by the SSEC—the survey of resources that are available in near-Earth space. The committee specifically has in mind the Moon and the Earth-approaching asteroids as the location of potentially useful resources. At this time the committee certainly has an open mind concerning the likelihood that resources in near-Earth space can be beneficially utilized in the near future. This recommendation should therefore be recognized as simply one of prudence for the world's leading space power: that we should determine what resources are available in space and what technologies would be needed to exploit them so that at some time in the future the nation can evaluate the benefits and costs of using near-Earth resources as an alternative to materials that have had to be lifted at great cost from the Earth's surface.

Based upon these recommendations of goals and upon the philosophy that the core-program missions should not demand new "enabling" technologies, but rather should use technology advances to cut costs, the SSEC proposed that NASA should build its Core Solar System Exploration Program around two types of missions:

1. *Observer missions* to the inner Solar System (out to the orbit of Mars), based upon spacecraft technology derived from commercially available, Earth-orbital spacecraft. The first mission recommended (on the basis of science priorities established by the National Academy of Sciences) is a polar orbiter about Mars designed to follow up on geoscience and climatological questions arising from the Viking missions. This mission is now in development toward a 1990 launch. Other Observer-class missions are also planned, all to be launched by the year 2000.

2. *Mariner Mark 2 missions* to the outer Solar System,

including the comets and main-belt asteroids, based upon spacecraft technology derived from the Voyager and Galileo projects (including outer-planet, atmospheric-entry probes). Following science priorities identified by the National Academy of Sciences, a rendezvous mission to a short-period comet has been recommended as a first mission. This first Mariner Mark 2 mission is a candidate for a new start in 1987, toward a 1991 launch to Comet Wild 2.

In the last three budget years, 1984 to 1986, NASA has supported the SSEC recommendations and, in turn, the implementing center (JPL) has exercised diligence in adopting a "new way of doing business" in the planetary exploration arena. One may, therefore, be optimistic in believing that the U.S. program of Solar System exploration is once again moving effectively.

The Augmented Program

Because the technological constraints (adopted to restrain costs) of the core program exclude some of the highest scientific priorities of the National Academy's recommendations, the SSEC also recommended that, at the earliest opportunity, two technologically challenging missions be added to the core-program mission set. Specifically, these are a Mars Rover/Sample Return mission and a Comet Nucleus Sample Return mission. Both will require considerable technology development—propulsion, aeromaneuvering vehicles, robotics, sample-acquisition techniques, and more. Both would benefit from international cooperation. (Several of the core-program missions are already being intensively studied for implementation as cooperative missions.)

The prospects for the near-term start of either of these augmentation missions are quite uncertain relative to the prospects for the core-program missions because of the large cost difference; much more work remains to be done to define these missions and to find innovative ways to implement them (including international partnerships).

Near-Earth Resources

In its first report (defining a core program), the SSEC identified the survey of resources available in near-Earth space as an important new responsibility of the NASA program of Solar System Exploration. In its second report (on augmentations to the core program, which is still in preparation at this time), the SSEC will examine in more detail the significance of this new program element. A brief summary is provided here.

The possibility of there being economic advantages to using the resources available in near-Earth space is based upon several factors. First is the enormous energy that must be expended to reach Earth orbit from the Earth's surface as compared to the energy needed to travel there from the lunar surface or from the surface of the Earth-approaching asteroids (a payload factor of 1.5 percent for the first case compared to perhaps 50 percent for the lunar and asteroid cases if the Earth's atmosphere is used as an aerobrake for the Moon-to-Earth part of the trip). A second factor is the long-term prospect for substantial growth of activity in space, including traffic from low Earth orbit (LEO) to geosynchronous

Earth orbit (GEO); obviously a large requirement for material would be needed to justify the investment involved in developing nonterrestrial mining, extraction, and delivery capability. With the recent U.S. decision to move ahead with the development of a permanently manned space station in LEO and with the burgeoning of the communications satellite traffic at GEO, the prospects for a continuously increasing amount of activity in space certainly must be taken seriously. The question then arises as to whether resources available on the Moon and asteroids can serve a useful purpose in an increasingly space-based economy and whether straightforward, and ultimately inexpensive, techniques for achieving access to those resources can be developed. There are, at present, many uncertainties, some of which can benefit from research and some of which must await the test of time.

Uses of Nonterrestrial Resources in Space

Some of the most immediately obvious possible uses of nonterrestrial resources in LEO and GEO are:

Bulk shielding against radiation and space debris
Liquid oxygen for propulsion and for life support
Metals and ceramics for structures

Solar flares are one unavoidable hazard of concern for long-duration human activity in space while debris impact is another that is beginning to be of some concern. If shielding becomes a requirement, then the amount of material needed (typically measured in tons for each astronaut) could soon become prohibitive if it had to be brought up from the Earth's surface. Raw dirt from the lunar surface would serve well for shielding and could be the first application for which an economic market might develop.

Likewise the requirement for liquid oxygen could develop relatively rapidly to meet the needs of LEO/GEO traffic; current projections indicate that 300 tons will be needed annually by the year 2000. Such an amount would call for ten Shuttle payloads of oxygen delivered to LEO each year. The additional possibility of supplying liquid hydrogen fuel from the Moon cannot be discounted; water ice hypothesized to be trapped in permanently shadowed craters at the lunar poles could be the source (the ice having been derived from impacting comets over the aeons).

Materials needed to build structures are also potentially available on the Moon and the asteroids. Lunar rocks are basically Earth-like in composition with aluminum, iron, titanium, and silicon being the most abundant useful elements in addition to oxygen. It seems unlikely that substantially enriched minerals—ores—will be found on the Moon because the processes that have concentrated minerals on Earth (and which depend on the aqueous environment and on life processes) are not applicable to the Moon. Nevertheless, plausible techniques to extract useful elements from the lunar soil have been proposed.

Plausible techniques for returning materials to LEO and GEO have also been discussed, including the construction of ablative shields from lunar materials to act as efficient aerobrakes on return to Earth orbit. Therefore, in principle, the use of nonterrestrial materials to support a developing space economy is certainly possible. Proponents of the concept would argue that commitment to the use of resources available in near-Earth space will be the critical event in making a real space economy viable.

From an environmental perspective, the key question to address may be when and how rapidly and within what framework such activity in space should occur. No one can confidently answer these questions today, for the pace will depend upon more than technological factors alone, as in the early days when political considerations fueled the activity more than the technical readiness. But the challenging nature of the technological steps does suggest that the large-scale use of nonterrestrial resources will not take place until well into the next century.

It seems likely that little of our terrestrial mining and extraction technology will pass over into the space-resource arena. We are not likely to be dealing with concentrated mineral deposits—ores—but rather with ordinary soils and rocks. And we will not be able to use large quantities of water in the extraction processes as is typically the case on Earth. All of our extraction techniques take for granted the relatively high Earth gravity for moving materials and also the Earth's atmosphere for heat removal. For space activity it will be necessary to start with a clean sheet of paper and an inventive mind to determine practical ways to deal with lunar and asteroidal resources.

Recognizing the major challenges that will have to be overcome, but also recognizing the human genius for grappling with such problems, one might ask what is a reasonable timescale for the utilization of space resources to become a reality. An optimistic scenario might go as follows:

By mid-1990s:	Permanent space station in LEO
By late-1990s:	Operational orbital transfer vehicle (OTV) to carry crews and cargo to and from GEO
Early 2000s:	OTV modified to achieve lunar and asteroidal transfer capability Early lunar base
2010:	Permanent lunar base with capability to supply liquid oxygen and bulk material to Earth orbit Small base on Mars
2025:	Developing space economy in Earth orbit and on Moon Autonomous Martian base

A more skeptical analyst might add 25 years to the time at which a permanent lunar base could be serving an economically useful role and might doubt that there will ever be a full-scale space economy able to justify substantial human activity on the Moon or asteroids. NASA's Solar System Exploration Committee does not presume to any particular clairvoyance, but it does recommend that the United States be prepared for the eventuality that space resources *may* be one of the keys to the future of our nation's economy. To this end the committee has recommended that a detailed survey of the Moon be carried out by a lunar polar orbiter; a telescopic discovery and survey effort for Earth-approaching asteroids (of which only 80 out of perhaps 1,000 have so far been discovered) be conducted using available research techniques; research into practical techniques for the processing of nonterrestrial materials be carried out; and a preliminary look be taken at the design of a lunar base oriented toward the utilization of lunar materials.

Some Environmental Issues

All human activities have some impact on the environment and activities in space will surely be no exception. Not all of the impact must necessarily be of a negative nature; it is to be hoped that, first, there will be increasingly beneficial effects for the terrestrial environment as space industrialization proceeds and that, second, the negative impacts will be minimal and carefully controlled. The negative impacts on previously pristine planetary environments could include the full range of problems we have experienced on Earth.

Some of the more obvious include nuclear wastes, because nuclear-energy sources may have crucial advantages for the early establishment of bases on the Moon, asteroids, and Mars. In the case of the Moon, which is steadily bathed in sunlight for two weeks at a time and has no atmosphere, it seems likely that photovoltaic energy sources will have natural long-term advantages that should make nuclear-waste disposal less than a dominant problem.

For the Moon, pollution of ground water and atmosphere will be avoided completely since both resources are lacking. Waste disposal would appear to be mostly an aesthetic problem that, one would hope, would be a tractable one. Working in favor of all waste-disposal problems is the considerable incentive not to waste anything because of the great cost of transportation. The rigorous demands of a clean environment to assure health also imply that the maintenance of a pristine (recycled) atmosphere and water supply will receive heavy engineering attention. In general one may hope and expect that the natural constraints imposed on space explorers will work to prevent the casual attitudes and unexamined economic incentives that have brought such harm to our own planet's environment.

Others in this book have raised some *really* long-term environmental questions related to the possibility of transforming the other planets for human habitation —*terraforming* as it has come to be called. I am not familiar with any technical studies of such an idea, but I am intuitively doubtful that we can even anticipate what kind of technology would be needed to accomplish such a Herculean task. Moreover, my personal reaction to the idea is very mixed; as someone who has been involved in a number of Mars missions as a scientist, I have come to like Mars very much just as it is—a beautiful red planet with stunning geological formations and with dynamic polar caps and clouds. So, I would intuitively prefer to leave Mars alone as a pristine planetary wilderness. Perhaps in the past it was an even more beautiful planet —the dried-up river channels presumably were real rivers once when Mars enjoyed a more Earth-like hydrological cycle. If it would be possible to recreate the earlier Mars (tapping water that is evidently abundant on Mars in the form of permafrost), then such terraforming might be an acceptable goal.

In the case of Venus, the other neighboring planet that might be transformed, my personal views are different; Venus, with its heavy, hot atmosphere and sulphuric acid clouds, does not delight me as it is. We must use radar eyes to examine its surface, and I am biased to prefer to use my own. Like Mars the early Venus may have been much more attractive to humans (the atmospheric composition has the signature of an early massive loss of water), so the prospect of terraforming Venus to an earlier, more Earth-like state is potentially quite appealing. But it is not clear that there is enough water left on Venus to ever allow this.

It seems to me, therefore, that individuals concerned about solar system environmental issues can reasonably leave the problem of terraformation for future generations to worry about, if and when it assumes a degree of reality. Issues associated with the use of near-Earth resources are also not pressing at present—a good reason why we should address them now.

Note

1. *Planetary Exploration Through Year 2000: A Core Program,* Report of the Solar System Exploration Committee of the NASA Advisory Council (Washington, D.C.: U.S. Government Printing Office, 1983).

Philosophical
and Environmental
Perspectives

———————

Space Exploration and Environmental Issues*

WILLIAM K. HARTMANN

Introduction

Space exploration has an interesting relation to the environmental movement. As predicted as early as 1948, a blossoming awareness of Earth's fragility came at the same time as the first voyages away from Earth. In 1948 the British astrophysicist Fred Hoyle predicted that "once a photograph of the Earth, taken from the outside, is available—once the sheer isolation of the Earth becomes known—a new idea as powerful as any in history will be let loose."[1] On Christmas Eve in 1968, astronauts orbiting the Moon televised pictures of the Earth rising over the lunar desolation and were moved to read a passage from Genesis to accompany their live broadcast into our living rooms. After astronauts' snapshots showed the Earth as a ball, poet Archibald MacLeish wrote that "to see the Earth as it truly is, small and

*This paper was originally published in *Environmental Ethics* 6, no. 3 (1984): 227–39.

blue and beautiful, in that eternal silence where it floats, is to see ourselves as riders on the Earth together. . . ."[2] Posters showing the blue globe of Earth hanging in black space became available during that period and are still popular.

It is no coincidence that the first "Earth Day," in 1970, came soon after these pictures became available. The image of the spherical Earth looking like a marble in space made the man on the street more profoundly aware that the Earth is truly finite. In the past, there was always some frontier that we could escape to—somewhere to start over again. Sweeping west and east from its early bases in Europe and the Middle East, Western man improved his standards of living (not in the sense of electric toothbrushes, but in the sense of hot and cold running water, warm dry houses, and adequate food) by consuming this frontier. America was founded and evolved on the premise of moving on to a new frontier. America's past success in the world may not be so much due to the inherent quality of our political system (as we like to believe), but rather to the fact that our politicians and economic system have been ideally suited to a rapacious exploitation and consumption of the resources of our young country.

Now the frontier has swept all around the Earth and closed on itself. By attempting to increase consumption and by dumping wastes into our now limited environment, we have strained international relations and are beginning to stew in our own waste juices. The realization of this has led to the environmental movement with its attempts to change perceptions.

Now, as during Renaissance times, a new frontier is opening. It is interplanetary. It may produce its own renaissance. The new lands are, from what we have seen so far, uninhabited. Mars lacks even organic molecules, according to Viking Lander soil tests, although meteorites have yielded extraterrestrial organic molecules that give us clues about the origin and evolution of life. The new lands of the Solar System have interesting materials. Thus, like it or not, the interplanetary frontier involves questions of exploration and exploitation that we are going to have to face.

Some Critiques of Space Exploration

The impact of space exploration on the maturing of environmental thinking has been ambiguous. Few environmentalists consider space as part of our environment even though it is beginning to be accessible to us, and even though the major energy source on Earth comes from space: the long-term renewable radiation from the nearest star, the Sun. Some environmentalists appear to view space exploration as a jingoistic boondoggle—the ultimate expression of a crazed technological society that insists on carrying through whatever mad schemes have become technologically feasible. Some environmentalists are concerned that even the possibility of space exploration, not to mention colonization, will result in our littering pristine planetary surroundings, like our roadsides, with our castoff junk.

A few years ago I was invited to write a chapter on space exploration and the environment for the second edition of the Friends of the Earth book, *Progress as if Survival Mattered*—a wonderful book with a wonderful title that expresses exactly our planetary predicament.[3] I submitted an earlier version of this article. An editor, facing a space problem of his own, dropped the chapter from the book, commenting that discussing opportunities for human benefits *beyond* Earth would create a "disposable planet mentality"—a tendency to squeeze our planet dry and then move on to the next.

It is unlikely that the disposable planet philosophy can ever gain wide conscious acceptance, in view of the latest findings in space. The only known planetary bodies are those in our own solar system, of which about twenty-five are larger than 1,000 kilometers across; innumerable others are smaller. Of all these the Earth is the only one with a breathable atmosphere and with liquid water trickling across its surface.

The Earth turns out to be a Hawaii in a solar system full of Siberias. This is not to say that Siberia is uninhabitable; it is just to say that Siberia lacks some of the attractions of Hawaii. Earth is the only known place where we can stand naked in the light of a nearby star and enjoy our surroundings. Unlike some early frontiersmen who exhausted one farmland and moved on to the next, we will find no rational motivation for destroying the planet to which we are umbilically linked and then attempting to move on. The plains of the Moon or Mars are, although beautiful, barren. To say that we should not even explore them for fear of writing off the Earth is akin to arguing that we should never hike into the wilderness, either out of curiosity to see what nature has produced there, or out of sheer reveling in our ability to do it, for fear we will *therefore* neglect our home environments. We may be messing up New York, but it's not because we're being lured by the deserts of Nevada.

A different opposition to space exploration appears to come from a subtle extension of the environmentalists' logic. A solid chain of reasoning leads from Earth's finiteness to a concern over the materials we consume and the wastes we exhaust into our atmosphere, oceans, and bodies. It leads to a concept of stewardship over the planet that we occupy and to our views that "small is beautiful," that we should pursue "progress as if survival mattered." A look at the rate at which we are altering Earth's atmosphere, waters, and urban environment leads to recognition that we cannot continue unlimited industrialization of the Earth. The momentum of these arguments, however, has carried some environmentalists on to the position that since technological discoveries have allowed overpopulation, pollution, and rapacious consumerism, technology itself is the culprit. In some quarters this idea has been carried beyond the rejection of technology (the application of discoveries about nature) to a rejection of science itself (the attempt to observe nature and learn the properties of the natural world). An undercurrent in late twentieth-century culture is a rejection of verifiable problem-solving approaches to daily life and of intellectual curiosity about the cosmic environment around us, as illustrated by the popularity of astrological superstitions and other subjective cults.

Environmentalists are still sorting out these competing modes of thought about the future directions of terrestrial civilization. Our general conclusion has been to espouse a simpler, less consumerist approach to daily life, but we have not abandoned the human intellect and its quest for new information, new understandings, new experience. Some environmentalists have been criticized for adopting an overly romanticized, Rousseau-like vision of rural agricultural homesteads planned "in harmony with nature." These visions lead to questions of how far back we are willing to go in abandoning such technological improvements as fabricated metal tools, hot and cold running water in our homes, indoor toilets, electricity, etc. The "small is beautiful" ethic espoused by many of us is simply a recognition that we must adopt the limited, simple levels of technology suitable to a pleasant and productive life style. It should not become a wholesale rejection of the technological base that has made our civilization possible and that provides the material foundation for artistic and scientific enterprises. The goal of learning about our natural surroundings on Earth and in space remains a valid and healthy goal. It is an expression of our innate human curiosity, our sense of adventure, and our hope of improving human life in a practical way. Having learned many basic facts about Earth's geography, we are now trying to learn some basic facts about the radiation and particle environment near Earth, the origin of our system of worlds, the evolution of their strange surface landscapes and atmospheres, and the causes of dramatic climate fluctuations that appear to have occurred in the past on some of them (including Earth).

All of this leads to two important points about space exploration. First, it should not be carried out as a technological boondoggle or expression of militaristic/nationalistic exhibitionism. Rather it should be viewed as an extension of the intellectual curiosity that makes us human in the first place. If we woke up one morning on an island in the midst of a vast sea dotted with other islands, our first enterprise after acquiring food and water would be to explore our own island and find out what resources or peoples might exist on the other islands. We were, in fact, born onto an island in the vastness of space; we know that there are other islands nearby and we want to find out about them.

Second, the opportunity to explore space changes one of the fundamental underpinnings of the environmental movement: it means the frontiers are not, after all, gone. There is an expanding frontier in the infinity of space if we choose to explore it. Of course, the amount of planetary surface in our solar system (that nearby part of space that we've been exploring for the last two decades) is not infinite, but is still large by Earth standards. The amount of land area on all known planetary bodies smaller than the Earth is over twice the total area of the Earth and about eight times the land area of the Earth. Of course, it is not as readily habitable as most of the Earth's land area, but it raises opportunities regarding the availability of resources. (The total area of the four giant planets is about 240 times the Earth's area or about 840 times the Earth's land area, but these surfaces are relatively inaccessible because of the extremely strong gravitational fields and uncertain surface properties of these planets, which make landings and takeoffs questionable.)

Space Exploration and Space Resources

Whether space materials will come to have practical importance depends on a number of factors such as the nature of the materials and their accessibility. Consider the following factors:

1. Humanity is rapidly gaining the ability to operate *in* space. This ability depends on a broad-based technological support and could be forever lost if Earth-based technological civilization burns its non-renewable resources and collapses before space travel is firmly established.

2. This capability is not accompanied by an immediate, known, economic justification in terms of a specific foreseeable return on investment. Rather, it is under-

taken for a complex mixture of reasons; it is viewed by some participants as a political enterprise, by some as scientific exploration, by some as a technological challenge, by some as human adventure, and by some as a long-term speculative economic investment.

3. In terms of energy expenditure, to transport materials from one small body (such as the Moon or an asteroid) to another nearby body or to a nearby orbit is more economical than it is to transfer materials from the Earth's surfaces to a nearby orbit, because of Earth's strong gravity. This means that if useful materials can be found on the Moon or nearby asteroids they could be brought to Earth orbit or to lunar stations more cheaply than similar materials could be delivered from the Earth.

4. Construction of large inhabitable structures in space, in part from extraterrestrial materials, is quite feasible.

5. Materials of economic value and basic practical interest are abundant in space. Although the surfaces of the inner planets, their satellites, and asteroids are primarily rock and the satellites of the outer planets are icy bodies, spectroscopic studies indicate that some asteroids are probably rich in pure nickel-iron similar to the pure nickel-iron in meteorites that fall on Earth from space. The iron meteorites were utilized as a source of iron in prehistoric times and their parent asteroidal materials could be so utilized in the future. It appears likely that the asteroid belt contains some bodies of nearly pure nickel-iron alloy many kilometers across, and other bodies of mixed composition, about half stone and half nickel-iron, of similar size. At least a few such bodies hundreds of meters across approach close to the Earth/Moon system, or cross Earth's orbit. Such smaller bodies could

be moved from their nearby orbits by using low-thrust engines over a period of months or years; they could be brought into orbit around Earth where they could be dissected for their metals. These could be used in making larger materials processing labs in orbit. Alternatively, the smaller asteroids could be shaped into "re-entry" vehicles and landed in remote areas of Earth to be cut up and utilized. The economic value of such masses of metal is enormous. As the costs of metals on Earth go up, and the costs of space operations go down, we can predict a time when the value of such objects will exceed the costs of retrieving them from space.

6. Judging from meteorite samples, asteroids have other valuable materials besides nickel-iron metal. One interesting class of such materials are the platinum-group metals. Unlike other resources, some of these are worth thousands of dollars per kilogram. The return of small shuttle-cargo-bay-sized payloads could have very high economic potential. Moreover, these are strategic materials, for which the U.S. depends heavily on the U.S.S.R. and other countries. Abundant sources in space could thus reduce geopolitical jockeying for their control on Earth.[4]

7. According to discoveries from the Viking Lander on Mars, the Martian soil contains about one percent by weight of water that can be easily removed by mild heating. Abundant frozen water has been detected in the polar ice caps of Mars. About three-quarters of the asteroids in the asteroid belt are believed to be composed of a meteoritic material, which, according to measurements of samples that fell on Earth, contain from a few percent to as much as twenty-two percent water. Comet nuclei are believed to be "dirty icebergs" with a large fraction of frozen water. The soil that covers the Moon contains a small amount of hydrogen loosely trapped from the solar wind that

can be removed by heating. These are potential sources of water and hydrogen that could be used by space explorers.

8. The energy required to transport materials from the asteroid belt to Earth orbit is roughly comparable to that required to transport the same kind of material from the surface of the Earth to Earth orbit. Even closer asteroids are known, where less energy would be required. Furthermore, the materials can be transferred in interplanetary space by solar sail spacecraft that are "pushed" by exposure to sunlight and consume no chemical energy resources, contrasted to the fuel-burning rockets used to launch materials off the Earth.

9. Feasibility studies indicate that oxygen, iron, sulfur, nitrogen, carbon, and helium could be extracted from lunar soils and rocks. It has been asserted that viable self-sustaining productive economies for lunar colonies or orbiting space colonies could be established.[5]

Whether we greet these facts and concepts with dismay ("Oh, my God! Now *they* are going to mess up the space environment as well as the Earth!") or with hope ("Now *we* have new options for survival off the Earth"), they will not go away.

We would not have admired some Neanderthal who refused to cross the next range of hills to see what was beyond. We do not admire the clerics who would not look through Galileo's telescope because the view of moons going around Jupiter demolished their conception of an Earth-centered universe. Similarly it seems premature and hardly admirable, in an era of population pressures and material shortages, to refuse to seek out further facts about the space environment around us. These indeed might present better options for humanity in dealing with questions of progress as if survival matters. The purpose of the environmental movement is not, after all, to prevent any further utilization of resources by humanity. That is impossible, even in a recycling society, due to the unaffordability of 100-percent recycling efficiency. Rather, we seek a more optimum interaction of mankind with nature, with the goal of preserving the Earth's environmental quality. We recall the slogan of the Friends of the Earth: ". . . dedicated to the preservation, restoration, and rational use of Earth and its resources."

Space exploration gives a potential option for implementing this slogan. Implementing such slogans, however, will be no easier than it has been for the rest of the environmental movement. In 1980, the governor of California became a presidential candidate who advocated a plank of "preserve the Earth, serve Mankind, explore the Universe," and was promptly ridiculed in the national press as "Governor Moonbeam," the "science-fiction candidate."

Rather than winding down the space program and crippling any possibility of learning more about the space options open to us, we should pursue a vigorous program of exploration of the space environment. For the next few years space exploration should be a reconnaissance designed to give us the facts we need to decide what to do next. It should be conducted in several parts similar to the programs pursued at NASA today. One part should be physical exploration by spacecraft and by humans. Another part should be a strong support program of Earth-based studies through astronomical, laboratory, and theoretical techniques. A third part should be engineering studies to reveal future human options on Earth and off Earth by means of space operations. For example, large space structures can intercept significant amounts of energy from the great nuclear power plant in the sky . . . the Sun. This collected energy can either be used in space colonies (which, once constructed, could process resources with absolutely no terrestrial pollution) or beamed down to the Earth (providing power sources with minimal terrestrial pollution). The principal objection to the latter has been the effects of the microwave radiation if the energy is beamed by microwave to Earth. In addition, there has been a philosophic objection to power being supplied by large centralized stations dependent on high technology. In spite of our push for decentralized power sources, such as solar collectors at the level of individual family consumers, some centralized, high-output power stations appear necessary for manufacturing. Therefore, trade-offs should be further considered between the solar-power satellite concept and other more polluting processes such as coal-burning power generators and nuclear generators.

Space Exploration and Space Wilderness Areas

Space exploration will reveal strange new landscapes and lead to problems of preservation. The solar system contains sites and sights that evoke awe for their historic importance or for their sheer physical beauty. In the same way we urge preservation of wilderness areas on Earth for future generations, we ought to preserve space wilderness areas of special interest. There are the first landing sites, such as the Tranquillity Base of Apollo 11. In the pristine desert landscapes of

Mars there are volcanoes bigger than Everest and canyons a hundred times bigger than the Grand Canyon. There are unvisited, geologically fresh craters on the Moon, with rugged rims 100 kilometers across, allowing monumental vistas across floors dotted with meteorite impact pits, volcanic outcrops, and central mountain massifs. There are strange-shaped asteroids twice as long as wide, tumbling end-over-end through space. The same human curiosity that led us to Yellowstone, and through the Sierras to Yosemite, will lead us inevitably to these sites.

There are already those who espouse the view that whoever gets into space first, in particular, whatever consortium of investors interested in mining nearby asteroids, should have the right to do whatever they want with the materials they find. In the worst case, this could lead to destruction of scientific information and unusual natural wonders. Some principles of compromise need to be found to allow identification of special sites, scientific sampling of important objects, and feasibility tests of resource utilization.

Identification of proposed space wilderness areas might meet this need. These would be a limited list of sites and objects open to scientific study, but closed to exploitation. The so-called Moon Treaty, drafted at the United Nations and considered for ratification by the United States, correctly speaks of solar system materials as a common heritage of humanity. However, it has been criticized as being too restrictive in these areas, putting space ventures of this sort under the ill-defined "regime" of national governments on Earth, which could hamstring efforts of exploration and feasibility testing. We need these efforts in time to provide new options for responding to environmental crises on Earth.

Space Exploration and Survival

Aside from effects on material resources and energy resources, and on human imagination, the exploration of space has much longer-term implications. Survival is the key word. In a very real sense, the absence of space travel absolutely guarantees nonsurvival of life on Earth. It is a question of time scales. To consider the longest time scale first, we know that in a few billion years (perhaps 5×10^9 years) the supply of hydrogen in the solar interior will be so reduced that the Sun will follow a type of evolution observed in certain other stars, increasing in luminosity and expanding its diameter until the Earth is engulfed and all life on it is destroyed. It is likely that other disasters will befall the Earth long before that. A dozen or more moderately large asteroids (one to nine kilometers in diameter) are known to cross the Earth's orbit; many more smaller ones do the same and supply the meteorites that fall on Earth. The time scale for individual bodies of this type to collide with Earth is on the order of a few tens of millions of years. We can predict confidently that catastrophic impacts of asteroids or comets (also typically a few kilometers in diameter) will occur on such time scales. The collision of the Earth with such a body would cause an explosion larger than the largest nuclear devices exploded on the Earth so far, creating a crater roughly ten kilometers or more across. This would cause devastating shock effects in a state-wide area and inject dust into the atmosphere, affecting the climate for years. Geologists have identified eroded craters several tens of kilometers across formed in this way millions of years ago. Growing geochemical and fossil evidence indicates that an impact of an asteroid roughly ten kilometers across sixty-five million years ago caused an episode of climate change and biological extinction that led to the demise of many species of plants and animals, including the dinosaurs.

Similar environmental changes might have been caused by other planetary phenomena, such as changes in atmospheric transmission of sunlight, triggered by volcanic eruptions or slight perturbations in the Earth's orbit. Similar perturbations are now widely believed responsible for the ice ages that are quite frequent in geologic history. All of these changes occur on time scales of tens of thousands of years to tens of millions of years and will probably be much better understood as a result of planetary exploration, since we are beginning to discover similar effects in other planet's histories. For example, Martian exploration has revealed what seem to be dry river beds, testifying that water once ran on Mars in a different climatic regime. Such planet-scale changes justify our desire as a species to understand planetary evolution better.

Returning to the effects of asteroid impacts, we can note that even on a time scale as short as the present century there have been several impressive examples of collisions between the Earth and the interplanetary debris. On 30 June 1908, an enormous explosion in Siberia exceeded the energy of the first atomic bombs. The object, which was probably a small comet nucleus, exploded in the atmosphere without striking the ground, but blew trees over as far as fifteen kilometers away. Because the impact occurred in a remote part of Siberia there were no casualties, although one observer was blown off a porch some sixty kilometers away. Decreases in air transparency were detected as far away as California. Again, on 10 April 1972, a house-sized interplanetary body entered the atmosphere almost tangentially over the western United States. The vivid fireball was widely photographed over the Grand Tetons and detected from above by a classified Air Force satellite, but it skipped back out of the Earth's atmosphere without crashing to the ground. A slightly different orbit would have led to an impact with an explosion approximating that of the Hiroshima bomb, probably somewhere in Alberta, Canada.

Thus, the asteroids that approach Earth are hardly an academic matter, and they provide an interesting test of environmentalist philosophy. On the one hand, a recent *Scientific American* article about them concluded by suggesting that they become an inviolable scientific and natural preserve.[6] On the other hand, there is a question of how to react to the occasional (one every few decades?) visitor that is small in interplanetary terms but large in terms of potentially devastating impact effects. We will soon have the ability to detect these in advance, and probably we will soon have the ability to do something about it. Altering the orbits of such asteroids or utilizing their materials for human benefit (i.e., mining of iron, construction of space habitats) may seem quite preferable to "living in harmony with nature" to the extent of letting them crash down upon the populated Earth.

Putting questions of natural disasters aside, there is a question of survival that involves political disasters. One can say with all good intention that we should work to solve our political problems on Earth before exporting ourselves to other planets. Nonetheless, such an attitude ignores a real possibility that nuclear warfare or accidental disaster (such as destruction of the ozone layer) could devastate life on Earth. The visionaries who discuss the possibilities of self-sustaining colonies of humans, either in orbit or on other planetary surfaces, are really increasing chances for survival of the human race against such disasters. Self-sustaining space colonies, if we create them, will have the side effect of giving humanity an extra insurance policy. This is not saying that it is all right to ruin the Earth because we can always go someplace else. This is merely recognizing that the space environment may provide the opportunity for self-sustaining colonies that could give humanity an extra option on survival.

Consider again our metaphor of being born on an island in a sea of islands. If we now perceive that we were born not on an island, but on a luxury liner—the spaceship Earth—which had had some fires on board, some smoke in the ventilator system, and some occasional food poisoning, we might be even more interested in assessing the passing islands. Islands may not be luxury liners, but they aren't about to sink in the near future either.

To argue against space survival insurance on the grounds that it fosters a disposable planet mentality is like a crazy man's response to the fire chief's warnings about fire hazards on the luxury liner. Instead of helping the passengers with lifeboat practice, he burns the lifeboats on the grounds that this will encourage the passengers to be more careful with matches.

Space Exploration and Alternative Societies

Finally, space exploration gives us an additional option that is of interest in environmental contexts. Many of the social conflicts that threaten the Earth arise from differences of opinion regarding the solutions to political and social problems. With the closing of the frontiers of the Earth there are no psychological "escape hatches" whereby groups can set up their own societies and try their own solutions. The future option of building orbiting space cities allows the possibility for alternative political systems to be tried. There can be experiments. No government need be threatened by a minority with a different idea if minorities are free to go away and try their own system in the same way that minorities were free to move to America a few centuries ago. For this reason the exploration of space should be conducted in a way that allows some freedom of expression. The United Nations' Moon Treaty can be criticized on these grounds since its vague proposal that future space endeavors be governed by a "regime" of terrestrial nations does not clarify questions of civil rights and freedom of choice. Encouragement of self-governing settlements of many kinds on the new frontier of space would provide a needed "pressure release valve" for those discouraged with the large bureaucracies of Earth.

Speculative Visions of the Future

If we don't change our rapacious consumption of Earth's resources soon, we are likely to do serious damage to Earth's climate and to ourselves.[7] One projection, assuming "business as usual," is that we simply exhaust our consumable resources, leading to a collapse of technological civilization, accompanied by widespread famine, economic desolation, etc. Another projection assumes that we achieve a steady-state economy, but as Herman E. Daly has pointed out:

> A [steady-state economy] is not a panacea. Even a [steady-state economy] will not last forever, nor will it overcome diminishing returns and the entropy law. But it will permit our economy to die gracefully of old

age rather than prematurely from cancer of growth-mania.[8]

Since both of these scenarios look forward merely to the collapse of our civilization and a return to pre-industrial rural isolation with shortages of iron, other metals, energy, etc., neither is scintillatingly attractive.

Of course, we cannot fully foresee the future, and to try to force the future into a restrictive plan is to lose the chance to develop unforeseen discoveries. We cannot guarantee consequences of space exploration, though it appears to be a form of research that has a likelihood of expanding our options. Consider this alternative scenario for the future. We use the remaining fossil energy resources to develop alternative energy technologies. We establish a capability of space operations. Our planet becomes recognized as a unique haven in the solar system, to be protected and cherished. A zero-growth population of passengers on the spaceship Earth maintains Earth's population consistent with the carrying capacity of Earth. As David Brower notes in his "Third Planet Operating Instructions": "The planet is self-maintaining, and the external fuel source will provide exactly as much energy as is needed or can be safely used."[9] We soon see an end to the gouging of ever-deeper layers of Earth in search of new raw materials and fossil fuels, because replacement materials are to be found outside the spaceship Earth. Self-sufficient space settlements, in orbit and on smaller planets, provide new resources in a viable economy based on trade with Earth, which comes to be viewed more and more as a haven from the other environments of the Solar System. The mining and refining of the new resources, and some manufacturing, are done in orbit. Only product, not pollution, is delivered to Earth's biosphere. If the space economy were as vigorous as one might hope, new settlements could be built with no consumption of Earth materials, since solar energy, metals, hydrogen, oxygen, and building materials are abundantly available in space. Humanity grows, not by crowding Earth, but by seeking adventure and life elsewhere.

In short, consideration of terrestrial civilization's evolution and its long-term relation to its space environment suggests only three broad classes of outcomes: (1) accidental or deliberate destruction of life on Earth through expanding consumerist technology or warfare; (2) slow decay of a civilization that restricts itself to a finite Earth and either runs out of materials or is irreparably damaged by a cosmic accident; or (3) expansion of civilization into the space environment with attendant diversification, utilization of space resources, and consequent greater insurance against accidents that could damage all of mankind at once. Space exploration is no panacea—there are no panaceas—but it holds promise for long-term amelioration of many problems we sense on a distressingly finite Earth.

Notes

1. Quoted in Oran W. Nicks, ed., *This Island Earth* (Washington, D.C.: NASA, 1970), p. 30.
2. Ibid.
3. Hugh Nash, ed., *Progress as if Survival Mattered*, 2nd ed. (San Francisco: Friends of the Earth, 1981).
4. John Lewis and Carolyn Neimel, "Asteroid Mining and Space Bunkers," *Defense Science 2000+* 2, no. 3 (1983): 33.
5. See David Criswell, ed., *Lunar Utilization* (Houston: Lunar Science Institute, 1976) and Gerard O'Neill, *The High Frontier* (New York: William Morrow, 1977).

6. George W. Wetherill, "Apollo Objects," *Scientific American* 240, no. 3 (March 1979): 65.

7. As made clear by economic projections of, for example, Donella H. Meadows et al., *Limits to Growth* (New York: Universe Books, 1972), and subsequent studies, such as Wassily W. Leontief, "The World Economy of the Year 2000," *Scientific American* 243, no. 3 (September 1980): 207–31, and H. E. Goeller and A. Zucker, "Infinite Resources: The Ultimate Strategy," *Science* 223 (1984): 456–62.

8. Nash, *Progress as if Survival Mattered,* p. 338.

9. Ibid., p. 27.

The Preservation
of Natural Value
in the Solar System

HOLMES ROLSTON, III

Set as a shining jewel in the dark abysses of space, Earth is a unique treasure, exuberant with life. Millions of species have evolved, increasing in variety and complexity over billions of years. By contrast, the space environment seems hostile, cold, empty. Earth is home, a fertile oasis; that is the good news. The bad news is that Earth is lost out there in the stars. A solar system, a galaxy, even a star, is mostly nothing, empty space; and where there is something, it is sterile—frozen or scorched, swirls of gases or inert rockpiles. But an ecosystem, especially one with persons, an Earth, this is something rich and significant, an intricate web of instrumental and intrinsic values.

Earthlings live neither at the range of the infinitely small nor of the infinitely large; but humans may well live at the range of the infinitely complex. In a typical handful of humus, which may have ten billion organisms in it, there is a richness of structure, a volume of information (trillions of "bits") enormously advanced over anything elsewhere in the solar system, or even, so far as we know, in myriads of galaxies. The human being is the most sophisticated of evolutionary and ecological products. In our seventy kilograms of protoplasm, in our single kilogram or so of brain, there may be more operational organization than in the whole of the Andromeda Galaxy. The number of possible associations among the ten billion neurons of a human brain, and the number of thoughts that can result from this, may exceed the number of atoms in the universe.

Out there, trillions of atoms spin round and yield nothing more than aggregated whirls of flaming gas, clouds of dust, raw energy, rotating and revolving chunks of brute matter. But here trillions of atoms spin in richly informed ways to yield life and mind, with sentience and cultured experiences. Space is barren, perhaps not entirely but almost so, seen in contrast with the fertility of Mother Earth. Michael Collins, a veteran astronaut, concludes, "The more we see of other planets, the better this one looks."[1]

Such an account—treasure-here/emptiness-there —is relatively true. But is it absolutely all that needs to be said? The last two decades have been productive for space exploration; we have visited and probed other worlds, mapped planets and moons, increased our knowledge by an order of magnitude. The same two decades have also been notable for the emergence of environmental ethics, with its rethinking of the philosophy of nature, its reformed appreciation of values carried on the ecosystemic Earth. We have increased our sensitivity by an order of magnitude. Now is the time for value explorations in space, for a philosophy of the solar environment to complement that of the biospheric environment. What follows is an ethical probe into the solar-planetary system.

1. Accidental Nature:
Earth as an Astronomical Accident

A moment's reflection introduces anomalies into this value-at-home/waste-elsewhere perspective. Except for activity dependent on radioactivity, Earth is solar-powered. The energy with which I write and that with which you read was supplied by a nuclear reactor 149,600,000 kilometers away. The ecosystem is the Sun/Earth, in some sense heliocentric even though the complexity is mostly earthbound. The solar sphere is as vital as the atmosphere. Once we start considerations like this, there is almost no stopping of them.

The Sun/Star is the right size and age. About its central star, Earth must (a physical requirement, if there is to be life) occupy an orbit that permits water to form and liquid water to circulate over most of its surface. Earth must be big enough to retain an atmosphere, small enough that the atmosphere can evolve from a reducing to an oxidizing one, with the proper gases to provide an insulating effect. Earth's tipped axis produces the diversity of seasons, and there is enough differential heating to drive favorable hydrologic and meteorological cycles, making weather and climate. Earth has a moon, which produces the tides and creates the crucial intertidal zone, where life later moves from sea to land. Earth has a thin, condensed crust surrounding an incandescent globe, a living skin over hot rock. There is enough radioactive heat buried in the core to keep the crust active, rechurning environments, while degassing an atmosphere "blessed" with hydrogen, carbon, nitrogen, and oxygen compounds, all becoming ingredients in a thin hot soup from which life can evolve.

All this makes the right setup for life. Recalling that

an ecosystem requires both energy and materials, we may first say that the materials are already here, only recycled, while the solar energy has to be resupplied daily. But the materials were not always here, and their history takes us back to the formation of Earth and solar system, and then back further and out of the solar system. The Earth is linked up to the solar system and beyond. In one way, we Earthlings have powers that exceed anything else found in the solar system; but in another way that system has powers we do not, since it generated us. We are first in complexity, last to arrive.

Alas, however, there is no scientific theory how, much less why, all these puzzle pieces should fall together so fortunately. Space exploration has not produced a scrap of progress on this issue, not even a promise of any lawlike, systemic headings in the solar system. So, fearing cognitive dissonance, the official doctrine is to affirm positively (lest the really negative character of the claim be heard) that the fortunate planetary setup is due to "astronomical accidents."[2] Those who speak of Earth as being an "accident," like those who say that life is an accident, are often not clear what they mean. "Accident" usually has two, conflated layers.

(1) The set of resulting characteristics, which on Earth are highly valued, result in significant part from the impingement of otherwise unrelated causal lines. That is, the productive factors, while fully causal at least in a statistico-deterministic sense, were tending nowhere; this is *relative randomness.* All events have followed small- or middle-scale causal laws; these causal laws, while everywhere operative, have no systemic unity, no governing integration. Causal events in their complicated interactions are a big mess, and there are no large-scale laws that determine that the nine planets will be

placed thus and so, with the third one at just the proper distance to make it a habitat for life. There is nothing holistic about the systemic organization. The necessities and beauties of celestial mechanics notwithstanding, the system is a chaotic jumble.

Such relative randomness is compatible with un-broken causation, but not with systemic organization at cosmic or solarplanetary levels. Events are causally determined, but accidental in that there is no principle producing high-order results, accidental in not merely a teleological sense, but accidental in any systemic sense. The unbroken causal lines are a jumble, not those of a system with tendencies to produce anything, certainly not tendencies to produce life or mind. Adapting the somewhat outmoded vocabulary of Aristotle, there are entirely sufficient efficient causes, but these neither necessitate nor make probable the operation of any formal causes. The system has no formative tendencies.

(2) There is a further kind of randomness that some-times also enters astronomy. The set of highly valued characteristics, though they result from many interjumbling causal lines, may have, further, some indeterminate points. The set of antecedent efficient causes were not sufficient for the set of resulting characteristics Earth has. There is some *absolute randomness* in Earth's past history. The various factors that resulted in the characteristics of Mercury, Venus, Mars, Jupiter, Saturn, Titan, Mimas, Ariel, and so on include some genuine dice throwing. The system is to some extent open, not fully deterministic.

This absolute kind of randomness first entered physics at the microscopic level in quantum physics; and many physicists think still that there are no macroscopic effects at everyday levels, much less astronomical effects at solar-planetary levels. All indeterminacies wash out in the averages, overwhelmed by the statistical odds, and big-scale events are fully statistico-deterministic. But others are not so sure. Thermodynamics has yielded some surprises in systems previously thought to be deterministic. Climates, once assumed to be fully causal, may be partially open systems. What goes on in so-called "naked singularities" and "black holes" is supposed by some to warp or destroy causal laws and constants, perhaps with some absolute randomness in result. Cosmologists even take the expanding universe back in time and shrink it in size until, in what they call the Planck Era, quantum indeterminacies become relevant in the subsequent placement of galaxies. In the oscillating universe—big bang, big squeeze, big bang squeeze—in each new epoch "the universe is squeezed through a knothole,"[3] and its features, causal laws, constants are destroyed and reemerge with some characteristics set by absolute randomness. One hardly knows what to make of such speculations.

Randomness of either kind, relative or absolute, is consistent with the official doctrine about what happens on Earth, after it is formed, during the evolutionary development. That course too has antecedents without headings; life's outcomes are matters of mutation, genetic drift, biological accidents, "chance riches."[4] The spectacular story that manages to happen first in chemical evolution and later in biological evolution is perfused with relative and absolute randomness. So why should anyone think the planetary evolution any less so? One way to confirm this is to see how fortunate Earth is by comparison with the unlucky planets. Planets come in great variety, but there are no interesting achievements on any others. They are unsuitable for life; they will be almost impossible places to visit. They are suspended in permanent deep freeze, or they boil in chaotic heat. Earth is paradise; they are hells.

This means for value theory that humans cannot value the causes that lie behind Earth as positively productive forces, for they were not. Earth is where and what it is by luck, causal forces notwithstanding. The most that humans can say, after we arrive and reflect about our circumstances, is that these lucky concatenations of intersecting causal lines, once dissociated and later scrambled, mixed also with absolute randomness, if such there is, are instrumentally valuable retrospectively. They did in fact happen to result in our being here, and one can certainly value good luck. But anyone is deceived who thinks he or she is valuing more than chance riches. The astronomical forces are not even valuable instrumentally in any systemic sense, for there is no coherent system, much less are such forces intrinsically valuable in themselves. Places where these kinetic forces have produced something unearthly are out of luck. Jupiter and Pluto, or the minor planet Chiron, are not even instrumentally valuable. None of the non-Earth places, unless they once stood in the causal chains that produced Earth or yet stand in support of Earth, are *of value*. They just *are*— brute matter or raw energy; they are only matter-in-motion; so never mind!

It seems at this point that a positive environmental ethic is also out of luck. Ecology, etymologically, is a logic of one's home, and our home is locally Earth. Regionally, our home is the solar system; cosmically, it is galaxies and beyond; and an environmental ethic might not seem finished until it has an account of the space environment. But no comprehensive account can be given; the solargalactic environment is, at bottom, a randomness, relative or absolute, because of the jumbled causal lines and mixed indeterminacies. The most that can be asked is whether and how we Earthlings, who have so resourcefully used Earth, can someday make *resources* of these non-Earth places, mining the Moon, doing experiments on Venus, taking a vacation touring Saturn —a secondary environmental ethic. But no primary environmental ethic is possible, no account of the productive *sources.* The question is whether this astronomical world can *belong to us;* there is no question how we *belong to it,* and no question whether it *belongs by itself.*

2. *Anthropic Nature: A Fine-Tuned Universe*

The route that space explorers have to follow, leaving *terra firma,* is to enlarge the circle of investigation little by little, exploring first the Moon, then nearby planets, then probing more distant ones. Even astronomers who stay at home and look outward have to push farther and farther, starting in our own galaxy, moving to galaxies beyond, and thence to the edges of the universe. This has been done sufficiently to permit a "space axiologist," puzzled about the astronomical accidents that put Sun, Earth, Saturn in place, to begin at the beginning. Cosmologists have already been doing these explorations, and I plan next to quit nearby value exploration and send a probe back to the beginning, down to the foundations. In the strange curvatures of space-time, which can bend logic as well, the longest way round can be the shortest way home.

We can put our valuational probe on board some experimental probes already underway investigating the formative astrophysical forces. These inquiries have yielded an impressive result with a rather unfortunate name—the *anthropic principle.* We cannot do experiments revising the universe, but we can do thought experiments to see what another one would be like. Contrary to the picture of accidental nature just sketched, the result is that the universe is mysteriously right for producing life and mind, demonstrably on Earth and perhaps just as well elsewhere, a result that would better be said to yield *biogenic* and *psychogenic* principles.

The universe is twenty billion light years across, twenty billion years old, staggeringly lavish in its size and age; and within it matter is very rarefied. Matter also condenses into complex formations, the most impressive of which are life and mind. But the rarity of any biological environment supports the previous picture that nature on the whole is a ridiculous swirl and empty waste. Together with our neighboring life forms on Earth, humans are puny and transitory phenomena having no essential relationships to these vast, dumb processes that constitute all but the tiniest fraction of nature. We are epiphenomenal; we are astronomical accidents.

Next, however, let us change this picture around, using some *if-thens. If* we remove the stars, *then* most of the story fails. In the astronomical world—galaxies, stars, space—nature mostly exists at the low structural ranges of micronature—as particles, electromagnetic radiation, electrons, protons, hydrogen. Yet in the stars nature energetically builds and steadily aggregates. The stars are the furnaces in which all but the very lightest elements are forged. Without such stellar cultures there can be no later evolution of planets, life, mind. Supernovae explode to disperse their matter throughout space. Earth and its humans are composed of stardust, fossil stardust! The stars cook up the dirt, which later becomes the humus, which later cooks up an ecology with its humans.

Interestingly, the mix of elements in the later stars,

despite their enormous heat, is as favorable for the future of life as is the mix of elements on Earth. Indeed, says George Wald, an evolutionary biochemist, "the proportions of the elements in living organisms is much closer to their distribution in later-generation stars than in the planets. . . . The stars are in every way closer to life."[5] So no one with a cosmic view can think that the stars play no part in forming ecosystems. They supply energy and materials for all that comes after.

If we make a substantial reduction in the number of particles in the universe, or in its total size, *then* what would be the consequence?[6] There is not enough material or enough cooking time for thermonuclear combustion, which requires several billion years to build the heavy elements. No universe can provide several billion years of time, according to the theory of general relativity, unless it is several billion light years across. *If* we cut the size of the universe by a huge reduction (from 10^{22} to 10^{11} stars), *then* that much smaller but still galaxy-sized universe might at first seem roomy enough, but it would run through its entire cycle of expansion and recontraction in about one year!

If the universe were not expanding, *then* it would be too hot to support life. Indeed, *if* the expansion had been a little faster or slower (especially since small differences at the start result in big differences later), *then* connections shift so that the universe would already have recollapsed or so that galaxies, stars, and planets could not have formed. The extent and age of the universe are not obviously an outlandish extravagance, if it is to be a habitat for life and mind at its middle ranges. Indeed, this may be the most economical universe in which mind can flower on Earth and perhaps elsewhere—so far as we can cast that question into a testable form and judge it by present physical science.

If the matter of the universe were not so relatively homogeneous as it is, *then* large portions of the universe would be so dense that they would already have undergone gravitational collapse. On the other hand, *if* the distribution of matter were entirely homogeneous, *then* the chunks of matter that make development possible could not assemble. Other portions would be so thin that they could not give birth to galaxies and stars.

Further, many physical constants and processes, both at microphysical and astronomical levels, strikingly fit together to result in what has happened. Change slightly the strengths of any of the four forces that hold the world together (the strong nuclear force, the weak force, electromagnetism, gravitation—forces ranging over forty orders of magnitude) or change various particle masses and charges, and the stars burn too fast or too slowly, or atoms and molecules, including water, carbon, oxygen, do not form or do not remain stable, or other checks, balances, cooperations are interrupted.

B. J. Carr and M. J. Rees, cosmologists, conclude, "The basic features of galaxies, stars, planets and the everyday world are essentially determined by a few microphysical constants and by the effects of gravitation. Many interrelations between different scales that at first sight seem surprising are straightforward consequences of simple physical arguments. But several aspects of our Universe—some of which seem to be prerequisites for the evolution of any form of life—depend rather delicately on apparent 'coincidences' among the physical constants. . . . The Universe must be as big and diffuse as it is to last long enough to give rise to life."[7]

If one undertakes thought experiments revising the ratios, constants, atomic sizes, and dynamics in the laws that govern these operations, then one runs into similar impossibilities, surprises, and unknowns. When we consider the first few seconds of the big bang, writes Bernard Lovell, an astronomer, ". . . it is an astonishing reflection that at this critical early moment in the history of the universe, all of the hydrogen would have turned into helium if the force of attraction between protons —that is, the nuclei of the hydrogen atoms—had been only a few percent stronger. In the earliest stages of the expansion of the universe, the primeval condensate would have turned into helium. No galaxies, no stars, no life would have emerged. It would have been a universe forever unknowable by living creatures. A remarkable and intimate relationship between man, the fundamental constants of nature and the initial moments of space and time seems to be an inescapable condition of our existence. . . . Human existence is itself entwined with the primeval state of the universe."[8] Concluding a study of energy processes on cosmic scales, Freeman J. Dyson, a physicist, writes, "Nature has been kinder to us than we had any right to expect. As we look out into the universe and identify the many accidents of physics and astronomy that have worked together to our benefit, it almost seems as if the universe must in some sense have known that we were coming."[9]

Fred Hoyle, an astronomer, reports that he was shaken by his own discovery of critical levels involved in the stellar formation of carbon into oxygen. Carbon only just manages to form and then only just avoids complete conversion into oxygen. If one level had varied by a half a percent, the ratio of carbon to oxygen would have shifted so as to make life impossible. "Would you not say to yourself, . . . 'Some supercalculating intellect must have designed the properties of the carbon atom, otherwise the chance of my finding such an atom through the blind forces of nature would be utterly minuscule'? Of course you would. . . . You would conclude that the carbon atom is a fix. . . . A common-sense interpretation of the facts suggests that a superintellect has monkeyed with the physics, as well as with chemistry and biology, and that there are no blind forces worth speaking about in nature. The numbers one calculates from the facts seem to me so overwhelming as to put this conclusion almost beyond question."[10] "Somebody had to tune it very precisely,"[11] concludes Marek Demianski, a Polish cosmologist and astrophysicist, reflecting over the big bang.

How the various physical processes are "fine-tuned to such stunning accuracy is surely one of the great mysteries of the cosmology," remarks P.C.W. Davies, a theoretical physicist. "Had this exceedingly delicate tuning of values been even slightly upset, the subsequent structure of the universe would have been totally different." "Extraordinary physical coincidences and apparently accidental cooperation . . . offer compelling evidence that something is 'going on.' . . . A hidden principle seems to be at work, organizing the universe in a coherent way."[12]

Mike Corwin, a physicist, looks over the evolution of the universe from chaos to consciousness, and concludes, "This 20-billion-year journey seems at first glance tortuous and convoluted, and our very existence appears to be the merest happenstance. On closer examination, however, we will see that quite the opposite is true—intelligent life seems predestined from the very beginning. . . . Life as we conceive it demands severe constraints on the initial conditions of the universe. Life and consciousness are not only the direct result of the initial conditions, but could only have resulted from a narrow range of initial conditions. It is not that changes in the initial conditions would have changed the character of life, but rather that any significant change in the initial conditions would have ruled out the possibility of life evolving later. . . . If initial conditions had been different, the universe would have evolved as a lifeless, unconscious entity. Yet here we are, alive and aware, in a universe with just the right ingredients for our existence."[13]

There are all kinds of connections between cosmology on the grandest scale and atomic theory on the minutest scale, and we may well suppose that we humans, who lie in between, stand on the spectrum of these connections. The way the universe is built and the way micronature is built are of a piece with the way humans are built. The shapes of the other regions of the universe, the shapes of all the levels above and below, are crucial to what is now taking place close at hand. In its own haunting way, the physical structure of the astronomical and microphysical world is as prolife as anything we later find in the biological urges. Prelife events can have, and have had, prolife consequences. George Wald says, "Life . . . involves universal aspects. It is a precarious development wherever it occurs. This universe is fit for it: we can imagine others that would not be. Indeed this universe is only *just* fit for it. . . . Sometimes it is as though Nature were trying to tell us something, almost to shake us into listening." "This universe breeds life inevitably."[14]

Manfred Eigen, a thermodynamicist, concludes a long mathematical analysis finding "that the evolution of life . . . must be considered an *inevitable* process despite its indeterminate course."[15] Eric Chaisson, an astronomer, agrees: "A central feature of cosmic evolution, then, is the developing realization that life is a logical consequence of known physical and chemical principles operating within the atomic and molecular realm, and, furthermore and more fundamentally, that the origin of life is a natural consequence of the evolution of that matter. . . . Subtle astrophysical and biochemical processes . . . enable us to recognize the cosmos as the ground and origin of our existence. . . . It's a warmer and friendlier scenario now. . . . We are not independent entities, alien to Earth. The earth in turn is not adrift in a vacuum unrelated to the cosmos. The cosmos itself is no longer cold and hostile—because it is *our* universe. It brought us forth and it maintains our being. We are, in the very literal sense of the words, children of the universe."[16]

3. Projective Nature: Formed Integrity

Overlaying anthropic nature on accidental nature, we can still paint a further picture, with some of the old pictures still showing through. I plan to conserve the facts under a different value theory, one neither accidental nor anthropic, but one portraying *projective nature.* Nature's "projects" are regularly valuable, as are its "objects" and its "subjects," sometimes more, sometimes less. True, Earth lies critically on a main sequence, complex with intrinsic values; but it does not follow that non-Earth places are wayward lines without intrinsic value. Analogously to the way in which it is arrogant anthropocentrism for humans to value themselves and disvalue jumping spiders, it is Earth chauvinism for Earthlings to value Earth and disvalue Jupiter. Both the jumping spider and Jupiter are formed in the wonderland of projective nature. There are disanalogies with which we must deal: a jumping spider has organic integrity; Jupiter has site integrity. But both are projects with their glory.

Nature is energetic and fertile, evidenced at length in

life and mind. That does involve some accident, but it cannot be all accident; it is an immanent property of systemic nature that natural history results. We live in what K. G. Denbigh calls "an inventive universe."[17] Projective nature is restless. There is a throwing forward of dynamic events that often culminate in natural kinds, products with wholeness—stars, comets, planets, moons, rocks, mountains, crystals, canyons, seas. The biological and psychological processes that on Earth culminate the astronomical and geological processes are still more impressive, but to be impressed with life in isolation from its originating matrix is to have but half the truth. The original meaning of *nature,* from the Latin *natans,* "giving birth," suggests that value in nature lies in its generation of life. A better cue lies in the meaning of *physics,* the Greek word for *nature,* a "bringing forth." Systemic nature is valuable as a productive system, with Earth and its humans only one, even if perhaps the highest in richness or complexity, of its known projects. Nature is of value for its capacity to throw forward all the storied natural history. On that scale, humans on Earth are latecomers, and it seems astronomically arrogant for such late products to say that the system is only of instrumental value, or that not until humans appear to do their valuing does value appear in the universe.

It is less short-sighted but still seriously myopic to value the system only for its production of life, although this is of great moment within it. Nonbiotic things have no information in them, no memory, no genome, much less sentience or experience. There are no cells, no skin, no centered control. Impressed with the display of life and personality on Earth, humans correctly attach an ethical concern to persons and to organisms, but we may incorrectly assume that mere things even on Earth, much less on Mars, are beyond appropriate and inappropriate consideration. The astronomical and geological phases in nature are, on some of their tracks, precursors of life. They are of value on that account, and when life is reached, everything else can seem far "down below," short of the fullness of being displayed in life, and thus without value. But their distance "down below" does not make them merely of instrumental value, nor does it make those places that are "sidetracked" of no value.

All the elevated forms have bubbled up "from below," and the basic stratum is of value for its projective tendencies, which are *value-able, able to produce value* wherever they result in formed integrity. Crystals, volcanoes, geysers, headlands, rivers, springs, cirques, paternoster lakes, buttes, mesas, canyons—these are also among the natural kinds. They are constantly being built, altered, and their identity is in flux. They do not have organic integrity or bounded individuality. They defend nothing. They do not have "character," and there seems in them no conflict and resolution. Nothing there can be afraid, disappointed, frustrated, hurt, or satisfied. So they may seem to have no integrity that can be valued.

But they are recognizably different from their backgrounds and surroundings. They may have striking particularity, symmetry, harmony, grace, spatio-temporal unity and continuity, historical identity, story, even though they are also diffuse, partial, broken. They do not have wills or interests, but rather headings, trajectories, traits, successions, beginnings, endings, cycles, which give them a tectonic integrity. They can be projects of quality.

Nature is not inert and passive until acted upon resourcefully by life and mind. Neither sentience nor consciousness is necessary for inventive processes to occur. There is genesis, Genesis, long before there are genes. Inventiveness in projective nature lies at the root of all

value, including sentience and consciousness, and nature's created products regularly have value as inventive
achievements. There is a negentropic constructiveness
in dialectic with an entropic teardown, a mode of working for which we hardly have yet an adequate scientific
much less a valuational theory. Yet this is nature's most
striking feature, one which ultimately must be valued and
is of value. In one sense we say that nature is indifferent
to planets, mountains, rivers, microbes, and trilliums.
But in another sense nature has bent toward making and
remaking them for several billion years.

These performances are worth noticing—remarkable, memorable—and they are not worth noticing just
because of their tendencies to produce something else,
certainly not merely because of their tendency to produce this noticing by our subjective human selves. They
are loci of value so far as they are products of natural
formative processes. The opening movements of a sym-
phony contribute to the power of the finale, but they are
not merely of instrumental value; they are of value for
what they are in themselves. The splendors of the heavens and the marvels of the geomorphic Earth do not
simply lie in their roles as a fertilizer for life. There is
value wherever there is positive creativity. It is *productive
power,* not merely *experiential power,* that produces value.

It is therefore unfortunate that this projective principle should be termed an anthropic principle, suggesting
that the point of the universe is to produce *Homo sapiens,*
with its corollary that other phases of the story are errant
worlds. It is hubris to believe that everything else in the
universe, in all its remotest corners, either has some
relevance to our being here or has no value. Nature
displays multiple fields of uncontained exuberance, and
why should the parts irrelevant to us trouble us? Nor is
there any need to cram the universe with other forms of

life and mind. Life and mind need only be among nature's interesting products. In truly cosmopolitan moods humans can find all these levels and regions equally required or fitting for the show. Our level is relative among many reference frames. The anthropic principle is a subset within, if also a pinnacle of, projective nature.

It is also inadequate to think of Earthlings as the only fortunate beings in a nature that uses accidents productively. One way of coupling the anthropic and the accidental components is to see Earth as valuable by accident, with Mercury through Pluto valueless by accident, although the system is valuable for its trial-and-error creativity. Those places had to be there for Earth to be here, in the sense that solar systems have to toss out many planets if there is, now and again, to be one right for life. The non-Earths are like mutants in biology; they are astronomical "permutants." Without mutation, life cannot evolve, but most mutants are worthless; only one in a thousand lies on a successful (well-adapted) track. So with the stars and their planets. Most are wastelands, wayward worlds. A few stars become supernovae and cook up elements that will later become planets. A few planets hit the right combination for the main sequence, for life to evolve. This is not luck at the systemic level, since the stochastic system is programmed for permutational experimenting, with statistically probable hits somewhere. But it is local luck. Where there is a positive hit, the life and mind for which the universe is (s)tumbling can be realized. But the other places? They are out of luck, stillborn worlds, dead residues, errors necessary so that there can be successes elsewhere. The universe is mostly full of miscarriages; rarely does it give birth to life and mind. The others are the "noise" that lies in the background of a "significant signal."

Again, without denying that randomness is there

with (and for) creative results, are these other worlds nothing but false starts, episodic by-places, valueless satellites because they are not in the main orbit? Whatever truth there is in these accounts, there is a truth more fundamental. The pluralism among planets and moons has an explanation in the principle of projective nature. An astronomer is perhaps entitled to think of these things as having only trajectory courses, but a philosopher can think further of projectory courses. That is, these worlds are thrown forward in a weak, nonteleological sense, yet still a spontaneously constructive sense. Part of the coherence of the system is that it invents diversity. So the diversity is not merely accidental. It is intrinsic to the system to spin off unique projects.

The display of planets and moons has indeed resulted from accidents and impingements of related and unrelated causal lines. The planets fell where they fell in their orbits, captured the moons they captured, collided with the meteoroids they accreted, with relative or even absolute randomness; but the cosmic panorama both is and is not accidental. The solar system is a kaleidoscope, and any particular display may mix related and unrelated causal lines, relative and absolute randomness. But that there will be a diverse display—this is not random but the inexorable outcome of a restlessly projective nature. The solar system is, like a "kaleidoscope" etymologically, a system that tumbles through formed beauty.

(1) In earthen *biological diversity,* mutations occur at random. Sometimes this is with absolute randomness; there is no set of sufficient causes in the quantum range when radioactive decay produces radiation that triggers a mutation. Sometimes this is with relative randomness; the causal chains lie all in place but were previously dissociated, as when accidentally ingesting a chemical mutagen precipitates a mutation. One may ask, "Why is

this mutation there?" and give only the reply, "It occurs randomly." But when one asks, "Why is randomness there?" one is less tempted to reply that it is only random that randomness is there. Randomness is as intrinsic to the system as are matter and energy, and biological systems have learned to use it as a diversifier, capturing by natural selection random events advantageous to specific lifelines, building from zero to five million species in as many billion years. Randomness is one of the formative principles.

(2) In human *psychological diversity,* ideas pop into our heads at random, bubbling up from our unconscious minds. Whether this is with absolute or relative randomness we hardly know enough brain physiology to say. These ideas mix with causal and logical lines operating within our psychology; they mix with sociological forces and ideologies, and the resulting achievements of thought and culture are quite diverse. There is rationality here, mixed with personal and social decisions and with related and unrelated interactions of cultural and biological lines. If one asks, "Why were transistors, or steam engines, or wheels discovered just when and where they were?" the answer will contain some causes, some reasons, some randomness. But if one asks whether personalities, societies, cultures will take diverse patterns, the answer is, "They are certain to do so, because psychological and social systems are intrinsically diversifying systems."

(3) In earthen *geomorphological diversity,* no two places are alike—no two mountains, canyons, rivers, islands, continents, tectonic plates, climatic regimens. Each has its distinctive individuality. Again, there are related and unrelated causal lines, there is relative and absolute randomness, so that any specific outcome is only partially predictable or even explainable in retrospect. If one asks

why the Colorado River meanders through the Grand Canyon as it does, with Hance Rapids here and not a half mile west on the same hard strata, the answer contains mixed elements of causation, initial historical conditions that no theory can supply, and perhaps even genuine indeterminacies. But that the Earth is varied topographically is no accident; it is intrinsic to the system to churn landscapes and seascapes, mixing geomorphic principles with enough openness that the resulting diversity never ceases from poles to equator, Paleozoic Era to the present.

(4) In the *solar-systemic diversity,* forerunning the geomorphic, biological, psychological, and social diversities, we confront a similar principle. The unconscious mind is a random idea generator; the genetic system is a random species generator; the geomorphic forces are random landscape generators. The solar-planetary forces are random world generators. The whole spectrum is random project generation. But the randomness is not chaotic; it is creative. Astronomical nature is *drifting through a project search,* simpler than but analogous to the way biological mutations and psychological trial and error are not worthless but a drifting through an information search. What is going on is systematic compositional permutation, the spontaneous appearance of collective order. Something is at work diversifying the material.

(5) In the *galactic diversity*, we can detect projective nature from the start. The energy unleashed at the big bang is turbulently formative; one peculiarity is how it clumps into galaxies and stars. Just where and why it clots this star, Alpha Centauri, and those galaxies, the Magellanic Clouds, we cannot say. Some suppose these locations result from random indeterminacies near the start. But star events in the number 10^{22} and galaxy

events in the number 10⁹, though each may have random factors involving precise location or size, cannot as a statistical tendency be random. This must reflect a law of nature.

A further peculiarity is how certain stars forge the heavier elements, iron, silicon, and the rest, with carbon just managing to form and just managing to escape complete conversion to oxygen. Again, factors here may be random, but that somewhere, sometime, the ninety-odd elements are produced in felicitous proportions—this process, which goes on in billions of stars, cannot be random. It is a formative principle immanent in matter and energy.

A further repeated tendency is for certain stars to explode themselves as supernovae yielding clouds of dust and gas, with such clouds falling in on themselves under their gravity, yet not entirely so. Some chunks get knocked out in the rotating collapsing mass, yielding a great platter about a star's equator. The forces that produced the rings of Saturn or the Galilean moons of Jupiter seem similar to those that produced the solar system, similar to those that rotate the galaxies. Something makes a platter, a protosun at the center; something sweeps up orbiting planets rather than plunges all into the sun. Humans have been ignorant, at least until recently, whether there exist any other solar-planetary systems; but the tendency to clot, differentiate, to collapse and nucleate, to spin and rotate is so pronounced in the universe that our solar system must be an instance of a more pervasive tendency. The dark companion to Barnard's Star, the ring thought to be planets around Fomalhaut, the preplanetary system around Vega, or the streaks of light around Beta Pictoris are beginning to supply empirical evidence that our solar system is not just a freak accident.[18]

One principle here is called a tendency to collapse, as when a galaxy, star, or dust cloud collapses on itself. But the "collapse" so called is matter prone to gravitational alliance with itself, yet in such a way that the swirling, differentiating result is a tendency to construct as much as to collapse. Gravitation couples dust to dust, clump to clump, and spins and heats the whole. The gravitating is counterbalanced by electromagnetic forces, tending to prevent overcollapse into black holes, and protracting the life of stars as sources of materials and energy. The result creates temperature differentials in aggregates kept in turbulence, energy irradiated over matter, all of which is order waiting to happen.

After moral consciousness arises, there can be evil creativity. Perhaps there can be disvaluable creativity within ecosystems, when a new organism evolves to ruin an ecosystem, although the principle that only the better adapted within their communities survive protects against this. But at astronomical levels, it is difficult to think what bad creativity would mean. Nor does a systemically projective nature suppose that all astronomical events are creative. Some are destructive, as when an asteroid crashes into a planet with highly developed landscapes, perhaps even one with ecosystems. Destructions may be inevitable if there is to be perpetually re-churning creativity, an astronomical parallel to the way that biological death is required for there to be ongoing evolutionary life. The destruction of stars as supernovae seeds the matter that later collects into planets. Things are perpetually destroyed, but their destructions are regularly preludes to re-creations. What the model of projective nature finds is a systemically positive creativity that moves events—at least at fertile locations and over significant stretches of time—higher upslope than the destructive forces move events downslope. At such

place-time locations there is recurrent formed integrity.
This does not have to be uninterrupted, and it will not
be unending. Yet if this stops at one place, it will reap-
pear elsewhere.

4. Solar-Planetary Nature: Distinctive World Histories

Now we can think more particularly of the
non-Earth places not so much as accidental mutants but
rather using a model of other "species," other world
kinds with alien integrity. We can appreciate the order
that has happened there for what it is in itself, and not
from a human point of view. The nine planets and thirty-
six moons, together with minor planets, Apollo objects,
comets, planetesimals, thousands of asteroids, and millions of meteoroids, are proving fascinating beyond expectation. The planets show an extraordinary diversity,
and their moons not less so. There are twenty-five
worlds larger than a thousand kilometers across, several
thousand worlds big enough to land a spaceship on.
Differences in body size, composition, density, mass,
gravity, magnetic fields, distance from the Sun, axial tilt,
rotation-to-orbit time ratios, thermal conditions, radioactivity, photodissociation by sunlight, clouds, circulation patterns, equilibrium mechanisms—all result in
complex interactions that make each place a different
story.[19]

The inner planets are rocky; the outer gaseous or icy.
Jupiter is over a thousand times the volume of the Earth.
The pressure at the surface of Venus is a hundred Earth
atmospheres; the temperature 400° C. Jupiter and Saturn
seem to have no surface at all, becoming gradually more

dense with depth. Only Earth seems to have tectonic plates, although Mars, Mercury, Europa, Ganymede, and probably Venus have crustal fracturing. The atmospheres of the planets (on all but Mercury and possibly Pluto) and even on some moons (Titan) vary widely. Some atmospheres (Earth, Venus, Mars) evolve dramatically. Wind velocities at Saturn's equator can reach 450 m/sec. In addition to Jupiter's array of moons, it has two sets of Trojan asteroids locked into its orbit, proceeding fore and aft. Io is bizarre, perpetually in volcanic convulsions, heated by an eccentric orbit around massive Jupiter, causing frictional tides. Orbiting in Jupiter's giant magnetic field, Io generates a massive electric current, 5 million amperes. The magnetosphere of Jupiter, a pulsing field, if we could see it in the night sky, would be several times as large as the moon. Ganymede and Callisto, which might have been thought similar, have quite different histories.

On Jupiter and Venus there are auroras and lightning. The F-ring of Saturn contains five components in irregular, interweaving orbits that no present theory of orbital dynamics adequately explains. Saturn displays 100,000 discrete rings. Earth and its moon are quite dissimilar companions; the Moon has proved more complex and evolved than expected, although waterless, airless, lifeless; and scientists are puzzled how these two came into their binary partnership. A fresh challenge to solar science is to explain why planets, moons, asteroids are as varied as they are.

Possibly we are dealing with a pluralism that has no principled unity. The solar "system" so called is not a coherent system; the planets and moons are isolated worlds with little in common, nothing past the physics, chemistry, and geomorphologies they share. They may once have had common causal lines or origins, mixed with many nonrelated causal lines. But these have since separated; each world goes its own, unrelated way. Never do they meet. After all, many other parts of our universe are out of causal contact with each other. We should not speak of astronomical *nature* in the singular; there are only local and multiple *natures* in unrelated worlds.

Possibly the sorts of questions later generated on Earth, a place of value, about whether these other worlds also have value is a misplaced question, an interplanetary category mistake. We ought not ask whether they have value; this is an earthbound question that cannot be asked there, something like asking whether it is 9:00 P.M. Eastern Standard Time on Pluto, or whether the enormous collision that nearly destroyed Mimas might have happened on a Tuesday. The value question, so far as it can be asked, is an exported question, which can only be related to Earthlings' needs or interests. It cannot be asked intrinsically, neither from the point of view of a planet-in-itself, nor systemically from the point of view of the Solar System. Alien planets and solar systems do not have value points of view; only Earthlings do.

But possibly we can learn to ask value questions in nonearthbound ways, and interpret what is happening on the planets as continued formative activity. Take cratering, for instance. This batters and saturates the terrestrial planetary landscapes and seems chaotic and valueless. But these collisions, which only leave meaningless scars from one perspective, are from another perspective the operation of the gravitational forces that swept up the planets in the first place. What is sporadic on short time scales (an occasional meteor crash) is systemic on larger time scales (the collecting of local worlds). These impacts fuse pacts of matter. Without this accreting of chunks, there would have been no Earth, no life, no persons. One cause of the emptiness in interplanetary space is that matter is swept up into planets and moons, and in this sense emptiness in space is the obverse of constructiveness in projective nature, which has gathered up the puzzle pieces. There is emptiness there because there is something here.[20]

With the manufacturing of land comes the manufacturing of landscapes. As the terrestrial planets are formed, impact cratering subsides, but enough continues to churn relief. Further, volcanism and tectonic movements appear, widespread and powerful. Olympus Mons, a volcano on Mars, approaches the size of Texas. Crustal fracturing is found on Mars and Mercury, on Europa and Ganymede, and probably on Venus. Planets and moons often have (or have had) internal heat engines, which further churn relief. Lava flooding is present on the Moon (the mare regions). Even the "dead" scenes have been active at previous times.

Weathering and erosion erase what volcanism, tectonic movements, and impact cratering have constructed, and yet these too are constructive forces. Where there is an atmosphere (Earth, Mars, Venus, Titan) moving over a surface, meteorological forces transport materials and erase landscapes (now combining with the gravity that, earlier, was crucial for accretion). Where there is liquid—water, methane, carbon-dioxide glaciers, lava—fluvial erosion can take place (on Earth, Mars, perhaps Titan). These morphological and orogenic forces interplay and carve landscapes. Anyone who appreciates rugged landscapes (cliffs, gorges, expanses) on Earth will delight in the Valles Marineris on Mars, with canyons four times as deep as the Grand Canyon and as long as the United States is wide. Any Earthling who enjoys watching weather fronts and storm clouds will find awesome the storms on Jupiter.

Each new world, each place in that world, will be a novel topography, more or less interesting, but never uninteresting, just as each landscape on Earth is a new twist to the kaleidoscope. Though the other planets are places of limited possibility, at least in their present states, they are also places where formative nature is creatively at work. Some things will be interesting because they are further expressions of familiar laws of nature extrapolated from Earth: the elements, the atomic table, chemistries, the 32 crystal classes, often the mineralogies and rock types. Yet each world will also be interesting because its particular phenomena actualize potential unknown on Earth. The language currently preferred (because it has a ring of scientific respectability) is of the "evolution" of each planet and place. What is really meant is that each location has its own history.

On the basis of what we know from chemistry, physics, geomorphology, meteorology, mineralogy, and petrology, solar scientists might think they can predict what we will find before we explore a new planet. But this will not be entirely so. Physicists and chemists have often anticipated what they would next find: the neutrino, helium in the atomic table. Astronomy is often a highly predictive science. Neptune and Pluto were predicted before they were seen, as was the bending of light near the Sun and the spiraling solar wind. Orbits and eclipses can be predicted centuries ahead.

By contrast biology has been a poorly predictive science. The organelles in the cell—the nucleus, chromosomes, mitochondria, plasmids—were surprises. One can never predict, before examining a new plant, what alkaloids it contains, and thus the vincristine in *Catharanthus roseus* came unsuspected. One can never say, before exploring a hitherto unknown lake, island, or tropical forest just what is there, especially if isolated from already known faunas and floras and speciation has been at work. The discovery of *Catagonus,* an "extinct" peccary alive in Paraguay, came as a surprise. This is because biology is full of history as physics and chemistry are not.

We are learning that solar science, too, despite its laws, is full of history. Each planet, moon, place is going to have its own story, a unique world that cannot be predicted in advance, not entirely, not in many interesting details, but which can be enjoyed only upon discovery. So it was with the odd orbits of Nereid and Triton, Neptune's moons, with the rings of Uranus, and its rotational axis in the plane of its orbit, with Pluto's companion, Charon, with the frenzied activity on Io, and so it will be with whether Saturn has D, E, and G rings. Bradford Smith, a team leader on the Voyager missions, said, "I don't think we could have been more wrong in predicting what we would see on the Galilean satellites."[21] What Voyager found that was unexpected was the equal of what Magellan found that was unexpected.

Celestial mechanics calculates results so beautifully just because it leaves out the "personalities" of the planets. Where and what size a planet is, its axial tilt, how many moons it has, whether these were spinoffs from the parent or gained by capture, what their orbits are, whether a planet or moon has an atmosphere, its meteorology, its magnetic field, its magnetosphere, what volcanic eruptions have taken place, whether a planet radiates more heat than it receives from the Sun—such characteristics can be suspected but are derivable from no theory plus initial conditions. Initial conditions, which are themselves history, couple with laws of nature and perhaps with genuine indeterminacies; knowns mix with unknowns to drive storied developments, kaleidoscopes of related and unrelated causal lines, relative and perhaps even absolute randomness, all products of interesting diversity. There will be order with spontaneity, constancy with contingency. We can predict only parts of the stories. We can predict that there will be surprises, and that many of the surprises will be worlds of strange integrity.

The technical way of saying this is that solar science, as well as interstellar astronomy, is going to be as idiographic as it is nomothetic. A plain way of saying this is that these planets, places, projects will routinely command proper names.

5. *Preserving Nature: Respecting Projective Integrity*

Humans ought to preserve projects of formed integrity, wherever found. Already operating in earthbound environmental ethics, this principle underlies respect for life, organic individuals, species, ecosystems, landscapes. Humans themselves are a lofty expression of this creativity; the mind and hand epitomize creativity, and our own continuing creativity (expressed in human capacities for space travel, for understanding alien places, for use of nonearthen resources) is also to be respected. This licenses the exploration and even the exploitation of space. But just as the human dominion on Earth is constrained by a respect for other forms of being, the human presence in space, which is neither our dominion nor our native domicile, ought to be constrained by a respect for alien forms of projective integrity. If an ethicist shrinks from the vocabulary of *duty* here, there will be *ideals of attitude* toward these places.

Can this be expressed in more detail? Two caveats follow, with six preliminary rules for nature preservation in the solar system. A first warning: Humans are now in a poor position to say what the formed integrities elsewhere in the solar system are. Speculating over what places, planets, moons should be designated as nature preserves would be more foolish than for Columbus to have worried over what areas of the New World should be set aside as national parks and wildernesses. All the same, in retrospect, our forefathers would have left us a better New World had they been concerned sooner about preserving what they found there, not as early as the fifteenth century but neither as late as the nineteenth and twentieth centuries. Let the twenty-first, the twenty-second, and the twenty-third centuries profit by the mistakes of the sixteenth, seventeenth, and eighteenth. Earthlings have little power to affect extraterrestrial places today, but then the Pilgrim Fathers posed little threat to the ozone layer with fluorocarbons, nor to genetic processes through plutonium radioactivity.

A second warning: Banish soon and forever the bias that only habitable places are good ones (temperature 0–30 degrees C., with soil, water, breathable air), and all uninhabitable places empty wastes, piles of dull stones, dreary, desolate swirls of gases. To ask what these worlds are *good for* prevents asking whether these worlds are *good* in deeper senses. The class of habitable places is only a subset of the class of valuable places. To fail as functional for Earth-based life is not to fail on form, beauty, spectacular eventfulness. Even on Earth humans have learned, tardily, to value landscapes and seascapes that have little or nothing to do with human comfort (Antarctica, the Sahara, marine depths). Just as there is appropriate behavior before Earthen places, regardless of their hospitality for human life, so there will be appropriate (and inappropriate) behavior before Martian landscapes and Jovian atmospheric seas.

These other worlds are not places that failed. Nature never fails. Nature only succeeds more or less with its projective integrity. We do not condemn a rock because it failed to be a tree, though we may value it less than a tree. We do not condemn a tree because it failed to be a person, though we may value it less than a person. We ought not condemn Mars because it failed to be Earth, although we may value it less than Earth. There may be fewer formed integrities on Neptune, but there will be some that do not exist on Earth. Learning to appreciate these alien places for what they are in themselves, not depreciating them for what they failed to be, will provide an ultimate test in nature appreciation. Only as we allow that it is good that Apollo asteroids are of no "earthly use" will we learn whether they are an outlandish good.

After these warnings, we can think more positively. The following rules probe toward an exploration ethic.

(1) *Respect any natural place spontaneously worthy of a proper name.* Projective nature is valuable at the systemic level; and there results a kind of baseline value in every rock and cloud, since even the simplest things are products of nature's creativity. But such value is so pervasive and relatively minimal (though absolutely impressive) that it cannot be made operational. Many products of nature (meteoroids, lava flows, dust clouds) have insufficient projective integrity to warrant particular respect or admiration. Others do, and one way to test for these is to see whether an entity commands a proper name. Proper names are often tags for the convenience of geographers and mapmakers (the Four Corners Area, the Hellas Basin) or needed for historical reasons (Plymouth Rock, Halley's Comet), and humans sometimes give their artifacts (cities, nations) proper names. Proper names given for other reasons are not sufficient to warrant protection. But some places seem to warrant proper

names for what they spontaneously are in themselves. If so, that signals our perception of enough topographic integrity to enter its protection into the calculus of trade-offs. This protection should be at something like the level of scope to which the proper name attaches. Such a place will have features, differentiation from elsewhere, peculiarity of form, ensemble of components, gestalt and mood, all of which are ingredients of formed integrity.

In this sense we will probably not come to feel that humans have duties to every crater on the Moon or to each solar flare because these places/events as such have little integrated process in them. But by the time we are drawn to attach a proper name to a place, there is enough particularity, differentiation and integration of locus, enough provincial identity to call for protection. This does not address the question how much these places count; it only locates one particular sort of thing that can come to count operationally in an extraterrestrial ethic. We might also want to preserve representative types, but what one is respecting here is not generic landscapes but particular locality.

As test cases, one might ask whether to preserve Phobas or the Great Red Spot on Jupiter. We can imagine (in the not-too-distant future) military commanders testing to see whether they had enough nuclear muscle to blow these places to smithereens. The rule here is that such testing should not, without overriding justification, destroy places with enough site integrity to command proper names.

(2) *Respect exotic extremes in natural projects.* On worlds elsewhere and elsewhen nature will give expression to potential that could not be realized on Earth. This will always be true more or less, but where true the more, where there is salient quantity, quality, or natural kind, that will be reason for appreciating notable formed in-

tegrity. Just as humans value diversity on Earth, humans should value diversity in the solar system, all part of the robust richness of nature. For instance, rock volcanoes and the basalt they spout will be common both on Earth and elsewhere, but volcanoes of ice, spouting lava made of ammonia and water, or liquid methane seas may exist on Titan and not elsewhere. Saturn's splendid rings may be unexcelled in many solar systems. Jupiter's ring may be dynamic, steadily lost into Jupiter's atmosphere and replenished, by material supplied from satellites just outside it, as Saturn's rings are not. That a formative event in nature is rare is, *prima facie,* reason for its preservation. At such places humans can learn something about the *nature* of things, the *nature* in things.

The second rule extends the first in that humans respect phenomena in addition to places, extremes in systemic expression, regardless of whether they call forth proper names. Such events are, to twist a phrase of astronomers, singularities—not naked singularities but idiomorphic ones. To play with a phrase of particle physicists, we ought to conserve strangeness. This can be interpreted, if one prefers, as an ideal of human excellence, but it can be interpreted as well in terms of respect for "excellences" (= exuberances) in projective nature. These are places where humans get flung into wildness and magnificence unbounded by earthly constraints. If Earthlings consider only whether these places have functional utility, our experience can be of futility or horror; but if we consider the expressions of which nature is capable, the experience can be of amazement in wonderland.

(3) *Respect places of historical value.* Some planets, moons, places do not merely spin; they spin stories. They have their "once upon a time," their "long ago and far away," their "fortunes." Some have more story than

others. History is nowhere even-textured and homogeneous. Although all events are contained in history, they are not equally critical or significant historically. In earthbound history, some decades, centuries, persons, nations, species, mutations have more import for the ongoing story. Astronomical nature too is historical, usually at a slower pace, at least from our inertial reference frame; but there too are flux and change, beginnings and endings, turning points.

Humans ought to preserve those places that have been more eventful than others. The places where water flows or has flowed (only on Mars?) will be of special interest. Some planets, moons, cratered plains, fault canyons, mountain ranges provide more complex books to be read. Some are palimpsests, canvases with the new painted over the old. Some provide fossil evidence for the history of the solar system in ways that others do not. Callisto is a 120-degree-K ice museum of a bombardment period four billion years ago. Some may once have had life, or have made near approaches to it, of which evidence is left. The Moon, Mars, and Mercury are senile landscapes. From the rule to follow, this provides a reason not to preserve them; but we have here to notice that they are museum places where the records have been kept from the first two-and-a-half billion years of planetary evolution, and that is reason for preserving their richest landscapes. So we might permit engineers to simulate a nuclear meltdown on Mare Imbrium, but not in Tycho, the great rayed crater, since the latter is of historical interest as the former is not.

This rule can, like the others, be interpreted humanistically as saving these stories for humans to read. But it can better be interpreted as recognizing that projective nature is a historical system, a book that writes itself, and that one human value is being let in on this valuable eventfulness, these histories spun entirely apart from the human presence.

In combination, the preceding rules should preserve places of high scientific value.

(4) *Respect places of active and potential creativity.* Some places, planets, moons will be more energetic than others, perhaps on geological scales, perhaps volatile and ephemeral. Others will be stillborn, quiescent, others senile. By this criterion, Earth's moon is inactive; Jupiter is dynamic. By contrast with the ancient surface of Callisto, the surface of Io is as young as yesterday. Some of these places may, in a future epoch, when the Sun explodes, become habitats for life. We want to respect the hot spots of projective nature. We protect generativity; we keep open the theatre. We mistreat nature to see it as inert and passive, as dumb stuff, unless and until activated and enlightened by mind. Rule 4 is the forward-looking complement to Rule 3, a retrospective rule.

Over perhaps five billion years, the evolutionary development on Earth has climbed from zero to over five million species. A deplorable thing that the lately arrived humans are doing is shutting down the speciation processes by habitat depletion and extinctions, at a rate that is potentially catastrophic. They are thwarting the formative biological processes. Similarly, we ought not to degrade the solar-planetary creativity. In the solar system, as much time lies ahead as behind us (perhaps five billion years in both directions). Perhaps Earthlings cannot greatly affect the solar-systemic evolution on broad scales; but perhaps they can shut down locales of active development, and that would be a pity.

All the planetary places are energy knots in a restlessly active space-time plasma/ether. Even the coolest of them—Pluto and Charon—are freeze-dried energy, coalesced in what is only an apparent void. The "hottest

The Planetary Environment

Space travelers will find a vast array of natural
resources ripe for commercial and industrial
exploitation buried within a stunning new realm
of scientific and aesthetic wonder and delight.

(ABOVE: *Mars from Phobos;* BELOW: *Saturn from its moon Rhea*)

Resource exploitation of the solar system will begin with the mining of asteroids in near-Earth orbit. Some experts believe that it will be possible to move these asteroids into orbit around the Earth before mining begins.

(Asteroid mining above Earth)

With the establishment of a station on the Moon and a colony on Mars, scenes like this one will become commonplace.

(Dust storm on Mars)

Kazuaki Iwasaki/Space Art International

Expeditions to more remote places like the moons of Jupiter and Saturn will bring back breath-taking scenes like these. They will gradually broaden our aesthetic appreciation of nature, encouraging and nurturing preservationist and conservationist concern for the solar system as a whole.

(ABOVE: *Io and Jupiter;* BELOW: *Iapetus*)

Michael Carroll

Just as the first pictures from space of our planet suggested the concept of Spaceship Earth, transforming forever our perceptions of the world we live on, images like this one, looking inward from the edge of our planetary system, may one day provide the foundation for a new vision of our solar environment and of the place of humankind in the universe— moving us well beyond the concept of Spaceship Earth.

(Our Sun from Pluto)

places"—not in terms of degrees Kelvin but in terms of energy irradiated over matter in formative thermal ranges—deserve special consideration. A planet, or a place on it, not less than a particle, is a manifestation of the great underlying process, and where that process is especially pregnant, humans ought to respect the pregnancy. This can, again, be an ideal of human excellence, but it can be a respect for "excellences," creativity in projective nature.

(5) *Respect places of aesthetic value.* Some planets, moons, comets will have more symmetry, harmony, elegance, beauty, grandeur than others, and this counts for their preservation. Aesthetic value is always present with formed integrity, although aesthetics is not the only category through which such integrity is to be interpreted. Complexity, fertility, rarity, information content, historical significance, potential for development, and stability are others. Nevertheless, aesthetic properties are high-order value properties and should be preserved in the degree to which they are present. Such scenes are the "pictures" that illustrate the historical "text." They provide the "poetry" that graces the "prose," excellences that register on sensitive beholders as they come under the sway of creativity inherent in solar-planetary nature. Out there experiences of the sublime hitherto unknown await us, and respect is demanded in the presence of the overwhelmingly sublime.

(6) *Respect places of transformative value.* [22] A major theme during the last four centuries has been widening human horizons. Humans have become modern as they have gained awareness of the depths of historical change, of the diversity and extent of creation, of the magnitude of time and space. Astronomers with their telescopes, biologists with their microscopes, taxonomists with their phylogenetic trees, geographers with

their travels, along with others such as geomorphologists, paleontologists, archaeologists, anthropologists, have widened our vistas. Space exploration is writing still a further chapter in the story of pushing back horizons.

Humans ought to preserve those places that radically transform perspective. Just as it was a good thing for medieval Europe to be dislodged from its insularity, challenged by the Enlightenment and the Scientific Revolution, it will be a good thing for Earthlings to be unleashed from the Earth-givens. We can reduce human provinciality with the diverse provinces of solar-planetary nature. In space, so much is scrambled—what counts as day or night, year or season, hot or cold, up or down, bizarre or normal, what counts as land, sea, sky, the feel of gravity. These disorienting, unsettling discoveries will expand our juvenile perspectives. For intellectual and moral growth one wants alien places that utterly renegotiate everything in native ranges. These will prove *radical* places to understand, not merely in the anthropic sense that our *roots* lie there, but in the nonanthropic sense that they *uproot* us from home and force us to grow by assimilating the giddy depths and breadth of being. Those who cannot be seriously confounded by nature have not yet seriously confronted it.

Some will say that this makes instrumental use of solar-planetary nature, finding its appreciation a means to larger human experiences. We preserve those places that act as intellectual fertilizer. That is true, but not the end of the account. Sooner or later, humans will concede that these places have high transformative value because they have exotic formed integrity. They fertilize the human mind because nature is creatively projecting something there. In this sense Rule 6 is the upshot of Rules 1 through 5.

A principal thing to get transformed in space is our

earthbound value system. Out there few places are warm or comfortable, there is no sentience, no pain, pleasure, interests, much less felt preferences satisfied. There is no resource use, no adaptation for survival, no genetic sets defended. Nothing seeks anything; there are no means to ends. There is neither love nor freedom. There is only indifference. All is blah! So we incline to judge, from our relative earthen reference frame, that these are valueless places. Values happen on Earth, not elsewhere, unless Earthlings go elsewhere.

But there are mysteries that ride on the Sun's rays, majesties in the swirling gases and chunks of matter, and humans will benefit by learning to see other worlds, other events where they are for what they are, as surely as they benefit by having air, water, and soil. The historical struggle, repeated now in ourselves, has always been to get a big enough picture; and we now stand at an exciting place: one world trying to figure out the others.

The human genius takes an interest outside its own biological sector. Nonhuman species take an interest (biological or psychological) merely within habitat, in prey or predator, in resource or shelter. Only the human species can value at a distance that which does not stand in its own lineage, underpinning, or life-support system. The initial challenge of environmental ethics has been to press that task in the earthen environment. A space ethic extends the challenge into the astronomical environment. We require a space metaphysics to go with space physics. Space exploration must also be value exploration.

Later on, humans become *excited* (in the psychological sense) when they get let in on these things. Earlier on, what is first happening is that these places, planets, moons, with their winds, clouds, tectonic movements, volcanism, electromagnetic fields, are getting *excited* (in the geophysical sense) by energy fluxing over matter, by heat engines within, by solar radiation, by radioactivity, by kinetic and other creative forces of nature. In the order of knowing, the excitement is first in the human beholder and then in the systems beheld. But the excitement, in order of being, is first in objective, energetic, material nature, and only much later in human subjectivity. It need not follow that every excitement of physical nature can or should excite value in a human beholder (not in more than foundational, baseline ways), but the more lofty excitements of physical nature will regularly produce valued excitement in human beholders. Until we have a value theory that takes things in proper order, we have not yet enjoyed the transformative value that solar-planetary nature has to offer.

Some will complain that all this is wrestling with shadows; there is no value in solar-planetary nature, only an illusion that appears when humans come on stage. But I think not; we are wrestling with creativity. Positive creativity is no illusion, but rather the principal value in the universe, from which all else derives, and which above all needs appreciation and protection. Some will complain that, even if there is extraterrestrial value, any present concern about preserving it is far-fetched. Perhaps so, but sooner or later the far-fetched can become farsighted.

References

1. Michael Collins, "Foreword," in Roy A. Gallant, *National Geographic Picture Atlas of Our Universe* (Washington, D.C.: National Geographic Society, 1980), p. 6.
2. LaMont C. Cole, "Man's Ecosystem," *BioScience* 16 (1966): 243–48, citation on p. 243. See also Freeman Dyson's puzzlement about nature's kind accidents cited below (note 9) and that of

P.C.W. Davies about extraordinary coincidences and apparently accidental cooperations (note 12).

3. C.W. Misner, K.S. Thorne, and J.A. Wheeler, *Gravitation* (San Francisco: W.H. Freeman, 1973), p. 1215.

4. Stephen Jay Gould, "Chance Riches," *Natural History* 89, no. 11 (November 1980): 36–44; "Perhaps our world really is only the result of randomness" (p. 36).

5. George Wald, "Fitness in the Universe: Choices and Necessities," in J. Oró, S.L. Miller, C. Ponnamperuma, and R.S. Young, eds., *Cosmochemical Evolution and the Origins of Life* (Dordrecht, Holland: D. Reidel Publishing Co., 1974), pp. 7–27, citation on p. 22.

6. For what follows see, in addition to following references, John A. Wheeler, "The Universe as Home for Man," in Owen Gingerich, ed., *The Nature of Scientific Discovery* (Washington, D.C.: Smithsonian Institution Press, 1975), pp. 261–96; also his "Genesis and Observership" in Robert E. Butts and Jaakko Hintikka, eds., *Foundational Problems in the Special Sciences* (Dordrecht, Holland: D. Reidel Publishing Co., 1977), pp. 3–33.

7. B.J. Carr and M.J. Rees, "The Anthropic Principle and the Structure of the Physical World," *Nature* 278 (1979): 605–12, quotations on pp. 605, 609. See also George Gale, "The Anthropic Principle," *Scientific American* 245, no. 6 (December 1981): 154–71; B. Carter, "Large Number Coincidences and the Anthropic Principle in Cosmology," in M.S. Longair, ed., *Confrontation of Cosmological Theories with Observational Data* (Dordrecht, Holland: D. Reidel Publishing Co., 1974), pp. 291–98; and John D. Barrow and Frank J. Tipler, *The Anthropic Cosmological Principle* (New York: Oxford University Press, 1986).

8. Bernard Lovell, "In the Centre of Immensities" (presidential address to the British Association for the Advancement of Science, 27 August 1975), published in part as "Whence?" in the *New York Times Magazine*, 16 November 1975, pp. 27, 72–95, citation on p. 88, p. 95. See also Bernard Lovell, *In the Center of Immensities* (New York: Harper and Row, 1978), pp. 123–26. On the other hand, if the same force (the strong nuclear force) were a few percent weaker, only hydrogen could exist.

9. Freeman J. Dyson, "Energy in the Universe," *Scientific American* 225, no. 3 (September 1971): 50–59, citation on p. 59.

10. Fred Hoyle, "The Universe: Past and Present Reflections," *Engineering and Science* 45, no. 2 (November 1981): 8–12, citation on

p. 12. See Hoyle's "On Nuclear Reactions Occurring in Very Hot Stars, I. The Synthesis of Elements from Carbon to Nickel," *The Astrophysical Journal,* Supplement Series, 1 (1954): 121–46.

11. Marek Demianski, quoted at the Conference on Quantum Theory and Gravitation, Loyola University, 1983, in Dietrick E. Thomsen, "In the Beginning Was Quantum Gravity," *Science News* 124, no. 10 (3 September 1983): 152–57, citation on p. 152.

12. P.C.W. Davies, *The Accidental Universe* (New York: Cambridge University Press, 1982), pp. 90, 110.

13. Mike Corwin, "From Chaos to Consciousness," *Astronomy* 11, no. 2 (February 1983): 14–22, citations on pp. 16–17, 19.

14. Wald, "Fitness in the Universe: Choices and Necessities," p. 8f.

15. Manfred Eigen, "Self-organization of Matter and the Evolution of Biological Macromolecules," *Die Naturwissenschaften* 58 (1971): 465–523, citation on p. 519.

16. Eric Chaisson, "The Scenario of Cosmic Evolution," *Harvard Magazine* 80, no. 2 (November–December 1977): 21–33, citations on pp. 29, 33.

17. K.G. Denbigh, *An Inventive Universe* (New York: George Braziller, 1975).

18. M. Mitchell Waldrop, "First Sightings," *Science 85* 6, no. 5 (June 1985): 26–33.

19. Most of the empirical facts in what follows can be found in J. Kelly Beatty, Brian O'Leary, and Andrew Chaikin, eds., *The New Solar System,* 2nd ed. (Cambridge, Mass.: Sky Publishing Co., 1982) or in G.A. Briggs and F.W. Taylor, *The Cambridge Photographic Atlas of the Planets* (Cambridge, England: Cambridge University Press, 1982).

20. In a still more fundamental sense, all matter and energy are a warp, crinkle, bubble in space-time, so that the space-time "emptiness" is really the "fullness" out of which everything appears.

21. Bradford A. Smith, "The Voyager Encounters," in Beatty et al., *The New Solar System,* 2nd. ed. (Cambridge, Mass.: Sky Publishing Co., 1982): pp. 105–16, citation on p. 109.

22. Adapting a phrase used by Bryan Norton in the context of preserving Earth's biological species. The author also appreciates the criticisms of J. Baird Callicott.

Wilderness and Space

PAUL F. UHLIR
and WILLIAM P. BISHOP

I. Introduction

*W*ilderness is a concept that is not new to mankind. Nor is the connection between the concept of wilderness and outer space revolutionary. There are, however, many opportunities and implications not obviously apparent that arise by placing space in the context of wilderness or by viewing the earthly wilderness from the vantage point of space.

Wilderness has meant and continues to mean different things to different cultures and individuals. It has been a frontier, a place for expansion and colonization, and a source of natural resources. It has also been a place of psychological renewal, of religious and metaphysical significance, and aesthetic pleasure. Most recently, it has been the object of legal definition and protection in U.S. and international law. Man has thus taken the first small steps to change from being a reckless exploiter of wilder-

183

ness to the steward of the wilderness that remains on Earth.

Outer space, and more immediately our solar system, is the last great wilderness or collection of wildernesses. It is already perceived as a new frontier and as a strategically important location, both militarily and economically. We have tried with mixed success to protect other vast wilderness areas, especially the polar regions and the seas. The opportunity to protect the space wilderness is before us in the next few decades. We can and should set up the framework now.

Regarding a matter of more urgent importance— the preservation of our planet's natural environment —a number of converging trends make it possible to provide better stewardship over the remaining earthly wildernesses. Space gives us a unique vantage point for viewing huge geographical areas. The recently developed remote-sensing technologies, the data-processing powers of computers, and the beginning of true scientific understanding of regional ecosystems provide the basis for a dramatically different management technique for wilderness areas.

We will therefore explore three themes: (1) the general concept of wilderness and how it relates to space; (2) managing the earthly wilderness from space; and (3) managing the space wilderness.

II. Wilderness in Space

Before we discuss the space wilderness we must briefly examine some of the background attitudes that have shaped people's perceptions of nature here on Earth. There are two opposing world views that largely frame the basic attitudes toward wilderness. These are grounded in rationalism, which is essentially a "West-ern" outlook, and mysticism, which is predominantly an "Eastern" perspective.

In general, rationalism fosters an adversarial attitude toward nature. Being anthropocentric and materialistic, rationalism defines mankind's role as making order out of the surrounding chaos. Man must battle nature and conquer it to serve human needs. Since wilderness is that part of nature not yet subjugated, its value to man is primarily as a repository of unexploited resources. Wil-derness has no intrinsic value and no inherent rights; its value is assigned and all rights belong to man.

Mystical religions and philosophies are less an-thropocentric and more spiritualistic. Nature is neither chaotic nor something to battle. All things and beings coexist in harmony, and man is an integral part of nature. Wilderness thus has intrinsic value, apart from any value assigned to it by mankind. All living beings and even inanimate objects have an inherent purpose and a con-comitant right to exist.

Another way of classifying attitudes toward wilder-ness is by objective and subjective values. An objective view of wilderness employs a cost/benefit analysis in de-termining whether a certain wilderness area ought to be preserved and how it should be used. The factors impor-tant to such an analysis are relevant to areas of material human welfare, and are therefore primarily utilitarian. Subjective wilderness values are intangible and highly personal. They cannot be evaluated under a cost/benefit analysis because they are not quantifiable. It does not make them any less significant, however. We have iden-tified four general categories of subjective values: psy-chological/experiential, metaphysical/religious, moral/ ethical, and aesthetic.

Psychological wilderness values are entirely experience-oriented. This has led some observers to define wilderness in terms of experience (that is, the wilderness of natural sounds undisturbed by any man-made noises), rather than as simply a certain geographical area.[1] In the past, wilderness was primarily a place of physical and mental challenge, a proving ground. It also provided a place for solitude, for introspection or inspiration, for experiencing a feeling of personal freedom.[2] As population and urbanization have increased, so has the need to "get away from it all." Wilderness provides that opportunity.

Aesthetic values are commonly associated with the concept of wilderness. They are often used to justify the preservation of some spectacular spot in nature. Although aesthetics form an important part of subjective wilderness values, it is necessary to recognize that wilderness is more than just a pretty face.

As a part of nature, wilderness has had tremendous symbolic significance in religious and metaphysical contexts. An example of the symbolic value of wilderness areas common to all religions is the concept of "geo-piety," or "sacred grounds."[3] It refers to an area in nature that possesses divine power, where a person can have a transcendental experience or where some supernatural event has occurred that is central to a religion's dogma. Such an area must be preserved in its natural condition.

A more modern expression of the values attached to wilderness by mystical religions can be found among "ecophilosophers" and adherents to the "deep ecology" movement.[4] Under their value system, wilderness has an inherent right to exist and it is immoral or unethical to destroy it.

Only two centuries ago, the earthly wilderness was almost beyond measure. Vast areas were unexplored and uncharted. The prevailing attitude toward wilderness in the United States was based on extreme rationalism and materialistic values. Armed with the "frontier spirit," our forefathers set out to "tame the wild west" and exploit the land's natural resources to the fullest. As the unprotected wilderness areas began to rapidly dwindle by the early part of this century, their increasing scarcity prompted a national debate on the desirability of officially protecting those areas.[5]

It was not until 1964, however, that the U.S. government passed the Wilderness Act,[6] which established a National Wilderness Preservation System. Section 2 (c) of the act defined wilderness as follows:

> A wilderness, in contrast with those areas where man and his own works dominate the landscape, is hereby recognized as an area where the Earth and its community of life are untrammeled by man, where man himself is a visitor who does not remain. An area of wilderness is further defined to mean in this Act an area of undeveloped Federal land retaining its primeval character and influence, without permanent improvements or human habitation, which is protected and managed so as to preserve its natural conditions and which (1) generally appears to have been affected primarily by the forces of nature, with the imprint of man's work substantially unnoticeable; (2) has outstanding opportunities for solitude or a primitive and unconfined type of recreation; (3) has at least five thousand acres of land or is of sufficient size as to make practicable its preservation and use in an unimpaired condition; and (4) may also contain ecological, geological, or other features of scientific, educational, scenic, or historical value.

There are two things worth noting about the Wilderness Act in terms of the present discussion. Prior to the act, all of our remaining wilderness areas had little legal protection and no means of preservation. The creation of officially designated, legally protected wilderness areas turned them into artifacts subject to human control, but within a framework of preservationist principles and standards. This brings us to the second important point, and that is the way the act defined wilderness. It recognized that wilderness has nonmaterialistic values that are worth protecting. The act thus merged subjective, nonmaterialistic values with an objective cost/benefit analysis in setting up a rational land-use framework. As such, the Wilderness Act was a precedent-setting, national policy statement. Subsequent U.S. legislation has expanded the scope of protected wilderness areas, using the same or similar policy guidelines.[7]

It is, unfortunately, much more difficult to define and protect wilderness areas on an international level. This is so for a number of reasons. One is that the international attitudes toward the concept of wilderness are not subject to the cultural homogeneity of a single nation. It is much harder to establish a common set of operative values in a situation that involves a large number of interested parties with competing views and interests. In terms of a cost/benefit analysis, the more benign scientific, educational, and sociocultural considerations generally play second fiddle to political, military, and economic interests. While this also tends to be true in a national context, governments perceive the stakes as being greater on the international level. For instance, barring military activities in a large international wilderness area can have a significantly greater adverse impact on the perceived or real security interests of a nation than a similar ban in a wilderness area within its own borders.

Despite these obstacles, international wilderness

areas on our planet, such as the Antarctic and the oceans, have gained some measure of protection, particularly since the end of World War II. Although the international community has stopped short of designating them as wilderness areas, a number of protective principles have been established through multilateral treaties. With varying degrees of applicability and success, these principles include nonappropriation,[8] nonpollution,[9] the preservation of living and nonliving resources,[10] the restriction of certain economic and military uses,[11] and freedom of scientific research.[12] If we use the U.S. Wilderness Act as a standard for comparison, we might consider international wilderness areas as only partially recognized and designated, and therefore only partially protected. This brief overview of some of the attitudes and factors that shape our relationship with the natural environment and our general understanding of the concept of wilderness establishes the reference points for the discussion that follows.

Our exploration and utilization of outer space invites us to reassess the fundamental questions regarding our existence. An important part of that reassessment centers on our relationship with nature, both on and off our planet.

The entire universe, beginning just outside Earth's atmosphere, may be viewed as a collection of exotic wildernesses. Within our own solar system there are two generic wilderness areas: the "high seas" of space and the celestial bodies that are islands in those high seas. These two classes of wildernesses have either exaggerated or radically different characteristics from Earth's wildernesses, which will ultimately determine how we perceive and interact with them.

Both the high seas of space and the celestial bodies of our solar system share three common physical features. The first is their primeval nature. They are truly "untrammeled by man," as the Wilderness Act puts it. The second is their superhostile environment. Man cannot survive in space without the most advanced technologies. Thus, man is still "a visitor who does not remain." The third common feature, which is related to the second, is that all the environments outside our own in the solar system appear to be devoid of any organic life forms, at least as we know them.[13] There is also one physical characteristic not shared by the two types of space wildernesses—the high seas of space are infinite and formless whereas celestial bodies are finite forms.

These special attributes of the outer-space environment present us with the opportunity for novel wilderness experiences. Many of the psychological aspects commonly associated with a wilderness experience on Earth are distorted in some way. For instance, space travel and exploration is an "unnatural" activity in the sense that the entire experience is dependent upon state-of-the-art technologies and the maintenance of an artificial environment. A person in space is thus disconnected from the surrounding environment, contrary to most wilderness experiences on Earth. This also limits the potential for aesthetic appreciation only to what can be seen.

The moral and ethical arguments for preserving the environments of celestial bodies are similar to those regarding the preservation of earthly wildernesses.[14] Nevertheless, the apparent absence of any life forms detracts from those arguments. In the case of the high seas of space, such a position becomes difficult to uphold.

Finally, the many metaphysical outlooks on earthly wilderness all acquire a different dimension in the outer-space context. Infinite, unknown, uninhabited, and hostile, the outer-space wilderness will never stop exciting the imagination nor satisfy our inquisitive spirit.

III. *Managing the Earthly Wilderness from the Vantage Point of Space*

The first weather-observing satellite, TIROS-1, was launched by the United States 25 years ago.[15] Since that time the technology for observing the Earth and its atmosphere has advanced dramatically. Two general types of remote-sensing satellites are used, geostationary and polar-orbiting. In the United States, the agency that operates these satellites is the National Oceanic and Atmospheric Administration (NOAA), a branch of the Department of Commerce.

Geostationary satellites are positioned approximately 36,000 km above the equator where they orbit the Earth at the same rate as the Earth rotates below. This allows them to continuously observe the same region. A variety of sensors provide images in the visible and infrared ranges of the spectrum every 30 minutes to three hours. The spatial resolutions of those images range from 1 km to 8 km; that is, we can discern objects or phenomena of that size in the images.

The geostationary satellites, known in the United States as GOES, which stands for geostationary operational environmental satellites, are particularly useful for monitoring large-scale atmospheric phenomena. It is these images that we see on the television weather reports each evening and in the newspapers each morning. The satellites also provide significant oceanographic data on sea surface temperatures, ocean currents, and sea ice. Land surface temperatures and the extent of snow cover or flooding can be determined as well. Finally, the GOES are used to relay environmental measurements that are transmitted by data-collection platforms from remote wilderness areas of the Earth.

Satellites located at 36,000 km above our planet understandably have limitations. A sensor that can simultaneously see an entire hemisphere cannot see many details in any one region. Moreover, it cannot see over the horizon to the polar regions except at a very sharp angle, too sharp to make the image useful. In order to make up for these deficiencies, several polar-orbiting satellites are used. These are referred to as POES, polar-orbiting operational environmental satellites.

The POES fly in orbits that pass nearly over the poles. The orbits precess around the Earth in a gyroscopic fashion at an altitude of about 850 km. Their sensors possess a spatial-resolution capability of approximately 1 km to 4 km, and they are able to obtain much more elaborate information than the geostationary spacecraft.

We will limit the discussion here to the POES' applications to the monitoring and managing of wilderness regions, although they perform many other functions as well. The ability to observe large-scale natural events in remote wilderness areas is important not only for learning more about such occurrences but for warning people of impending danger and protecting wildlife. The POES can identify and track the progress of volcanic eruptions. They can monitor the development and advance of all severe storms, such as sandstorms, tornadoes, hurricanes, and cyclones. They are able to determine forest and wildland conditions that pose an increased risk of fire and can detect and follow wildfires when they occur.

They can also warn of coming droughts or floods by assessing the extent of snow cover and its depth.

All of these capabilities facilitate the process of managing wilderness environments. Other POES functions used for this purpose include the monitoring of vegetation growth, especially useful for the rain-forest crisis; cartography; wildlife supervision, both on land and in the oceans; and pollution control, including the surveillance of oil slicks on large bodies of water, identification of such atmospheric pollution problems as the arctic haze and ozone depletion, and location of the sources of pollution.

A different type of polar-orbiting satellite is used for viewing the geology and biology of smaller land regions. The U.S. version of this kind of spacecraft is called "Landsat." Landsat flies at an altitude of 706 km, and its sensors can detect objects as small as 30 meters in size. The satellite can therefore supply much more detailed environmental information than the POES. One significant drawback, however, is that the higher-resolution capability of Landsat also means that the amount of area it can cover in a day is significantly smaller. Whereas a POES can cover each part of the Earth once a day at the equator and more often than that near the polar regions, Landsat repeats its view of any given area only once every 16 days.

Other kinds of orbiting, remote-sensing spacecraft are being developed, both in the United States and elsewhere. Indeed, one of the most important aspects of remote sensing from space is the high level of international cooperation. Geostationary environmental satellites are operated by the United States, the European Space Agency, Japan, and India. Polar-orbiting, remote-sensing satellites have thus far been flown on an operational basis by the United States and the Soviet Union. By the end of

this decade, however, polar-orbiting environmental satellites will be flown by the European Space Agency,
France, Japan, India, and the People's Republic of
China. Canada, Brazil, and Indonesia have plans to
launch their own spacecraft by the beginning of the next
decade. All of these systems are being coordinated
through several international organizations and com-
mittees, including the International Polar-Orbiting Meteorological Satellite (IPOMS) group, the Coordination on
Geostationary Meteorological Satellites (CGMS), the
Committee on Earth Observations Satellites (CEOS), the
Landsat Ground Station Operations Working Group
(LGSOWG), and the World Meteorological Organization, a specialized agency of the United Nations.

NOAA and NASA are also in the process of coor-
dinating the development of polar-orbiting, remote-
sensing platforms with the European Space Agency,
Japan, and Canada. Planned for deployment in the early
1990s as a separate component of NASA's Space Station
Program, polar platforms promise to revolutionize
Earth-observation activities and our ability to better understand and manage our Earth's environment. The
platforms will provide guaranteed continuity of envi-
ronmental-satellite data, establish multidisciplinary/
multisensor coordination, improve data management capabilities, and foster international cooperation. Moreover, the increased remote-sensing capabilities will be
provided with greater reliability and less cost than the
current expendable satellites because the platforms will
be serviced in space by our Shuttle crews.

The currently operating remote-sensing satellites already generate large amounts of environmental data.
The launching of all the additional spacecraft mentioned
above will vastly increase the amount of data available.
Presuming that data processing and management diffi-

culties can be overcome, this mass of information will enable scientists to study our planet's environment on a global basis. A multidisciplinary, holistic approach to environmental sciences will change our perceptions and awareness of our impact on our natural environment. Man's relation to nature will be brought sharply into focus.

More specifically, our knowledge of individual wilderness areas will also increase tremendously. This will allow us to effectively manage both designated and undesignated wildernesses. The remote-sensing space systems will serve as electronic "park rangers." They will continue to monitor enormous wilderness areas for signs of potentially dangerous environmental conditions, and they will warn of natural disasters as they develop. With regard to designated wilderness areas, remote-sensing technologies will identify human misuse and thereby assist in the enforcement of existing legislation or treaties. Finally, and perhaps most importantly, they will focus greater attention on the vanishing undesignated wilderness areas, such as the tropical rain forests.

IV. Managing the Space Wilderness

In the previous section we saw how space can be used to help us understand and protect the remaining earthly wildernesses and our environment, in general. A significant feature of the space-based, remote-sensing activity is that it poses practically no environmental hazards of its own, either on our planet or in space. Unfortunately, other human activities in outer space are not as harmless. Moreover, the environmental risks are certain to grow along with our space capabilities. This section provides an overview of current international legal provisions, practices, and principles that are relevant to the protection and management of the space wilderness.[16] We then examine the areas that need to be addressed in constructing an adequate environmental legal regime for outer space.

The existing body of space law regarding environmental protection and resource utilization is a hodge-podge of ill-defined or conflicting provisions and principles. The linchpin of the present legal framework is the 1967 Treaty on Principles Governing the Activities of States in the Exploration and Use of Outer Space, Including the Moon and Other Celestial Bodies, known simply as the Outer Space Treaty.[17] This treaty includes a number of provisions that are normally associated with the protection and use of earthly wildernesses.

Nonappropriation. Article I of the Outer Space Treaty establishes space and everything in it as "the province of all mankind." Article II goes on to say that "outer space, including the Moon and other celestial bodies, is not subject to national appropriation. . . ." Prohibiting private ownership of wilderness areas is, of course, a fundamental wilderness principle.

Demilitarization. Article IV prohibits "nuclear weapons or any other weapons of mass destruction" from outer space and celestial bodies. Also, the Moon and other celestial bodies must be used "exclusively for peaceful purposes," and "the testing of any type of weapons and the conduct of military maneuvers on celestial bodies shall be prohibited."

Freedom of scientific investigation. This right, generally associated with public use of wilderness areas, is protected in Article I of the Outer Space Treaty.

Noncontamination. Article IX stipulates that "States Parties to the Treaty shall pursue studies of outer space, including the Moon and other celestial bodies, and conduct exploration of them so as to avoid their harmful contamination and also adverse changes in the environment of the Earth resulting from the introduction of extraterrestrial matter and, where necessary, shall adopt appropriate measures for this purpose." This provision, though vague, is significant in calling for additional environmental safeguards to be developed in the future.

Despite these laudable attempts at protecting the outer-space wilderness, the provisions fall short of creating any designated wilderness areas. Nor do they establish adequate guidelines or set up the institutional framework for preserving the outer-space environment. Absent from the treaty's provisions or even from its preamble are any of the nonmaterialistic wilderness values discussed in Part II, above. The Outer Space Treaty simply tries to set forth the basic principles necessary for the orderly exploration and exploitation of space.

Unfortunately, the treaty fails even in establishing the minimum acceptable standards of conduct. This is largely because of the vagueness of terminology and disagreement in interpretation of the provisions. For instance, an important definitional dispute concerns the term "harmful contamination" in Article IX. A broad range of possible interpretations exists.[18] A narrow interpretation would obviously be less protective of the space environment than a broad one. Additional problems with the Outer Space Treaty include the lack of adequate enforcement capabilities[19] and the fact that the Moon and other celestial bodies are all lumped together with outer space in applying the principles.[20]

There are five other treaties presently in force and ratified by the United States that are relevant in the space-wilderness context. The first three are arms-control agreements that restrict certain military activities in space. The multilateral Nuclear Test Ban Treaty of 1963 prohibits the testing of nuclear weapons in the atmosphere and in outer space.[21] The 1972 Anti-Ballistic Missile (ABM) Treaty[22] between the United States and the Soviet Union states: "Each Party undertakes not to develop, test, or deploy ABM systems or components which are sea-based, air-based, *space-based*, or mobile land-based" (Article V, Paragraph 1, emphasis added). An ABM system is defined as "a system to counter strategic ballistic missiles or their elements in flight trajectory . . ." (Article II, Paragraph 1). The final arms-control agreement is the 1977 Convention on the Prohibition of Military or Any Other Hostile Use of Environmental Modification Techniques.[23] Article I prohibits the "hostile use of environmental modification techniques having widespread, long-lasting or severe effects as the means of destruction, damage or injury to any other State Party." Article II defines environmental modification techniques as "any technique for changing—through the deliberate manipulation of natural processes—the dynamics, composition or structure of the earth . . . , or of outer space." The convention, however, expressly does not forbid "the use of environmental modification techniques for peaceful purposes . . ." (Article III) and therefore offers only nominal protection to the outer-space environment.

The other two agreements are potentially significant from an enforcement point of view. The 1973 Convention on International Liability for Damage Caused by Space Objects[24] assigns absolute liability to a launching state "to pay compensation for damage caused by its space object on the surface of the Earth . . ." (Article II). Although the liability convention does not contemplate any sanctions for damage caused to the outer-space envi-

ronment, this does not preclude the future amendment
of that agreement to include such a provision. The 1975
Convention on the Registration of Objects Launched
into Outer Space[25] provides that launching states must
register all space objects by supplying the Secretary-
General of the United Nations with the following
information: the name of the launching state(s); an appropriate designator of the space object or its registration number; the date and location of launch; basic
orbital parameters; and the general functions of the
space object (Article IV). This could become an important mechanism for assuring compliance with future environmental standards and will be discussed in more
detail below.

There is also one treaty that has not been ratified by
the United States that could have substantial ramifications in the context of the present discussion. This is the
1979 Agreement Governing the Activities of States on
the Moon and Other Celestial Bodies,[26] generally referred to as the Moon Treaty. This document closely
parallels many of the provisions set out in the Outer
Space Treaty. With regard to the environmental protection of the space wilderness, however, the Moon Treaty
goes considerably further than any previous agreement.
Article 7, paragraph 1, states, "In exploring and using
the Moon [and other celestial bodies], States Parties
shall take measures to prevent the disruption of the existing balance of its environment, whether by introducing adverse changes in that environment, by its harmful
contamination through the introduction of extra-envi-
ronmental matter or otherwise." This provision broad-
ens the parameters set by Article IX of the Outer Space
Treaty, which limited the proscribed conduct to the
avoidance of only "harmful contamination." Article 7,

200 Philosophical and Environmental Perspectives

paragraph 3, of the Moon Treaty nearly endorses the creation of legally designated wilderness areas in outer space. The paragraph proposes the following:

> States Parties shall report to other States Parties and to the Secretary-General concerning areas of the Moon [and other celestial bodies] having special scientific interest in order that, without prejudice to the rights of other States Parties, *consideration may be given to the designation of such areas as international scientific preserves for which special protective arrangements are to be agreed upon* in consultation with the competent bodies of the United Nations. [emphasis added]

Although the language is completely noncommittal, it is significant as an indication of a developing international consensus on the potential desirability of establishing such areas on celestial bodies. In this regard, it goes much further than Article IX of the Outer Space Treaty. The Moon Treaty also contains provisions on demilitarization (Article 3), freedom of scientific investigation (Article 6), and nonappropriation (Article 11) similar to the Outer Space Treaty, but in greater detail. Article 11 includes the controversial "common heritage of mankind" principle and sets forth a socialist framework for resource exploitation on celestial bodies. It is primarily the concepts and wording of Article 11 that have dissuaded the United States from signing the treaty.[27]

Notwithstanding the apparent improvement in environmental protection offered by the Moon Treaty, it is open to many of the same criticisms as the Outer Space Treaty. First, nonmaterialistic values are excluded from the document. Second, no institutional framework for protecting the space environment is proposed or established. Third, the treaty's effectiveness is undercut by the same vagueness in terminology suffered by the Outer

Space Treaty. Finally, the Moon Treaty does not distinguish between the different environments of our solar system's celestial bodies, although the focus is more specialized than that of the Outer Space Treaty.

The deficiency of existing treaties in establishing a legal regime for the protection of outer-space environments is not augmented by current international custom. Human exploration of space has been and continues to be governed by the materialistic policy goals of nation-states. These goals have been set in three main areas: military/national security, economic/commercial, and scientific. By their very nature, neither the military nor the economic objectives support the notion of preserving the outer-space wilderness. It is only the scientific goals that have produced any positive environmental practices.

Perhaps the most important environmental-protection standards that have been established to date for space are the planetary quarantine requirements developed by the international scientific community. The question of extraterrestrial contamination has concerned scientists since the launch of Sputnik. The first international effort at dealing with this issue came in 1958 when the International Council of Scientific Unions (ICSU) formed the Ad Hoc Committee on Contamination by Extraterrestrial Exploration (CETEX).[28] CETEX studied the various questions concerning experimentation and protection of celestial bodies as scientific preserves, and issued four principle directives:[29]

Freedom of activity should be maintained for experimentation and exploration of celestial bodies, limited only for compelling reasons, such as planetary quarantine requirements.

The Committee on Space Research (COSPAR) should be informed as soon as possible about any proposed experiments in outer space.

Experiments in space should be performed only if they are likely to yield useful scientific data.

No soft landings requiring the use of large quantities of gas should be made on the Moon before the completion of extensive studies, and all nuclear detonations on or near the surface of celestial bodies should be prohibited.

In 1964, COSPAR published its recommended planetary quarantine requirements, which were subsequently adopted by the United States.[30] The requirements were based on a quantitative approach that attempted to establish the probability of contaminating the target planet(s) of any given space mission. Appropriate precautions, such as decontamination or sterilization of the spacecraft, were taken according to the outcome of the statistical analysis.

By the beginning of this decade, however, this quantitative approach was found to have certain inherent weaknesses. These included the uncertainty in the required input parameters and the fact that all data obtained by planetary exploration have been consistently negative regarding the existence of any life forms on other planets in our solar system.[31] As a result, NASA proposed to revise COSPAR policy to limit the use of quantitative criteria to only a few select cases.[32]

The last category of existing law includes the general principles of environmental law that are internationally recognized. Although a review of this category of law is far beyond the scope of this paper, one important point should be made. There is a significant problem associated with applying general environmental law principles to the outer-space context. Space has radically different physical characteristics from the Earth's environment, not the least of which is that, for the most part, environmentally harmful acts in space have no tangible effects on our planet. In addition, the fact that no nation can claim sovereignty over any portion of outer space means that no public or private entity has any legal standing to claim damage to its environment. Thus many of the principles commonly associated with international environmental law on Earth lose their legal justification when transferred to the space context.[33] Perhaps the greatest difficulty encountered with this situation is with regard to the enforcement of principles and standards specifically designed to protect the space wilderness. This issue is addressed below.

The preceding discussion has served to illustrate the lack of legal protection now afforded the outer-space environment. There are several areas that need to be addressed in order to develop an adequate legal regime. The first is the promulgation of formal, internationally recognized and supported environmental principles. Those space treaties that are presently in force or are pending ratification are insufficient. The negotiation of an environmental space agreement by the leading space powers would be an important beginning. One author has already suggested a set of five principles that could guide the codification of environmental law for outer space.[34] These include the following:

The principle of environmental balance. This would use a cost/benefit analysis, but with substantial weight given to intrinsic environmental values.

The principle of conserved resources. The natural resources of outer space must not be exploited in a wasteful or environmentally damaging way.

The principle of responsibility. Absolute liability for wrongful or negligent acts to the space wilderness and the duty to restore conditions to *status quo ante* would be an important though difficult principle to implement. Although alluded to in the Outer Space and Moon treaties and implied by the planetary quarantine requirements, this principle would need an institutional framework for enforcement and is unrealistic in the near term.

The principle of demilitarization. This principle has already gained considerable support and expression in several treaties, as noted above. Given the highly politicized nature of the debate and the strategic importance placed on the effective military control of space by the superpowers, it is unlikely that this principle will get the approval of either the United States or the Soviet Union.

The principle of space exploitation. All states have the right to use and explore outer space, but they must do so pursuant to the first principle of environmental balance.

Implicit in these principles are certain standards of conduct. These standards would have to be articulated in a meaningful manner. For instance, it might be useful to formally adopt the planetary quarantine standards on a worldwide basis.[35] In a different vein, the "harmful contamination" standard set in Article IX of the Outer Space Treaty would need to be reworded, or at least interpreted much more broadly. The problem of setting adequate environmental standards is exacerbated by the vagueness of terminology and lack of accurate definitions in the present treaties. Unfortunately, this is a problem that plagues most international agreements and is motivated by a desire to reach the necessary consensus. The effectiveness of the agreement is thus undercut by political expediency and Machiavellian tactics. A future environmental-protection treaty for the outer-space wilderness would have to carefully define its operative principles and standards.

Another important element in establishing a legal

regime for the space wilderness is the specialization of provisions to meet the different requirements of each environment. While the principles must be broad enough to have universal applicability, the standards implementing those principles have to be tailored to meet the needs of the specific environments that they are designed to protect. Both the Outer Space Treaty and the Moon Treaty attempt to apply generic standards to all the celestial bodies in our solar system. This may be an adequate approach during the dawn of the space age, but as our technological capabilities increase and we extend our reach to more distant lands we will have to continually reassess the standards according to the information we obtain from each celestial environment. Some degree of flexibility will therefore have to be institutionalized to accommodate this process, perhaps through a system of zoning. Certain areas could be zoned for certain uses or nonuses. A standing consultative committee of experts could make the initial determinations, which could then be updated periodically to reflect our increased knowledge regarding each specific environment.

We now come to the most thorny issue of all, the problem of enforcement. Without effective enforcement mechanisms, the principles and standards set out in treaties are useless. But in order to accept vigorous enforcement provisions in international agreements means that states parties must voluntarily give up a certain amount of sovereignty. Thus the more stringent the compliance standards and applicable sanctions, the greater the potential infringement on a state's sovereign status. Governments are understandably reluctant to encumber their sovereignty unless they perceive they are getting significant advantages in return. Unfortunately, the protection of the outer-space environment is not a high political priority, at least for the foreseeable future.

There is an old adage that says that an ounce of prevention is worth a pound of cure. This is sound advice. Environmental calamities in space are and will continue to be difficult, if not impossible, to rectify. Further, governments simply will not agree to a provision that demands that restitution be paid for damage to an environment that does not belong to some other state. The extension of the strict liability principle to cover damage caused to the space environment is unrealistic. Existing provisions in the Outer Space Treaty (Article IX) and the Moon Treaty (Article 15) that call for consultations in the event of some breach are merely cosmetic.

Meaningful enforcement provisions should therefore focus on preventive measures. We have already noted several of these, including the informal planetary quarantine requirements, the various demilitarization and weapon-testing ban provisions, and the 1975 Convention on the Registration of Objects Launched into Outer Space. Other existing preventive measures include the rights of states to inspect other states' stations, installations, equipment, and space vehicles located on the Moon or on other celestial bodies. Both the Outer Space Treaty (Article XII) and the Moon Treaty (Article 15) include this right, although in practice it may be impossible to implement. Additional preventive provisions might formally recognize the planetary quarantine requirements, or expand the registration convention to use something akin to our Environmental Impact Statements. The establishment of various zones by uses, including wilderness zones, could be effective as well. Even here, though, the problem of enforcement will prove nettlesome.

Finally, we should not overlook the potential role of remote-sensing space systems in helping us manage the outer-space wilderness. There is no reason to doubt that such systems will prove invaluable in educating us about space environments and in identifying future problems in our solar system.

Notes

1. Philip M. Smith and Richard A. Watson, "New Wilderness Boundaries," *Environmental Ethics* 1 (1979): 61–64.
2. Edward B. Swain, "Wilderness and the Maintenance of Freedom," *The Humanist,* March–April 1983, p. 27.
3. Linda H. Graber, *Wilderness as Sacred Space* (Washington, D.C.: Association of American Geographers, 1976), p. 5.
4. See Donald Scherer and Thomas Attig, eds., *Ethics and the Environment* (Englewood Cliffs, N.J.: Prentice-Hall, 1983). For a contrary view see Scott Lehmann, "Do Wildernesses Have Rights?" *Environmental Ethics* 3 (1983): 129–46.
5. Lloyd C. Irland, *Wilderness Economics and Policy* (Lexington, Mass.: D.C. Heath, 1979), p. 31. See also Craig W. Allin, *The Politics of Wilderness Preservation* (Westport, Conn.: Greenwood Press, 1982).
6. Public Law 88–577, 88th Congress, S.4, 3 September 1964.
7. Irland, *Wilderness Economics and Policy,* pp. 35–42.
8. Article 2 of the Convention on the High Seas states: "The high seas being open to all nations, no State may validly purport to subject any part of them to its sovereignty." 13 U.S.T. 2312, T.I.A.S. 5200, 450 U.N.T.S. 82, 29 April 1958 (entered into force on 30 September 1962).
9. See Articles 24 and 25 of the Convention on High Seas; also see the Convention on the Prevention of Marine Pollution by Dumping of Wastes and Other Matter, 26 U.S.T. 2403, T.I.A.S. 8165, 29 December 1972 (entered into force on 30 August 1975).
10. See the following: Article IX (1) of the Antarctic Treaty, T.I.A.S. 4780, 1 December 1959 (entered into force 23 June 1961); Convention on Nature Protection and Wildlife Preservation in the Western Hemisphere, 161 U.N.T.S. 193, 12 October 1940 (entered into force 30 April 1942); Convention on Fishing and Conservation of Sea Resources, 559 U.N.T.S. 285, 29 April 1958 (entered into force 20 March 1966); Convention Concerning the

Protection of World Cultural and Natural Heritage, 16 November 1972 (entered into force 17 December 1975); Convention on International Trade in Endangered Species of Wild Fauna and Flora, 993 U.N.T.S., 6 March 1973 (entered into force 1 July 1975).

11. See notes 9 and 10 above; Articles I, V, and VII of the Antarctic Treaty; Treaty on the Prohibition of the Emplacement of Nuclear Weapons and Other Weapons of Mass Destruction on the Seabed and the Ocean Floor and in the Subsoil Thereof, 955 U.N.T.S., 11 February 1971 (entered into force 18 May 1972).

12. See Articles II and IX of the Antarctic Treaty.

13. D.L. DeVincenzi and P.D. Stabekis, "Revised Planetary Protection Policy for Solar System Exploration," in *Proceedings of the 25th COSPAR Meeting*, Graz, Austria, 25 June–7 July 1984, p. 1.

14. See note 4.

15. This section was written without the use of any reference materials. The reader interested in more information on the topics covered in this section should contact User Affairs Unit, Code E/ER2, NOAA/National Environmental Satellite, Data, and Information Service, Federal Building #4, Room 3301, Washington, D.C. 20233.

16. The overview follows the same analytical procedure used in deciding international disputes as set forth in Article 38 of the Statute of the International Court of Justice, 59 Stat. 1055, T.S. 993, 3 Bevans 1179, 1945.

17. Treaty on Principles Governing the Activities of States in the Exploration and Use of Outer Space, Including the Moon and Other Celestial Bodies, 18 U.S.T. 2410, T.I.A.S. 6347, 610 U.N.T.S. 205, 27 January 1967 (entered into force 10 October 1967).

18. See Amanda L. Moore and Jerry V. Leaphart, "Manipulation and Modification of the Outer Space Environment: International Legal Considerations," in *Proceedings of the Twenty-fifth Colloquium on the Law of Outer Space*, American Institute of Aeronautics and Astronautics, 27 September–2 October 1982, Paris, France, pp. 15–22.

19. See Articles VII, XI, and XII of the Outer Space Treaty. Article VII assigns international liability for damage caused by a launching state to another state party to the treaty. No liability is contemplated for damage caused to outer-space environments. Article XI requires states parties to inform the Secretary-General

of the United Nations about the nature, conduct, locations, and results of any activities in space. This is merely informational and, while necessary for adequate enforcement, provides no enforcement standards or sanctions. Article XII allows inspection of facilities, equipment, and vehicles on the Moon and other celestial bodies on the basis of reciprocity. This is subject to the same criticisms as Article XI above. In addition, it is very unlikely that states will allow such inspections to take place.

20. In general, the more specialized the provisions for each different environment, the more effective the protection.

21. Treaty Banning Nuclear Weapon Test in the Atmosphere, in Outer Space, and Under Water, 14 U.S.T. 1313, T.I.A.S. 5433, 480 U.N.T.S. 205, 5 August 1963 (entered into force 10 October 1963).

22. Treaty on the Limitation of Anti-Ballistic Missile Systems, 23 U.S.T. 3435, T.I.A.S. 7503, 26 May 1972 (entered into force 3 October 1972).

23. Convention on the Prohibition of Military or Any Other Hostile Use of Environmental Modification Techniques, T.I.A.S. 9614, 18 May 1977 (entered into force 17 January 1980).

24. Convention on International Liability for Damage Caused by Space Objects, 24 U.S.T. 2389, T.I.A.S. 7762, 29 March 1972 (entered into force 9 October 1973).

25. Convention on the Registration of Objects Launched into Outer Space, 28 U.S.T. 695, T.I.A.S. 8480, 14 January 1975 (entered into force 15 September 1976).

26. Agreement Governing the Activities of States on the Moon and Other Celestial Bodies, A/RES/34/68, 14 December 1979.

27. See Kevin B. Walsh, "Controversial Issues Under Article XI of the Moon Treaty," *Annals of Air and Space Law* 6 (1981): 489–98.

28. Patricia M. Sterns and Leslie I. Tennen, "Protection of Celestial Environments Through Planetary Quarantine Requirements," in *Proceedings of the Twenty-third Colloquium on the Law of Outer Space,* American Institute of Aeronautics and Astronautics, 21–28 September 1980, Tokyo, Japan, p. 111.

29. Ibid.

30. Ibid., p. 112.

31. DeVincenzi and Stabekis, "Revised Planetary Protection Policy," p. 1.

32. Ibid., p. 3.

33. For an excellent review of international environmental-law principles see Jeffrey Maclure, "Acid Rain and International Law," *The Fletcher Forum,* Winter 1983, pp. 132–54.

34. Harry H. Almond, Jr., "A Draft Convention for Protecting the Environment of Outer Space," in *Proceedings of the Twenty-third Colloquium on the Law of Outer Space,* American Institute of Aeronautics and Astronautics, 21–28 September 1980, Tokyo, Japan, pp. 101–102.

35. Nevertheless, the question of planetary quarantine requirements may not be optimally resolved through a treaty. See Sterns and Tennen, "Protection of Celestial Environments," p. 116.

Environmental Ethics and Extraterrestrial Ecosystems

FRANK B. GOLLEY

Introduction

*D*evelopment of extraterrestrial ecosystems or space colonies is a major element in the space adventure. As far as we know space is hostile to life. If we are to live in space it will be necessary to design and construct ecological systems or ecosystems that can support humans indefinitely. In this essay I intend to address two questions. First, can we design a space-colony ecosystem? And, second, should we design space-colony ecosystems?

Ecological systems or ecosystems are the focus of much ecological research. The term *ecosystem* was coined by the English ecologist, Sir Arthur Tansley (1871–1955), in 1935 to describe natural systems composed of living and nonliving components. Tansley used the word system to stress the physics-like character of his conception and the importance of equilibria in ecosystem dynamics. Since the 1950s ecosystems have been intensively studied by ecologists and the word has become part of our technical vocabulary. Ecologists believe that ecosystems are organized hierarchically.

We can begin with the planet Earth as an ecosystem containing an atmosphere, hydrosphere, lithosphere, and biosphere. The Earth system or ecosphere can be disaggregated into a variety of subsystems, each of which is an ecosystem. These subsystems might include oceans, tundra, and forest ecosystems. Disaggregation can be continued until one recognizes systems associated with single leaves or puddles. In these ecosystems there is usually a producing component that converts solar energy into chemical energy through the process of photosynthesis. There is also a decomposing component that breaks down organic materials into molecules that can be recycled to other components. And we can identify consumer components that help maintain system stability and development. The dynamic behaviors of these components are frequently described as ecosystem production, decomposition, and stability—three features of ecosystem performance.

Unfortunately this beguilingly simple model is entirely unrealistic when we begin to link the abstract idea of a system component with living organisms. First, an ecosystem such as a lake or patch of forest contains thousands of species populations. Each species is a genetically distinct assemblage that has been selected through interaction with other organisms and the physical environment as that species suitable for the conditions at that time and place. The production component may contain tens to hundreds of species, and the consumer and decomposing components may contain hundreds to thousands; the actual inventories have never been completed. Second, if we trace the flows of materials, energy, or information from one individual organism to another through the complex networks of relationships, we discover that the indirect effects that feedback influences through multiple links may be more important in overall system performance than the direct feedforward effects we follow with a tracer or marker.

The result of this experience with ecosystems is that many ecologists have in their minds both a simple physical model of an aggregated, hierarchically organized, stable system and a complicated, dynamically changing complex of living and nonliving linked components. These two models provide very different guidance when we begin to reason from our experience with Earth ecosystems toward the design of extraterrestrial ecosystems and space colonies.

Humans did not design or build the Earth ecosystems we live in, yet we depend upon these systems for life. The problem of design has both a direct utilitarian and a metaphysical aspect because we understand *ecosystem* to mean a complex of living beings and environment that cannot be dissected; that is, the ultimate unit of ecology is an ecosystem. A living system cannot be operative and, indeed, is not conceivable alone. No living being exists separately from an environment. And thus, man cannot be treated separately from an environment. Design of a space colony means designing both for man and environment; one or the other is influenced reciprocally. Since we do not truly understand our terrestrial ecosystem, nor our relationship to our environment, we are limited in our capacity to design an extraterrestrial ecosystem. There is no immediate possibility of our obtaining full knowledge of ecosystems, and therefore we must approach the design problem experimentally. Experimentation may involve design of an Earth-like ecosystem to support a colony of humans or reforming the environment of a planet to accommodate human life. This latter approach is called terraforming.

Let us consider each of these two methods briefly to determine if there is a feasible way to design and construct a human colony in space.

Design of a Space Colony

One can define space colony in many ways. According to G. S. Robinson, a space vehicle in orbit around the Earth is a colony (or at least a protocolony) since it successfully holds man (and an infrequent woman) in a physico-chemical system for days and months.[1] At the other end of a range of possible states is an independent colony (a star colony in the fictional sense depicted by Keith Laumer) functioning all by itself in space or on another planet.[2] In between are all sorts of scenarios. The object is to create a space system in which humans can live a full life and reproduce with no (or minimal) material and energetic inputs from Earth. What would be required to accomplish this goal?

This question has received a large amount of technical attention in the United States and the Soviet Union. I have not reviewed all of the relevant literature, but based on the reports I have reviewed, I can confidently say that we are taking a scientific-engineering approach to space-colony design. Whatever the perspective, individual human needs are identified and solutions are devised to satisfy these needs.

As an example of the scientific-engineering approach, Frieda Taub quotes Whisenhunt's description of the daily balance of humans under normal conditions.[3] About two pounds of oxygen are required, and about 2.2 pounds of carbon dioxide are expelled daily; requirements for ingested water are about 4.5 pounds; and so forth. The question then phrased is how does one supply these weights of oxygen and water and absorb carbon dioxide at an appropriate rate to support humans? The initial approach was to create a mechanical system to supply humans their requirements. As Howard Odum has pointed out, a mechanical solution is the instinctive approach of the engineer and has dominated the NASA discussions of space colonies.[4] The problem with the mechanical approach is that resupply of parts, repairs, and fuel are required so that while it is obviously possible to sustain humans in space, it is probably not possible to supply them with the requirements to sustain life (food, waste removal, water, and so on) while maintaining the mechanical system at a tolerable cost. Such a space colony would function as a parasite on Earth and would never be independent.

In the 1960s ecologists suggested that this problem could not be solved over the long term by mechanical, physico-chemical devices. Rather, biological organisms need to be coupled to man in some way. The biological part would supply food, gases, water, and process wastes. Protection from the space environment, control and monitoring of biological resources, the built environment, recreation, work, and so forth are all supplied and maintained by physico-engineering methods. Current space technology has moved in this direction and experiments have shown that at least the initial steps are feasible. For example, Taub discusses a mixed algae-invertebrate-fish system using dried human feces as the only additional source of nutrients.[5] Odum and Beyers have discussed the requirements for maintaining closed systems in a balanced situation.[6] More recently, MacElroy and Averner have examined the problems of buffering changes within closed systems and concluded that physico-mechanical methods are required to maintain the space ecosystem in the desired state.[7] They state:

"The temptation to develop a closed ecosystem mimicking man's terrestrial environment becomes very strong. However some generally unappreciated aspects of the real world become obvious when closure is attempted: because of lack of sufficient buffering capacity and the absence of certain energy requiring functions, such as atmospheric circulation and rainfall, closed systems over long or short time periods become sterile. Recognition of this fact strongly suggests that mechanical or physico-chemical methods must be used to maintain an ecological system in a desired state."

It is important to recognize that all of these scientific engineering studies rest upon several assumptions that affect their application to space-colony design. First, the search for links between cause and effect (for example, between human need for food and food production) assumes that the indirect effects coming from linked system components would be unimportant or sufficiently well enough known that they could be accounted for. Second, systems are in a balanced or equilibrium condition over space and time and, therefore, one could detect deviations from the nominal state and correct the system. The first assumption may be true only for very limited cases and short time intervals. Indeed, most ecologists are aware of the difficulty of accounting for the influence of indirect effects in their experiments and observations. Unlike experimental laboratory sciences, ecologists seldom can control the environment and eliminate its effects. Similarly, the second assumption also may be true for a limited case, but it not only depends on the definition of balance but also contradicts our earlier observation of continual change in both the physical part of the planet and in the biological and cultural parts. In general I think that many ecologists would feel uncomfortable with these assumptions.

Neither the physical scientists-engineers nor the biological-ecological scientists have considered the human part of the ecosystem. In these studies humans are a separate element outside of the problem and are not treated as either a dynamic subsystem or as a dynamic linked element in a larger system. However, social scientists, humanists, and novelists have considered the human aspect of space colonization. For example, Robinson has examined some aspects of the social process in space colonies, especially from a legal point of view.[8] Social processes also are frequently a major element of space science fiction. The technical environment of main concern to the engineer-biologist is the passive stage on which the all too familiar behaviors (romantic, violent, competitive) of space persons are acted out. Clearly the confined, homogeneous, and highly controlled space environment, even on a large space colony, differs from our familiar Earth environment. The monitoring of each entity, from the molecule to individual, in each part of a colony and the control of performance of the parts to sustain the whole produces such a Draconian vision that one wonders how the adventure of space travel could ever compensate for the loss of the freedoms we enjoy on Earth.[9] And most seriously for survival, how does one maintain the creative-innovative impulse in an environment where every process and action is known and controlled for today and every day into the future?

Ecologists have been led by these problems to argue that a colony ecosystem needs to be large enough and to contain sufficient biological diversity for the essential processes of production and regeneration to be carried out by evolving, adapting biological organisms operating in ecological systems.[10] As mentioned above, this suggestion cannot be expressed in cause-and-effect or linear terms. Even accurate models of components and links are not available. The Earth systems are too complex, and our study is too young to approach the problem in this way. Thus, the suggestions of the ecologists are not operationally feasible for the space engineer-designer. This is probably the reason why NASA generally stopped support of ecological studies of closed space systems in the early 1970s.

Nevertheless, how could we approach the design problem, without total knowledge of the system? Rather than designing a complete system, we could experimentally change a system in small steps to discover how it responds. It is a long way from the orbiting space station to a space colony, but, as several ecologists have suggested, a series of experiments could be employed to create a space ecosystem.[11] Taub suggested a "detailed design of a regenerating laboratory ecosystem including man." Woodwell's committee stated that "if a serious effort is to be made in the development of livable space colonies, research should be started on the design and construction of closed agro-industrial ecosystems on Earth." Odum suggested multiple seeding experiments where collections of apparently useful organisms would be placed in appropriate colonies and allowed to evolve and reproduce, with cross-seeding across colonies. In this way organisms may evolve a system that could provide the services a space colony would require. Cooke, Beyers, and Odum have described expected trends in development from the initial seeded assemblage to an interacting system of organisms.[12] I can see no other way to develop space colonies than by this incremental, experimental approach, coupled with the recognition that experimentation requires failures. This approach could lead to organisms capable of living in a space-colony environment.

Thus, our answer to the question of the feasibility of space-colony design is a tentative yes. Given adequate resources and singleness of mind, it is conceptually possible to design a series of experiments that would lead ultimately to a colony in space. However, scientists have suggested another way called terraforming. Let us turn to this alternative.

Terraforming

Terraforming means wholesale rearrangement of a planet's environment by modifications of its energy balance or its material composition so that the planet can be made habitable to life. Oberg's vision conveys the nature of the idea exceedingly well:

> For Mars, a goal would be to provide the planet with thicker, breathable air, at temperatures high enough for lightly protected human beings to venture forth on its surface. Plant and animal life would spread across the now-barren surface, tingeing the red rocks with green, and turning the red sky into a beautiful dark blue. Liquid water would flow again on the surface and the eons-dry channels and gullies would become wet with new rains. Rainbows would appear in the sky, symbolizing not the restraint of floodwaters (as in *Genesis* after the Flood) but their *release* from eons of imprisonment within the permafrost.[13]

The methods of terraforming require a threshold or critical point where application of energy or materials within the capability of Earthlings would tip the physical processes into a different pattern. The idea, for example, of transforming the crushing atmosphere of Venus, which is largely composed of carbon dioxide and a surface temperature in excess of 900 degrees F, by seeding the clouds with algae depends upon conversion of the atmospheric carbon dioxide into carbon and oxygen by the algae. If the oxygen is chemically combined with the crust of Venus, the total pressure would decline, decreasing atmospheric infrared absorption, reducing the greenhouse effect, and lowering the temperature.[14] It is difficult to evaluate these scenarios. They seem imaginary in the extreme. For example, how many algae would need to be released on Venus, how would they be transported, how would they be grown, held, and packaged on Earth, and so on? Would there be an impact on Earth? Yet the idea has proponents.

As a biologist, it would seem to me that terraforming might be best accomplished by contamination of appropriate planets or moons with lower forms of life such as bacteria, algae, or protozoa. If the conditions were favorable for life, these organisms would survive, grow, and begin the evolutionary process that transformed this planet into a habitable one. If contamination was successful, possibly we could guide the process into directions congenial to human goals and also speed the process. Whatever the method, terraforming provides an alternative to direct space-colony design.

Motivation and Purpose

The question, Should we design a space colony? seems to have been answered in the affirmative as far as public support of NASA and the widespread interest in science-fiction themes indicate. Apologetics for space colonies take a variety of forms. These include the utilitarian interests of obtaining resources in space, escaping from Earth, building utopian societies, and the psychosocial interest in meeting a challenge or pursuing an adventure. Certainly development of space colonies is an acceptable theme in Western, as well as other, human societies. Why should there be such widespread support for an idea that seems technically very difficult, even problematical, and very expensive?

I feel that this question is very important, and I will speculate about some of the motivations for public interest in space colonization. First, while the space-colony concept has a variety of utilitarian values I think that public support in terms of tax dollars to fund research and experiment is more a response to the idea or concept than to the resources or industrial possibilities involved in space colonization. Space colonization fits our culture. (By culture I mean a system of explanation of our role on a living Earth that is complex, multifaceted, contradictory, multilayered, and expressed by individuals through actions and behaviors. In an ecological sense this is an expression of our human subsystem.) While there are many elements of our culture that are germane to space colonization, I will focus on four elements that may suggest why we want to create space colonies and why we are willing to devote such a large share of our resources to the task.

First, we want to construct a space colony to escape from Earth. The problems that man faces on Earth seem insurmountable. The intensity of concern mounts as humans become more and more tightly tangled in webs of exploitative, often violent interactions. Security is impossible in some great cities, such as Beirut, and our preoccupation with personal security in all cities grows. Governments everywhere seem to practice folly, in Barbara Tuchman's sense of the word.[15] In such a dilemma escape is attractive. The situation is not new to Western cultures. First, we escaped to America, then Africa and Australia. Now there is no land with weaker or more vulnerable inhabitants left to be conquered, but we continue to dream. Space beckons. Laumer in his space novel *Star Colony* has a character say, "Maybe here on Omega we'll have the chance to try it all again—and get it right this time."

Getting it right is the second cultural element to consider. Our culture tends to organize reality into simple dichotomies. Right-wrong is one of these. In a sense appropriate to this discussion, right fits an ideal. The ideal is when all the right things happen. It is a utopia. Utopian thinking has guided Western cultures for centuries. In the age of discovery and conquest Western cultures had numerous opportunities to experiment with ideal societies. While utopias have almost always failed, the ideal, especially in the context of facing the real unsolvable problems we mentioned above, persists. The Marxist ideal is a dominant social paradigm present in the world today, and it represents a typical pattern within this tradition. It can accept control of individuals for larger social ends, it has a vision of the ideal state, and it is willing to design a path to get from here to there. This must be one of the reasons why the government of the Soviet Union has so enthusiastically developed a space program and why the space adventure figures so prominently in Soviet society. To a much greater degree than here, space is interpreted by the artist, poet, novelist, schoolteacher, musician as a great human adventure leading toward a better world.

With "Star Wars," our own peaceful but contradictory space program has been corrupted and now takes on more of the military character of the armed camp. Its controlled life fits the military pattern. Thus, in our terms too space provides a place where an orderly human system can be developed. Yet this solution leads to a contradiction with traditional American ideals of free individual action. Space represents mechanical control, order, social versus individual ends. Can the contradictions between ideal order and free action be overcome?

The third cultural element concerns the mechanical focus in the space colony. We live in an increasingly machine-dominated world. Machines wake us, feed us, transport us, provide us work and entertainment. We have faith in machines. We have even interpreted our biological nature in machine language; witness the TV documentary on the human body entitled "The Magnificent Machine" and the "Spaceship Earth" metaphor of the environmentalist. Machines are created and maintained by scientists and engineers, who have high status in our society. Thus, we are not repelled by a machine world in which man must function as part of a machine. Our faith in machines leads us to overlook the implications of such a world.

And finally, this machine focus stresses one other element in our culture. The space colony is antinature. The living nature that we experience on Earth does not exist in space. Space is only physical. As far as we know life does not exist anywhere else in the universe. The space colony designer aims to recreate life in space, but the form of life is narrow and constricted. In contrast, this Earth is exceptionally complex and interacting; the level of noise, in a cybernetic sense, is very high; randomness seems important. Living nature is also ever changing. It reacts to environmental forces by evolution and adaptation.

Our only way to know and interact with the natural world is to directly experience it, and to evolve with it.

Built environments and machines are static and discontinuous. They limit our capacity to experience and evolve. And thus, they break our links with life. The space colony is the ultimate step in this progression— all links with life are lost, and man and his domesticated creatures become adjuncts to machines. Through the space adventure man overcomes life and recreates it in his own terms. The space colony is the modern city extended over the entire Earth. In a sense, this is the ultimate challenge to man, and it is not hard to understand why we are attracted to such Faustian opportunities.

These various examples suffice to show how the space-colony metaphor fits into our mythical world of imagination. Our children are raised before images of space men and women on television and in the comic book. The violent and strange worlds portrayed do not bother us since they actually represent our conception of Earth and mirror our own fears, hopes, and beliefs faithfully. But even so, the action of designing and experimenting with space colonies raises ethical questions.

For example, the space effort of the United States and the Soviet Union is frightfully expensive. From 1969 to 1979 space research in the United States cost about $33,829 million as compared with $30,341 million for health and $10,819 million for environment.[16] While these funds represent a massive expression of public support for the program, they come, of course, from the soil, water, rock, and labor of the world. A concentration of funds for the space adventure represents an extreme concentration of power and an aggressive monopoly of resources. Now that space is forever linked to military activity, support will grow ever larger. Space thus provides a further reason to demand greater flows of the world resources to the center. The modern pyramids grow larger and larger and the world community becomes more organized to provide the resources and labor for their construction. What problems on Earth could be solved with these funds?

Frankly, I can see no turning back from this adventure. It is built into our very bodies and souls, and it will perish only when we do. It represents in a particularly clear way the mythos of Western cultures. To change it, to focus on the Earth, human relationships with the natural world, and so on, requires a fundamental re-orientation of the culture. While such a change may be occurring, it is slowly adaptive and is not a conscious effort of government.

Conclusion

Is it possible to build a space colony? No one knows for sure, but we can visualize how a colony could evolve through a sequence of experiments. Should we build a space colony? That is quite a different question. Ecologists considered it in the mid-1970s and stated the answer as follows:

> Yet the problems of expansion into space also seem nearly insurmountable. If these challenges were to be solved on Earth, one might be considerably more optimistic about the possibilities of a space colony. To solve them first in space seems highly unrealistic.[17] [18]

Notes

1. G.S. Robinson, *Living in Outer Space* (Washington, D.C.: Public Affairs Press, 1975).

2. Keith Laumer, *Star Colony* (New York: Ace, 1981).

3. Frieda B. Taub, "Some Ecological Aspects of Space Travel,"

American Biology Teacher 25, no. 6 (1963): 412–21, citation on p. 412.

4. Howard T. Odum, "Limits of Remote Ecosystems containing Man," *American Biology Teacher* 25, no. 6 (1963): 429–43, citation on p. 430.

5. Taub, "Some Ecological Aspects of Space Travel," pp. 418–19; quoted from Garland B. Whisenhunt, "A Life Support System for a Near Earth or Circumlunar Space Vehicle," *Astronomical Science Review*, July–September 1960, pp. 13–20.

6. Odum, "Limits of Remote Ecosystems"; Robert J. Beyers, "Balanced Aquatic Microcosms—Their Implications for Space Travel," *American Biology Teacher* 25, no. 6 (1963): 422–29.

7. R.D. MacElroy and M.M. Averner, *Space Ecosynthesis: An Approach to the Design of Closed Ecosystems for Use in Space,* NASA Technical Memorandum 78491 (1978).

8. Robinson, *Living in Outer Space.*

9. C.J. Cherryh, *Downbelow Station* (New York: Daws Books, 1981).

10. Odum, "Limits of Remote Ecosystems."

11. G.M. Woodwell, "Ecological Considerations for Space Colonies," *Bulletin of the Ecological Society of America* 58, no. 1 (1977): 2–4; Odum, "Limits of Remote Ecosystems"; Taub, "Some Ecological Aspects of Space Travel."

12. G.D. Cooke, R.J. Beyers, and E.P. Odum, "The Case for the Multispecies Ecological System, with Special Reference to Succession and Stability," in *Bioregenerative Systems* (Washington, D.C.: NASA, 1968).

13. James E. Oberg, *Mission to Mars: Plans and Concepts for the First Manned Landing* (Harrisburg, Pa.: Stackpole Books, 1982), p. 193.

14. Carl Sagan, *The Cosmic Connection* (Garden City, N.Y.: Anchor Press, 1973), pp. 151–53.

15. Barbara W. Tuchman, *The March of Folly* (New York: Knopf, 1984).

16. National Science Foundation, *An Analysis of Federal R & D Funding by Function,* Survey of Science Resources Series, NSF-78-320 (Washington, D.C.: National Science Foundation, 1978).

17. Woodwell, "Ecological Considerations," p. 2.

18. I acknowledge with thanks the critical comments made on this manuscript by Susan Power Bratton and Monica Goigel Turner.

Moral Considerability
and
Extraterrestrial Life

J. BAIRD CALLICOTT

I.

*L*et me first ask what extraterrestrial life is and then go on to ask upon what conceptual foundations its moral considerability may be based.

In the still vital mythic human mind of the present age, the Space Age as it is often called, space exploration is portrayed essentially as a geometrical and technological projection of the European expeditions to the New World in the fifteenth, sixteenth, and seventeenth centuries—just as those explorations were mythically portrayed by the explorers themselves and their contemporaries in terms of still earlier paradigms.[1] Columbus, Cortez, and De Soto saw themselves as knights embarked upon a quest—if not for the Holy Grail, for the fabulous wealth of the Orient, the Fountain of Youth, or the lost Eden. They traversed a relatively vast ocean in relatively primitive and puny craft. The bold imagination and heroic temerity of the discoverers paid off, though not in terms of what they themselves actually sought. In fact they found vast new lands, populated by exotic flora and fauna and strange human beings. The fabulous medieval-biblical mythic portrayal of the discovery of the New World eventually gave way to the pedestrian reality of conquest, colonization, domestication, exploitation, and intercontinental commerce.

Today we see interplanetary space as a larger, emptier ocean, our current spacecraft as the Nina, Pinta, and Santa Maria and the planets as so many new continents. We expect to find no fountains of youth, cities of gold, or Edenic paradises (silly illusions of a bygone age) on Venus, Mars, or the moons of Jupiter and Saturn, but we do seriously entertain farming, mining, and colonizing our Sun's planets or those of some other. We project routine transport and commerce between worlds.[2] Why? Partly just because we can, or think we can, but more practically because we must if our civilization is to have the resources and the real estate to continue to grow. Just like Europeans of the previous centuries who, after overpopulating Europe and overtaxing the natural resources of that continent, moved their operations to the Americas and Australia and so avoided the consequences, we will, upon overpopulating and exhausting Earth's resources, move our operations to new New Worlds with the same impunity.

I personally regard the prevailing notions of routine space travel and extraterrestrial-resource and real-estate development with their implicit supposition of a throwaway Earth as no less vacuous and no less potentially tragic illusions than those of the most extravagant Spanish conquistadores.[3] The reality our adventures in space will disclose, I predict, and the sooner we realize it the better, is that we are, for all practical purposes, earthbound. Human life is evolved from, specifically adapted to, presently embedded in, integrated with, and utterly dependent upon the exact and unimaginably complex physical, chemical, and biological conditions of the planet Earth. The realization and affirmation of our earthiness, our inseparability from the Earth, should be, and hopefully soon will be, the biggest payoff of space exploration. Europeans readily adapted North America to European patterns of settlement, methods of agriculture, and manufacturing. South America and Australia have been somewhat less tractable. Humans will not find the Sun's other planets remotely so hospitable and submissive.[4] And interstellar exploration, discovery, and colonization is, as I shall explain, ruled out by the limitations of physical laws, the statistical improbability of Earth-like planets in accessible regions of the galaxy, and the sheer immensities of cosmic spatiotemporal dimensions in proportion to the relatively brief duration of a human lifetime.

I begin with this prevailing contemporary mythic representation of space travel and planetary exploration as a projection of earlier ocean navigation and continental exploration, because I believe it substantially shapes our uncritical expectation of what it would mean to find and interact with extraterrestrial life. In the most puerile and jejune science fiction—the pervasive popularity of which suggests, however, an implicit general credulity of its structural premises—our "starships" (with such revealing names as Enterprise) island hop among an archipelago of planets inhabited by only slightly strange-looking *people* in futuristic get-ups, or period costumes as the case may be. These planets and their unfortunate populations are often ruled by merciless, unearthly Oriental potentates or beautiful, but bad, Eurasian seductresses. Our guys vanquish theirs and thus help make the universe safe for democracy and either native or colonial bourgeois developers and entrepreneurs.

But these silly fantasies occur only in the Buck Rogers, Flash Gordon, Star Trek, and Star Wars type of science fiction, don't they? They also occur in the supposedly more sophisticated specimens of the genre, of which *Dune* is the most celebrated representative.[5] What is more astonishing and irresponsible, since it is not represented as science fiction but as science *per se,* is that equally fantastic notions are rife at the highest levels of scientific inquiry into the possibility of extraterrestrial life. Notice how A. Thomas Young, then Deputy Director of NASA's Ames Research Center and now Director of Goddard Space Flight Center, conflates life with human life:

> We know of only one existence of life in the universe —that being ourselves on planet Earth. We know that our Earth is an enormously small part of our Universe. A perplexing question evolves as to whether life abounds [in the universe] or are we unique.[6]

Actually, it is most probably the case *both* that we— human beings—are unique *and* that life abounds elsewhere in the universe. Young seems not only not to have thought of this possibility, but he gives no thought either to the ten to thirty million other species that with us comprise life on this planet. The explanation for this omission, I conjecture, lies probably in Young's participation in the now obsolete mechanistic world view pioneered by Descartes, whose conceptual segregation of living mankind from merely mechanical plants and animals has been compounded by subsequent militant humanism and human technological self-insulation from nature.

John A. Billingham, Chief of the Extraterrestrial Research Division of NASA's Ames Research Center, acknowledges the possible existence of other-than-human extraterrestrial life but seems to think of it as it may exist on other worlds only as the staging ground for the organic evolution of humanoid intelligence and, upon that, the cultural evolution of "technological civilizations." Writes Billingham:

> Modern astrophysical theory predicts that planets are the rule rather than the exception. Planets are therefore likely to number in the hundreds of billions in our Galaxy alone. Given a suitable location and environment for any single planet, current theories of chemical evolution predict that life will begin. And given a period of billions of years of comparative stability life will sometimes evolve to the stage of intelligence. The next step may be the emergence of a technological civilization, and it is possible that civilizations may be in communication with each other.[7]

If so, of course, we want to be in on the fun.

In the face of this sort of giddy enthusiasm for communicating with "intelligent life" on other planets, it is both sobering and irritating to observe that those involved in SETI, the search for extraterrestrial intelligence, have not first established—as a kind of preliminary benchmark or data base, so that they would have some idea of what communicating with an exotic intelligence would be like—communication with nonhuman forms of intelligent life on Earth. Cetaceans carry the biggest brains on this planet, with richly fissured cerebral cortexes and a brain-to-body weight ratio comparable to that of humans.⁸ Like us they are social mammals. But they live in an environment, relatively speaking, very different from ours. Hence, theirs is a world apart from ours, a terrestrial analog of an extraterrestrial environment. And they engage, apparently, in complex vocal communication, of which we to date understand not one word—or rather click, grunt, or whistle.⁹ What this omission reveals is not only an arrogant disregard for nonhuman terrestrial intelligence; it also clearly shows that by "extraterrestrial intelligence" those involved in SETI mean something very like, if not identical to, human intelligence.

The distinguished Harvard astrophysicist Eric J. Chaisson takes us from Billingham's idle but relatively modest proposal—to search the skies in hopes of eavesdropping on the interstellar communications of extraterrestrial technological civilizations—to the stock, infantile, science-fiction fantasies of universal conquest and dominion. Chaisson points out that in the moments following the big bang, radiation dominated matter and then, after a relatively short time, matter became predominant over energy. Now, listen to what will follow this:

> [O]ne thing seems certain [certain?!]: we on Earth, as well as other intelligent life forms throughout the Universe, are now participating in a fantastically important [fantastic, indeed!] transformation—the second most important transformation in the history of the Universe. . . . Matter is now losing its total dominance, at least in those isolated locations where technologically intelligent life resides. . . . Together with our galactic neighbors, should there be any, we may be in a position some day to gain control of the resources of much of the Universe, rearchitecturing it to suit our purposes, and in a very real sense, ensuring for our civilization a measure of immortality.¹⁰

One wants to know how it is possible for these scientists to say such things among their colleagues and maintain their professional credibility. Some might contend that Young, Billingham, Chaisson, Carl Sagan, and others who write in a similar vein do so deliberately to pander to our vanities of glory and greed in order to dupe us into allocating public funds to finance their very expensive but very speculative research and development projects. Without the prospect of rearchitecturing the universe and ensuring ourselves a measure of immortality, public support for astrophysics, exobiology, and NASA might dry up. But I just cannot bring myself to believe that such simple, base, and cynical motives are really the explanation.

I rather think that what we find here is a sincere and not uncommon mixture of science and myth. In addition to the mythic projection into outer space of the heroic adventures of Renaissance European mariners and the complementary post-Renaissance doctrines of mechanism and humanism, we can identify several deeper strata of obsolete dogma, in these conceptual core samples, mined from past Western culture. Oparine and Fessenkov have identified one key element—essentially a residue of Aristotelian and Thomistic teleology—namely, the belief that somehow we ourselves, intelligent (human) life, are the telos, the goal of God's creation now transposed into the (no doubt divinely planned and directed) evolution of the universe.[11] Hence, given the spatiotemporal vastness of the universe, it would be surprising, indeed, if nature did not at every suitable location achieve its natural purpose: us or something very like us—intelligent (humanoid) life.

In addition to the tendency to assume that the probable existence of life on other worlds must eventuate in human or humanlike intelligent life, there is the tendency to assume that human or humanlike intelligent life on other planets will inevitably be culturally similar to twentieth-century Western civilization or some more "advanced" version of the same. The myth of teleological organic evolution is compounded, in other words, by the myth of teleological cultural evolution. The theoretical paradigm of teleological cultural development is E. B. Tylor's Victorian anthropological scenario according to which mankind began its tenure on Earth in a state of abject "savagery," progressed through "barbarism," and arrived at last at a state of civilization (of which, of course, Anglo-American civilization is the most perfect stage) now, in the inevitable course of things, become technological.[12]

One thing we can be sure of, I suggest in sum, is that extraterrestrial life, if found at all, will not be found to be anything resembling human life. The embarrassingly wide supposition to the contrary seems attributable to unconscious residues of earlier Western religious and philosophical notions of teleological evolution, both natural and cultural, to Western religious and philosophical humanism, to Western cultural chauvinism, and to an uncritical extraterrestrial extrapolation of recent terrestrial history. Furthermore, to the extent that the hypotheses of the existence of "intelligent" extraterrestrial life and extraterrestrial "technological civilization" are either defined or tacitly understood in anthropomorphic terms (and how else could they be defined or understood?) we can also be confident that such life does not exist beyond Earth.

Anthropologist C. Owen Lovejoy has elegantly and authoritatively summed up the case against the existence of extraterrestrial humans (and with it intelligent, technological, anthropomorphic civilizations) as follows:

[M]an is a highly specific, unique, and, unduplicated species. If we wish to make probability estimates of the likelihood that cognitive . . . life has evolved on other suitable planets, the simplest and most direct question we may pose is: What is the probability that cognitive life would evolve on *this* planet, were not man already a constituent of its biosphere? From what we know of the human evolutionary pathway and of the critical elements that have directed it, the odds against its reexpression are indeed remote, if not astronomical. . . . What is the probability that any named species, be it mammal, reptile, or mollusk, would evolve again on this planet [let alone some other]? . . . I think it is quite reasonable to suppose that despite the immensity of the known Universe, the specificity of the physiostructure of any organism is so great and its immensely complex pathway of progression so ancient that such probabilities are simply infinitesimal.[13]

Thus, not only is it very unlikely that there are any other people out there, and in the absence of people or people-like creatures any other "technological civilizations" (not to mention the improbability that even if there were humanlike extraterrestrials, their cultural sequence would duplicate the Western model and culminate in a technological civilization), it is also, by exactly the same evolutionary-ecological reasoning, very unlikely that there are any Earth-like species whatever on other planets. It is therefore unlikely that there are and almost a certainty that we shall never find uninhabited (by humanlike creatures) Earth-like planets (analogous to lush, uninhabited tropical islands in the contemporary mythic mind), that is, planets with familiar species (absent *Homo sapiens*) interacting in familiar ecological patterns on which we might establish colonies.

II.

Having thus dispelled the science-fiction aura from the question, What is extraterrestrial life? let us consider a less fictional, more scientific approach to its answer.

Biology, the science of life, has been heretofore confined to the study of terrestrial life. Unlike physics and chemistry, which are, historically, cosmic in scope and compass, biology is a local science.[14] Therefore, to the extent that life is a well-defined scientific term in biology (the science of life, which has so far been limited to a study of terrestrial life), the very concept of extraterrestrial life is problematic, even paradoxical.

However, there is a certain unity in the sciences generally and, more particularly, continuity between chemistry and biology, both historically (or evolutionarily) and conceptually (or theoretically). Life on Earth, in other words, evolved upon a chemical base, and, as systematic conceptual constructs, organic chemistry and biology are bridged by biochemistry. Life, therefore, may be generically characterized without prejudice to its location or accidental specificity.[15]

Yale biophysicist Harold Morowitz has provided, in the concept of negentropy, perhaps the most general parameters for exobiology:

> Life as we know it . . . is not a property of the universe as a whole, but of planetary surfaces. These surfaces are not at equilibrium . . . because they constantly receive radiant energy from their central star and re-radiate energy to outer space. . . . Therefore . . . the molecular organization of planetary surfaces, which we know as evolution, involves no violation of thermo-dynamic principles.[16]

As Morowitz points out, however, the concept of life involves something more than mere molecular order that every planetary surface would, to one degree or another, exhibit. Self-organization (growth and development) and self-replication (reproduction) are, perhaps, the most general characteristics of a minimally "living" concatenation of molecules.[17]

We might also wish to add self-disintegration (death), if self-organization and self-replication themselves would not quickly end in self-stultification. Self-disintegration or death, in other words, seems to be a condition for the indefinite duration of self-organization and self-replication.

A planetary surface on which there existed growing, reproducing, and dying complex molecular structures would also be one on which there could occur natural selection, evolutionary elaboration, and ecosystemic complication and integration.[18]

If we go further and require that a properly living structure be cellular with a membrane and well-articulated nucleus, we would almost certainly price ourselves out of the solar system. Such life would be possible only on a liquid water planet, and the only such planet in the solar system is the Earth.

The remarkable bonding properties of carbon provide the most general chemical basis for the emergence and evolution of the complex self-organizing and self-replicating structures on Earth. But even to define life in terms of hydrocarbon polymers may be too restrictive. As early as 1940, English astronomer H. Spencer Jones pointed out that in certain extraterrestrial environments silicon could play a role similar to carbon on Earth.[19] Life on other planets, particularly on other planets in our solar system, then, if it exists at all, may not only be rudimentary or primitive, it may be, depending upon how generous we wish to be with the concept of life, based upon an altogether different biochemistry than life as we know it on Earth.

III.

Ethics is more a *normative* than descriptive study of human behavior. That is, in ethics we want to know less how people might than how they *should* or *ought to* act, do, treat, or live. The sense of norm in normative is not the sense of norm in the vulgar meaning of normal—that is, average, mean, lowest common denominator. Rather, norm in normative (and in the medical meaning of normal) connotes a benchmark, a standard, an ideal.

The *ethical* question of this paper is how to treat extraterrestrial life—if there is any and if we ever find any. As an ethicist, I am not competent to predict how we will *in fact* treat extraterrestrial life if and when we encounter it. However, as it seems to me, an untrained observer, the human track record—average, or in that sense, normal human behavior—does not bode well for any extraterrestrial life unfortunate enough to be discovered by us. I am not at all sure that, as an ethicist, I can even address with confidence the question how we *ought to* treat extraterrestrial life. The question is made remote and speculative by two general uncertainties, one meta-ethical, the other epistemic.

Firstly, while today almost everyone of sound mind and good will agrees that *human* life without qualification is the subject of unambiguous and incontrovertible moral concern, there is by no means general agreement that other-than-human *terrestrial* life should be the subject of a similar concern. The suggestion that other-than-human terrestrial life possesses moral value—value, that is, apart from its utility to serve human ends—is greeted at best with skeptical indulgence and at worst with impatient ridicule, not only by popular moralists and their constituents, but more especially by mainstream Western moral philosophers.[20] In the prevailing contemporary ethical climate, the hypothesis that we might even entertain just the possibility of human moral obligations to *extra*terrestrial life, assuming that it is not anthropomorphic, therefore will likely be regarded as so absurd as to be beneath contempt.[21] Animal liberation/ rights moral philosophers, who attempt to extend moral considerability to a narrow range of our closest terrestrial nonhuman relatives, are by their own estimation at the leading edge of ethical theory and, by the estimation of their mainstream philosophical critics, muddled sentimentalists.[22]

The chilly reception greeting even such comparatively modest proposals as animal welfare ethics for a more generous and expansive provision of moral considerability for nonhuman life forms cannot be attributed simply to the churlishness and/or niggardliness of reactionary guardians of the Western moral tradition. Rather, Western moral thought from Plato and St. Paul to Tillich and Hare provides few conceptual resources theoretically to underwrite such generosity of spirit and rigorously to effect such an expansion. But a more embracing ethic to be a proper ethic must have a sound conceptual basis and logical rigor, and it must somehow connect with historical moral theory. A life-centered— a literally biocentric—ethic discontinuous with traditional moral philosophy would not be recognizable as a species of ethics, and so could not be seriously entertained or critically appraised.

Secondly, not only is the very concept of extraterrestrial life problematic—because of the aforementioned local character of biology—but a critical exploration of the hypothesis that extraterrestrial life exists leads to an even more confounding paradox. Venus and Mars, the most likely planetary hosts for extraterrestrial life in our solar system, have been visited by unpeopled probes with disappointing results.[23] If life, however broadly defined, does not exist in the solar system—and it now seems more probable that it does not than that it does —may we suppose that it exists in the galaxy of which our solar system is a member?[24]

We know that our galaxy alone contains literally billions of stars. Thus, if our star, the Sun, is not unique or especially extraordinary in possessing a family of planets, and if we assume that life (defined so as not to be conceptually too terramorphic) is a natural, perhaps inevitable, stage in the progressive ordering of mature, suitably endowed and situated planetary surfaces, then the probability that extraterrestrial life exists in our galaxy beyond our solar system approaches unity and, thus, certainty.

But what of our chances to positively or empirically confirm this convincing *a priori* argument? Our spiral galaxy, the Milky Way, is on the average approximately 100,000 light years wide and 5,000 light years thick.[25] Exobiologist Valdemar Firsoff estimates there to be about two life-supporting planets per million cubic light years.[26] Let us now imagine ourselves actually setting out to find the other life-supporting planet in our million-cubic-light-year district. It ought to be only forty to sixty light years away.

The speed of light, however, is a limiting velocity —nothing can exceed it. And only particles of zero rest mass can actually attain the speed of light. Massy objects

like spaceships are limited in principle to several fractional factors less than the speed of light. For purposes
of calculating a time and energy budget for interstellar
space exploration, Hewlett-Packard engineer Bernard
Oliver suggests we generously posit a ship speed "far
beyond our present technology," of $\frac{1}{5}$ the speed of
light.[27] At that rate an expedition sent to our nearest
stellar neighbor, Alpha Centauri, four light years away,
would arrive in twenty years. In the forty-year working
lifetime of a highly trained crew the next closest star
beyond Alpha Centauri, regardless of its qualifications,
could be visited and examined—and this assumes that
our astronauts would be willing never to return home,
would be willing to undertake, in effect, a suicide mission.[28] A search of a few more stars might be undertaken
in a century by unpeopled probes, depending upon how
many we sent and how far away their targets were. What
would be the probability of finding in this way the other
life supporting planet in our million-cubic-light-year district in a thousand years or a hundred thousand or a
million, and at what expense of energy and other terrestrial resources?[29] My guess is that it would be very small,
and prohibitively expensive.

Hence, and here is the epistemological paradox, we
may take it as very nearly certain—given our knowledge
of the size and stellar population of the galaxy, our understanding of biochemistry and organic evolution, and
the reasonable assumption that our solar system is neither unique nor extraordinary—that life abounds in the
galaxy. But this knowledge has no, or very nearly no,
positive significance or operational translatability. To
the extent that scientific epistemology remains positivis-
tic, the seemingly very innocent and reasonable hypothesis that life abounds in the Milky Way turns out to be as
scientifically nonsensical as the hypothesis that an elec-

tron has both a definite location and a definite velocity. The hypothesis is unverifiable *in principle* primarily because of the limitations on our autopsy imposed by Einstein's constant c, the speed of light, which functions in the large arena of interstellar space somewhat like Planck's constant, h, the quantum, in the small arena of subatomic space. An uncertainty principle, in other words, is operative in very large dimensions of space-time as it is in very small, at least in respect to the search for extraterrestrial life.

The metaethical and epistemological uncertainties surrounding the ethical question posed here lead to a third, more practical uncertainty: Can there be, really, any serious justification for this exercise? If animal-welfare ethics are controversial, if terrestrial biocentric and ecocentric environmental ethics are contemptuously ignored or ridiculed, isn't the construction of an ethic for the treatment of something we know not what or whether it may be more than just a little fatuous?

Right now, right here on Earth, anthropogenic species extinction grinds on at a catastrophic pace.[30] While we are wondering how to treat hypothetical life that may, for better or worse, lie forever beyond our ken, let alone our actions, the life we do partially understand and certainly know to exist is being stamped out—often without notice or comment and with very little remorse or protest—under our noses. Shouldn't we get our intellectual priorities straight and worry first about the treatment of terrestrial life, which is presently under such extreme and actual duress? Once we've got a persuasive ethic worked out to help address the more pressing real-world problem of wholesale terrestrial biocide, then maybe we can think about how we ought to treat extraterrestrial life —if there is any, if we should recognize it when we see it, and if we should ever encounter it!

I am not convinced by this criticism of the present enterprise, even though I have stated it as strongly as I can. It sounds a lot like the stock liberal diatribe against the Apollo project in the sixties: As a nation, so that argument went, we are allocating huge sums of money to put a man on the Moon, while here on Earth socioeconomic conditions for the urban minority underclasses in affluent America grow daily more desperate, and in the oppressed and impoverished Third and Fourth Worlds the "wretched of the Earth" die daily of preventable disease and outright starvation. Shouldn't we put our moral and financial resources to work addressing these earthly social problems before we consider a hollow technological vanity like putting a man on the Moon?

I thought then, and still think now, that even so the Apollo project was morally defensible and economically worthwhile, not so much because of the official rationale —the technical and scientific harvest forthcoming from lunar exploration—but primarily because of the impact of Apollo on human consciousness here on Earth.[31] We have known since the centuries of Copernicus and Galileo that the Earth is a planet and the Moon its satellite. But for one of us to stand on the Moon, look upon a distant Earth, and return to the rest of us photographs of our own small and very precious planet translated heretofore mere propositional knowledge into palpable human experience. We all participated vicariously in that experience. It was, indeed, a most signal event in the collective mind of mankind. Neil Armstrong was the Archimedes of human consciousness. Given the Moon to stand on, he moved the Earth. His lever was a camera. More than any other single phenomenon, those photographs of a soft, lake-blue planet, coyly swirled about with flouncy clouds, floating in empty space—with the utter desolation of the moonscape in the foreground

—precipitated the ecological and environmental decade that immediately followed.[32] The photographs of the Earth taken from the Moon also helped bring to the forefront of social consciousness the concept of universal human community. We could all *see* our world as one. The concept of universal human rights immediately became public-policy rhetoric. We were all fellow citizens of a single small world, fellow passengers with all the other water-planet creatures on what then became spaceship Earth. Our indivisible collective dependency on Earth and its luxuriant life forms was made poignantly visceral by the empathy we all felt for the ill-fated Apollo XIII astronauts—their tenuous and precarious existence in space modules and spacesuits—on their desperate journey home to Earth.

The discussion of environmental ethics in the solar system, if not in the cosmos beyond, in a less far-reaching and certainly less dramatic way, might have a similar reflexive impact. To seriously entertain the ethical question, How ought we to treat extraterrestrial life? may put into proper perspective the more immediate and pressing question, How ought we to treat life on Earth? To entertain a noble moral stance toward extraterrestrial life might help to shame us into taking more seriously a noble moral stance toward terrestrial life. And, as I have elsewhere argued, the Copernican revolution (made palpable by the Apollo project) is as much a conceptual foundation of environmental ethics as the subsequent Darwinian and ecological revolutions in thought.[33] Hence, reminding ourselves from time to time of these larger spatial and temporal parameters may be conceptually important for terrestrial environmental ethics.

And who knows, somewhere in the solar system we just might find some extraterrestrial life. In case we do, it would be better for us, wouldn't it, to be morally prepared for our first close encounter with extraterrestrial life than to shoot first and ask questions later?

Let me conclude these penultimate observations with the following ethical thought experiment. Imagine our astronauts finding something that seems to be more than just a mineral configuration of matter somewhere off the Earth. After performing some tests and consulting some criteria, they determine that they have indeed found extraterrestrial life or "living things." They then systematically eradicate all of it (or them) within reach. There seems to be something wrong, something morally wrong, with such an act of destruction—something more wrong than if the astronauts had found, say, some interesting patterns etched by solar winds on a planet's lifeless surface and erased them. Let us begin with this hopefully shared moral intuition as a touchstone and ask ourselves why we feel that the former act of otherworldly vandalism would be morally worse than the latter.[34]

IV.

The most popularly known but philosophically least cultivated environmental ethic, the Leopold land ethic, provides little help for conceptually articulating our hopefully shared moral intuition respecting extraterrestrial life. The land ethic conceptually bases moral considerability for Earth's complement of animals, plants, waters, and soils upon evolutionary kinship and ecological community.[35] In other words, the land ethic confers moral standing on terrestrial plants and animals in part because they share with us a common evolutionary heritage. They are "fellow-voyagers . . . in the Odyssey of evolution"—indeed, perhaps we and they ultimately evolved from a single parent cell.[36] And Earth's plants and other animals along with the elemental components of Earth's biosphere are all, in Leopold's representation, also presently working members in good standing of Earth's biotic community. That is, terrestrial plants, animals, soils, and waters are ecologically integrated and mutually interdependent. This wholesale symbiosis of Earth's biota, by a moral logic that I have elsewhere elaborated, generates for us, according to Leopold, ethical duties and obligations to the ecosystem as a whole and to its members severally.[37] Extraterrestrial life forms, assuming that they were not of Earthly origin and inoculated somehow on some foreign body, or *vice versa,* would not be our kin—that is, descendants of a common paleontological parent stock—nor would they be participants in Earth's economy of nature or biotic community. Hence, they would lie outside the scope of Leopold's land ethic.

Pursuant to the general reflexive motif of this discussion, the consideration of the moral standing of extraterrestrial life sheds an interesting and very valuable light on Leopold's land ethic. It reveals the limitations of its conceptual foundations and thus highlights and more sharply defines its outlines. With our imaginations limited, as they often are in ethics and more especially in environmental ethics, by terrestrial horizons, Leopold's land ethic, which "enlarges the boundaries of the [biotic/moral] community to include soils, waters, plants, and animals, or collectively: the land," may seem to include everything "under the Sun" and thus to effectively include nothing, to be, in other words, impossibly dilute.[38] However, from the point of view of the Copernican spatiotemporal dimensions of our present discussion—the solar system, the galaxy, and the universe at large—the land ethic seems almost parochial in extent and even tribal in nature because it restricts itself to local —that is, terrestrial—beings and rests their moral value on kinship and mutual dependency. The very failure of the land ethic to provide moral considerability for extraterrestrial life reveals at once its strength for Earth-oriented environmental ethics—which is of course the only variety of environmental ethics with any genuine practical interest or application.

The land ethic, thus, could fairly be called a case of Earth chauvinism or terrestrialism. But unlike male chauvinism and racism, the land ethic is not anti-anything—extraterrestrial life in this case. It would not, in other words, encourage or necessarily sanction the suppression, enslavement, or destruction of extraterrestrial life. The land ethic simply has nothing to say about extraterrestrial life. If pressed to respond to the possibility that extraterrestrial life may exist in the solar system, that it may be found by human beings, and that it may be affected by human actions, an exponent of the land ethic might suggest that something analogous to diplomatic relations between autonomous and independent gens would be implied by it. But such an extension of the land ethic to moral problems with which it was not designed to deal is too speculative a matter to be pursued with confidence.

The advent and academic notoriety of the animal liberation/rights ethics set in motion an intellectual dialectic that led to the development of an apparently novel life-principle ethic by Kenneth Goodpaster, building on suggestions of Joel Feinberg, and a revival of interest in Albert Schweitzer's popularly known reverence-for-life ethic.[39]

Animal liberationist Peter Singer argued that animals ought to be extended the same moral consideration as people because animals have the same capacity as people for suffering.[40] For Singer, sentiency, the capacity to experience pleasure and pain, should be the criterion for the moral considerability of beings.[41]

As this was obviously an inadequate basis for an environmental ethic, since most environmental entities are not sentient—all forms of plant life, for example, and many kinds of animals are not—Goodpaster attempted to extend Singer's moral logic a step further.[42] Sentiency, he argued, ought not to be the criterion for moral considerability, since sentiency exists in some beings only as a means to another end—life.[43] Life, therefore, being the end in reference to which sentiency evolved as a means, ought to be the characteristic in reference to which moral considerability should be conferred.

As I have elsewhere pointed out, Goodpaster's life-principle ethic and Schweitzer's reverence-for-life ethic, though they differ primarily in vocabulary, rhetoric, and historical resonance, have in the abstract a common metaethical foundation.[44] In the last analysis, both defend the moral considerability of living beings because they are conative (a capacity logically parallel to sentiency).

The Goodpaster life-principle and Schweitzer reverence-for-life ethics urge that we extend moral considerability to (and/or reverence for, in Schweitzer's case) only terrestrial life. I do not mean to suggest that either Goodpaster or Schweitzer expressly exclude extraterrestrial life; it is just clear that, quite naturally, the only life they are thinking about is terrestrial life, since that's all the life anyone knows to exist or imagines that s/he might actually affect.

But extraterrestrial life would be conative. I mean I guess it would be minimally conative—that is, in Feinberg's by now classical definition of conative, in possession of at least one of the following characteristics:

"conscious wishes, desires, and hopes; *or* urges and impulses; *or* unconscious drives, aims, and goals; *or* latent tendencies, directions of growth and natural fulfillments."[45] Anything having the minimal characteristics of life sketched in Section II of this essay—a growing, reproducing, dying thing—would have, it would seem necessarily, at least latent tendencies, directions of growth, and natural fulfillments if not unconscious drives, aims, and goals or conscious wishes, desires, and hopes. Such a thing would have therefore a " 'good' of its own, the achievement of which can be its due," in Feinberg's words, and thus moral rights, as Feinberg grounds rights, or at least moral considerability, in Goodpaster's terms—if there is any significant difference between the possession of moral rights and moral considerability.[46]

Similarly, upon Schweitzer's more voluntarist and mystical rendering of conativity, I would suppose that extraterrestrial life, no less than terrestrial life, would be possessed by the will to live and therefore, according to Schweitzer, "[j]ust as in my own will-to-live there is a yearning for more life, . . . so the same obtains in all the will-to-live around me, equally whether it can express itself to my comprehension or whether it remains unvoiced." Schweitzer then goes on to say, "Ethics thus consists in this, that I experience the necessity of practising the same reverence for life toward all will-to-live, as toward my own."[47]

The life-principle/reverence-for-life ethics are, as it were, tailor-made for conceptually articulating and grounding our hopefully shared moral intuition that extraterrestrial life should be treated with respect, or reverence, if and when we may encounter it. The life-principle/reverence-for-life ethics, however, have a foible symmetrical to but opposite that of the Leopold land ethic. The land ethic is, because of its holistic or ecosystemic value orientation, practicable as a terrestrial environmental ethic, but, because of its conceptual foundations and logical structure, incapable of transference to life off the Earth. The life-principle/reverence-for-life ethics are, because of their conceptual foundations and logical structures, capable of transference off the Earth, but, because of their individualistic or atomic biases, impracticable as terrestrial environmental ethics.[48] In other words, the life-principle/reverence-for-life ethics are serviceable as extraterrestrial environmental ethics, but, ironically, fail miserably as terrestrial environmental ethics.

Let me elaborate. Only individual living things are conative, at least as Feinberg and Schweitzer variously understand this shared basic idea. Populations, species, biocoenoses, ecotones, biomes, and the biosphere as a whole are not. Hence, only individual living things are properly rights bearers (Feinberg), morally considerable (Goodpaster), or objects of reverence and respect (Schweitzer). To consistently practice the life-principle/reverence-for-life ethics at home on Earth would require a life style so quiescent as to be suicidal, as Schopenhauer clearly recognized and affirmed.[49] To live is necessarily to exploit other living beings. Since we are integrated members of the terrestrial bioeconomy in which the life of one thing is purchased by the death of another, the exponents of life-principle/reverence-for-life ethics at home on Earth are caught in an unavoidable practical conundrum at every turn. However, since our astronauts would not be integrated members of some extraterrestrial ecosystem and would be bringing with them their own terrestrial foodstuff and other necessities of life, the life-principle/reverence-for-life ethics would be practicable, without continuous compromise between principle and necessity, in respect to life on other bodies in the solar system—should there be any and should our astronauts ever encounter it. Without the need to eat or otherwise exploit extraterrestrial life our astronauts could categorically respect and/or revere it.

But there is both a rational philosophical demand and a human psychological need for a self-consistent and all-embracing moral theory. We are neither good philosophers nor whole persons if for one purpose we adopt utilitarianism, another deontology, a third animal liberation, a fourth the land ethic, and a fifth a life-principle or reverence-for-life ethic, and so on. Such ethical eclecticism is not only rationally intolerable, it is morally suspect as it invites the suspicion of *ad hoc* rationalizations for merely expedient or self-serving actions.

Let me therefore recommend an environmental ethic that is sufficiently inclusive and consistent to provide at once for the moral considerability of extraterrestrial as well as for terrestrial life without neglecting the practical primacy of human life, human needs, and human rights.

Bryan Norton has distinguished between strong and weak anthropocentrism.[50] Anthropocentrism is the view that there exists no value independent from human experience. Whether such a view is ultimately justifiable or not, it seems to be the prevailing view in Western axiology.[51] In Norton's terms, strong anthropocentrism takes any valued human experience as in principle equal to any other—push-pin is as good as poetry, bird-shooting as botanizing, and dune-buggying as desert pup-fish habitat restoration. Nonhuman beings are merely resources for valued human experiences, and no constraints—except essentially economic constraints—are warranted when those resources are consumed or destroyed in the process of using them to satisfy human preferences. From the point of view of strong anthropocentrism, if when human astronauts encounter life on another planet they are more amused to eradicate it than leave it alone, and a majority of the rest of us feel better off or at least no worse off for their having done so, then that is what they should do.

Weak anthropocentrism on the other hand, the *locus classicus* of which Norton finds in Thoreau, regards certain uses of things as transforming and ennobling human nature.[52] Some human experiences, therefore, are better than others because they expand and enlarge human consciousness, in short because they make better human beings of us.[53] Thus it is better to botanize than bird-shoot, save desert pup-fish than dune-buggy, and write poetry than play push-pin because push-pin, bird-shooting, and dune-buggying stultify the human spirit and stupefy the human mind while literature, science, and species conservation elevate the human spirit and enlighten the human mind.

Now, as it seems to me, weak anthropocentrism would apply to our use of extraterrestrial as well as terrestrial life all to the greater good of mankind. I can think of nothing so positively transforming of human consciousness as the discovery, study, and conservation of life somewhere off the Earth. It would confirm experientially, palpably, viscerally what we presently believe in the abstract: that life is the expression of an inherent potentiality in physical nature. Such an event would immeasurably advance the ongoing process of the naturalization of human consciousness, which is presently progressing all too slowly. And to find life off the Earth, to discover a wholly exotic biology, to cherish it, and try to understand something about it would, I believe, transform our present view of life on Earth. In relation to extraterrestrial life, terrestrial organisms, ourselves included, comprise one great family, one gens. The current myopic prejudices regarding terrestrial species as somehow alien or exotic forms would perforce melt away in comparison with truly alien or exotic life forms. In short, the Archimedean adventure of the Apollo project would thereby be completed.

Notes

1. See for example, Charles L. Sandford, *The Quest for Paradise* (Urbana, Ill: The University of Illinois Press, 1961) and Daniel S. Boorstin, *The Discoverers: A History of Man's Search to Know His World and Himself* (New York: Random House, 1983) for an account of the self-image of Renaissance discoverers. See William K. Hartmann, "Space Exploration and Environmental Issues," *Environmental Ethics* 6 (1984): 227–39, for an explicit, self-conscious projection of the Renaissance discovery, exploration, and exploitation of the New World into a new interplanetary frontier.

2. See William Hartmann, "Space Exploration and Environmental Issues," pp. 119–39 of this anthology, for a recent example of seriously entertaining these things. Ian McHarg, *Design With Nature* (Garden City, N.Y.: Doubleday, 1969), rather elaborately and very convincingly makes the point that to successfully design a self-sustaining space colony, which Hartmann also envisions, we would have to recreate the Earth.

3. Ibid. Hartmann denies that extraterrestrial resource development and colonization, which he enthusiastically recommends, would lead to a " 'disposable planet mentality' " (p. 122 of this anthology). Yet he apparently forgets this disclaimer and later writes, "The possibilities of self-sustaining colonies of humans . . . on other planetary surfaces are really increasing the chances for survival of the human race against [political and environmental] disasters" (p. 134 of this anthology). If we think we can escape these disasters by emigrating off the Earth, we shall have less incentive to try to avert them.

4. Ibid. Hartmann calls Earth "a Hawaii in a solar system of Siberias" (p. 122 of this anthology). More apt, but not nearly apt enough, would be a Hawaii in a solar system of Antarcticas. Hartmann goes on to say immediately, "Earth is the only known place where we can stand naked in the light of a nearby star and enjoy our surroundings." It is the only known place we can stand

wearing anything less than a spacesuit, and most other known planets provide either no place to stand or, if they do, even a spacesuit would not be protection enough from solar radiation.

5. Frank Herbert, *Dune* (New York: Chilton Books, 1965). In *Dune* we are to imagine a desert planet without oceans or extensive forests but with, nevertheless, an apparently breathable atmosphere containing, we must therefore suppose, free oxygen— and this is touted to be an ecologically well-informed science fiction! Irving Buchen, "The Future of the Future," *L & S* (Fall, 1984) points out that science fiction can have a very positive reflexive value in respect to our perception of the Earth and our lives on it. Among these is a collective identity for human beings, a globalized nationalism. The major motif of this paper is borrowed from Buchen. My discussion expands the point introduced in his article.

6. A. Thomas Young, "Conference Overview," in John Billingham, ed., *Life in the Universe* (Cambridge, Mass.: Massachusetts Institute of Technology Press, 1982), p. xi.

7. Billingham, "Preface," in *Life in the Universe,* p. ix.

8. See Peter Morgane, "The Whale Brain: The Anatomical Basis of Intelligence," in Joan McIntyre, ed., *Mind in the Waters* (New York: Scribner's, 1974), pp. 84–93.

9. See Peter Warshall, "The Ways of Whales," in *Mind in the Waters,* pp. 110–40.

10. Eric J. Chaisson, "Three Eras of Cosmic Evolution," in *Life in the Universe,* pp. 15–16.

11. A. Oparine and V. Fessenkov, *La Vie dans l'Universe* (Moscow: Editions en Langues Etrangères, 1958), translated from the French and quoted by V.A. Firsoff, *Life Beyond the Earth: A Study in Exobiology* (New York: Basic Books, 1963), p. xii.

12. E.B. Tylor, *Anthropology: An Introduction to the Study of Man and Civilization* (New York: Appleton, 1897).

13. C. Owen Lovejoy, "Evolution of Man and Its Implications for General Principles of the Evolution of Intelligent Life," in *Life in the Universe,* pp. 317–29. It should be pointed out that Carl Sagan, in *The Dragons of Eden: Speculations on the Evolution of Human Intelligence* (New York: Ballantine, 1977), asserts that "evolution is adventitious and not foresighted" (p. 8), but he remains undaunted in his belief in the existence of anthropomorphic extraterrestrial intelligence, even though he "would . . . not expect their brains to be anatomically or physiologically or perhaps even

chemically close to ours" (p. 243). How then could their functions be close to ours? Sagan's answer is "they must still come to grips with the same laws of nature" (p. 242). The laws of nature are objective realities, like Platonic forms—as opposed to Kantian descriptions of our own subjective ordering of experience—Sagan seems to think, and evolutionary development from widely divergent points of departure and following radically different pathways will converge upon a mental representation of them, not as target, but as a selective end result: "Smarter organisms by and large survive better and leave more offspring than stupid ones" (p. 241). Granted. But Sagan's argument turns on an ambiguity in the concept of "smarter organisms" coming "to grips with the same laws of nature." Cetaceans, who own brains very like ours in chemistry, anatomy, and physiology, have come to grips with the laws of nature governing the propagation, reflection, and detection of sound waves, but no one supposes that their evolution and intelligent deployment of echolocation entails that they have mastered the science of wave mechanics. Birds do not need to know aerodynamics to fly or optics to see. Survival intelligence, the evolutionary equivalent of street smarts, is not necessarily the same as theoretical intelligence. In sum and short, it is not necessary, in order to come to grips with the laws of nature on a practical basis, that an organism theoretically represent the laws of nature or even be cognizant that natural laws as such exist if in fact as such they do exist.

14. See J.D. Bernal, "Molecular Structure, Biochemical Function, and Evolution," in T.H. Waterman and H.J. Morowitz, eds., *Theoretical and Mathematical Biology* (New York: Blaisdell Publishing Co., 1965), chap. 5, for an explicit comparison of biology with physics and chemistry in this context.

15. See Peter Shuster, "Evolution Between Chemistry and Biology," *Origins of Life* 14 (1984): 3–14, for a recent summary discussion.

16. Harold J. Morowitz, "Biology as a Cosmological Science," *Main Currents in Modern Thought* 2 (1972): 153.

17. See Firsoff, *Life Beyond the Earth*, p. 4.

18. See Sherwood Chang, "Organic Chemical Evolution," in *Life in the Universe*, pp. 21–46; and F. Raulin, D. Gautier, and W.H. Ip, "Exobiology and the Solar System: The Cassini Mission to Titan," *Origins of Life* 14 (1984): 817–24.

19. See Sir H. Spencer Jones, *Life on Other Worlds* (London: English Universities Press, 1940).

20. For an extended discussion ranging from skeptical indulgence to impatient ridicule see John Passmore, *Man's Responsibility for Nature: Ecological Problems and Western Traditions* (New York: Scribner's, 1974).

21. I was interested to learn that Michael Tooley, "Would ETIs Be Persons?" in James L. Christian, ed., *Extraterrestrial Intelligence: The First Encounter* (Buffalo, N.Y.: Prometheus Books, 1976), provides, by applying the usual ethical categories of mainstream Western moral thought, moral considerability for extraterrestrial intelligent beings of sci-fi fantasy, provided that they are also conative, self-conscious, and can envisage the future. Tooley does not address and his discussion suggests he could not philosophically support moral considerability for mere life—extraterrestrial or otherwise.

22. Peter Singer, *Animal Liberation: A New Ethics for Our Treatment of Animals* (New York: The New York Review, 1975), writes, "Philosophy ought to question the basic assumptions of the age" (p. 10), as if his extension of moral considerability to animals were really radical. See H. J. McCloskey, "Moral Rights and Animals," *Inquiry* 22 (1979): 23–59, for a humanistic rejection of animal liberation/rights.

23. Paul M. Henig, "Exobiologists Continue to Search for Life on Other Planets," *BioScience* 30 (1980), quotes physicist William G. Pollard as saying of exobiology that it is " 'a branch of science so far without content' " (p. 9). Exobiologist Richard S. Young, "Post-Viking Exobiology," *BioScience* 28 (1978), makes the essentially logical (and thus largely formal) point that "the absence of evidence of life [on Mars] should not necessarily be construed as evidence of the absence of life" (p. 502).

24. For a discussion of the shift of informed opinion toward skepticism regarding extraterrestrial life, see Paul M. Henig, "Exobiologists Continue to Search for Life on Other Planets."

25. These dimensions are supplied by Firsoff, *Life Beyond the Earth*, p. xi.

26. Ibid.

27. Bernard M. Oliver, "Search Strategies," in *Life in the Universe*, p. 352.

28. Ibid. Oliver entertains the possibility of a search voyage spanning several generations requiring thus "nursery and educational facilities [which adds weight and increases energy requirements]. . . . The longer time," he realistically reminds us, "also

increases the risk of disaffection or actual mutiny by the crew: the parents were presumably screened for psychological stability; the children are not" (pp. 354–55). Incidentally, Oliver's calculations do not neglect the time-dilating effects of speeds approaching the speed of light in relativity theory; his time calculations are given in the ship-time reference frame.

29. Ibid. Oliver calculates the energy required to accelerate a starship of 1,000 tons to ⅕ the speed of light in multiples of units of millennia of U.S. energy consumption—that is, in units equivalent to 1,000 years of total energy consumption by the United States (p. 354)!

30. See Norman Myers, *The Sinking Ark: A New Look at the Problem of Disappearing Species* (New York: Pergamon Press, 1979), for an authoritative scientific account. For a philosophical-ethical response, see Bryan Norton and Henry Shue, eds., *The Preservation of Species* (Princeton, N.J.: Princeton University Press, 1986).

31. Hartmann, in "Space Exploration and Environmental Issues," very nicely summarizes and documents this impact. Hartmann's central practical concern seems to be that environmentalists not add their opposition to that of socialists, fiscal conservatives, and others who hope to see space-exploration projects scrapped. Although I do not share Hartmann's mythic vision of space colonies and space resource development, I am not opposed to space exploration, since I think that the more we explore space, the more deeply impressed we will be with our embeddedness in and dependency upon Earth.

32. Ibid. Hartmann agrees, "It is no coincidence that the first Earth Day, in 1970, came soon after these pictures became available."

33. See, for example, J. Baird Callicott, "On the Intrinsic Value of Non-human Species," in Norton, *The Preservation of Species*, pp. 138–72.

34. The role of intuition in ethics is controversial. Tom Regan, *The Case for Animal Rights* (Berkeley: University of California Press, 1983), p. 133ff., provides a recent summary, a sorting of the issues, and a defense for the utility of moral intuitions such as this one as a point of departure for further ethical analysis.

35. For a schematic analysis of the land ethic, see J. Baird Callicott, "Elements of an Environmental Ethic: Moral Considerability and the Biotic Community," *Environmental Ethics* 1 (1979): 71–81.

36. Aldo Leopold, *A Sand County Almanac and Sketches Here and There* (New York: Oxford University Press, 1949), p. 109. Lewis

Thomas, *The Lives of a Cell: Notes of a Biology Watcher* (New York: Viking Press, 1974), p. 5, notes that there is a "high probability that we derived from some single cell, fertilized in a bolt of lightning as the Earth cooled."

37. See Leopold, "The Land Ethic," in *A Sand County Almanac,* and J. Baird Callicott, "Elements of an Environmental Ethics," and "The Search for an Environmental Ethic," in Tom Regan, ed., *Matters of Life and Death,* 2nd ed. (New York: Random House, 1986).

38. Leopold, "The Land Ethic," p. 204.

39. Joel Feinberg, "The Rights of Animals and Unborn Generations," in William T. Blackstone, ed., *Philosophy and Environmental Crisis* (Athens: University of Georgia Press, 1974); Kenneth Goodpaster, "On Being Morally Considerable," *Journal of Philosophy* 22 (1978): 308–25; Albert Schweitzer, "The Ethic of Reverence for Life" in Tom Regan and Peter Singer, eds., *Animal Rights and Human Obligations* (Englewood Cliffs, N.J.: Prentice-Hall, 1976): 133–38. For a discussion of the dialectic see Kenneth Goodpaster, "From Egoism to Environmentalism," in K.E. Goodpaster and K.M. Sayre, eds., *Ethics and Problems of the 21st Century* (Notre Dame, In.: University of Notre Dame Press, 1979): 21–35.

40. Peter Singer, *Animal Liberation,* p. 1ff.

41. Ibid.

42. Kenneth Goodpaster, "On Being Morally Considerable."

43. Ibid., p. 316.

44. J. Baird Callicott, "On the Intrinsic Value of Non-human Species."

45. Joel Feinberg, "The Rights of Animals and Unborn Generations," p. 49. Italics added.

46. Ibid., p. 50. Goodpaster, in "On Being Morally Considerable," wisely steers clear of the intellectual quagmire of the nature of rights and the qualifications of rights holders.

47. Albert Schweitzer, "The Ethic of Reverence for Life," p. 133.

48. Kenneth Goodpaster, in "From Egoism to Environmentalism," provides a very clear and illuminating discussion of the moral reasoning, the logic, of all ethics that rest on a criterion for moral standing/moral rights, such as rationality, sentiency, conativity, etc.

49. Both Schweitzer and Goodpaster admit the strict impracticability

of their conation-centered ethics. Goodpaster, in "On Being Morally Considerable," writes, "the clearest and most decisive refutation of the principle of respect for life is that one cannot *live* according to it, nor is there any indication in nature that we were intended to." And Schweitzer, in "The Ethic of Reverence for Life," writes, "It remains a painful enigma how I am to live by the rule of reverence for life in a world ruled by creative will which is at the same time destructive will. . . ." For a fuller discussion see J. Baird Callicott, "On the Intrinsic Value of Nonhuman Species."

50. See Arthur Schopenhauer, *The World as Will and Idea,* trans. R.B. Haldane and J. Kemp (Garden City, N.Y.: Doubleday, 1961), p. 297ff.

51. Bryan G. Norton, "Environmental Ethics and Weak Anthropocentrism," *Environmental Ethics* 6 (1984): 131–48.

52. Ibid., p. 136.

53. For a historical analysis see J. Baird Callicott, "Intrinsic Value, Quantum Theory, and Environmental Ethics," *Environmental Ethics* 7 (1985): 257–75.

The Human
Dimension

The Social and Physical Environment of Space Stations and Colonies

PAUL C. RAMBAUT

Introduction

*A*s earlier life forms once left the sea and evolved to live on land, so modern man has left the Earth and is learning to live in space. Whereas the migration from sea to land spanned the course of aeons, the transition into space will occupy but a few more generations. While random genetic change enabled earlier adaptations, the intellectual prowess of man and his machines underlies his deliberate mastery of space. In this paper I discuss current physiological evidence and, where there is no evidence, theorize about whether man will indeed be able to live in space, generation after generation. This discussion is intended as preparation for a discussion of the ethical issues involved, the subject of the next paper in this volume.

The Space Environment

The space environment is a hostile one indeed. It contains no air nor water nor any elemental substance in sufficient quantity to be useful. There is however particulate material in the form of micrometeorites travelling at extremely high velocity. There is radiant energy that can heat exposed surfaces to very high temperatures and do substantial damage to organic material placed in its path. Most importantly, from a physiological point of view, a microgravity environment normally prevails in any spacecraft orbiting the Earth or bound between one celestial body and another.

The Spacecraft

A house, in the words of Le Corbusier, is a machine for living in. Man's house in space must be, more or less, a miniature replica of the world he has left. The fidelity with which the life-support machinery must replicate the earthbound environment depends both on the length of time individuals will remain in space and upon the ease with which they wish to transition between the Earth and space. In several ways, as will be discussed later, the changes that accompany transition by humans to a weightless world would be of no consequence were it not for the fact that they must someday return to Earth.

The Spacecraft's Atmosphere

A spacecraft must and can provide an atmosphere of the right composition and at the right pressure to support respiration and to maintain the integrity of tissues. Earlier U.S. spacecraft, such as Mercury, Gemini, and Apollo, provided atmospheres consisting of almost 100 percent oxygen at a pressure of only one-third that existing at sea level on Earth. The longest of these flights lasted only 14 days, a time apparently insufficient to elicit any untoward signs of oxygen toxicity or other effects. From the beginning, Soviet spacecraft have maintained more Earth-like atmospheres with partial pressures of oxygen and nitrogen matching those on Earth. Following the oxygen-fanned fire that occurred in the Apollo spacecraft on the launch pad in 1967, U.S. designers introduced nitrogen into the spacecraft atmosphere. Nitrogen was first used only during the launch phase, then on orbit at reduced pressure in the Skylab space station, and finally at full Earth-like pressure in the Space Shuttle.

In the future all spacecraft will probably contain atmospheres at near normal pressure and composition. The moisture content of this atmosphere and its temperature will match a comfortable living room on Earth, and carbon dioxide and other contaminants will be removed by mechanical means. For the next few years atmospheric gases will be carried into space in liquid form, consumed, and eventually vented into space. Later, spacecraft will be equipped to recycle oxygen after it has been reduced to carbon dioxide. This will be done by physico-chemical processes at first and then perhaps by plants, much as is done on Earth.

There is, as far as we know, no impediment to human respiration in space. Measurements made on Skylab and on Salyut showed no significant differences between respiratory processes on Earth and in space. While improvements might be expected on theoretical grounds in the perfusion of the lungs in zero gravity, measurements to verify this will not be carried out for several years.

Nutrition

Like the atmospheric gases, food and water are carried into space as expendable supplies. Although water is produced on the Shuttle as a by-product of the operation of the fuel cells used to produce electricity, the elemental constituents of this water must be carried into space as oxygen and hydrogen gas.

From experiments carried out on the earliest flights of Gagarin and Glenn, it was apparent that food and water could be consumed in space without difficulty. Insufficient data exist to describe completely how food, and specifically nutrient material, is absorbed and utilized by the body in weightlessness. It suffices to say, however, that the expectation that humans would be able to live in weightlessness with far fewer food calories than on Earth has not proved correct. Careful measurements made on the one-, two-, and three-month Skylab flights demonstrated that energy expenditure in space was very similar to that on Earth in a person performing approximately the same amount of work. Differences have been noted in the efficiency with which such minerals as calcium are absorbed from the gastrointestinal tract, and there are data to indicate that some changes in nutritional intake should be made to counteract loss of bone and muscle substance. In general, however, there is no reason to suppose that adult human nutritional requirements in space should differ from those on the ground. As with oxygen, nutrients and water will eventually be recycled in space, using human waste as raw material.

Light

In space the radiant energy of the Sun is unattenuated. This energy can be collected and used to power spacecraft systems and to provide a spectrum of light suitable for human habitation and for the growth and sustenance of plants. The periodicity of Earth's light-and-dark cycle can be artificially mimicked in space so that this important cue to circadian rhythm can be properly provided. Harmful ultraviolet radiation from the Sun can be shielded and transmitted in benign form so that it can support vitamin-D production and other functions.

Micrometeorites

Particles of matter ranging in size from the microscopic upward through many orders of magnitude traverse the space environment. While millennia may separate the arrival of kilometer-sized bodies in the vicinity of the Earth, millimeter-sized particles appear much more frequently. Special shades had to be installed to protect the windows of the Salyut 7 space station from the particles that had so severely degraded the optical quality of the windows of its predecessor Salyut 6. Damage to man from micrometeorites is prevented by the spacecraft and by the spacesuit. Catastrophic damage is eventually inevitable but exceedingly improbable. Space stations and space colonies would undoubtedly incorporate sufficient redundancy to survive any projected occurrence.

Ionizing Radiation

There are several sources of ionizing radiation in space. Some radiation is trapped in belts around the Earth extending from several hundred to many thousands of kilometers above the surface. Other forms of radiation come from the Sun, and still others come from beyond the solar system. Only when a spacecraft orbits the Earth roughly parallel to the equator and at low altitude can most of this radiation be avoided. At high altitudes and inclinations the spacecraft encounters more and more high-energy protons and electrons from the radiation belts. Excursions toward the poles or to very high altitude take the spacecraft away from the protective influences of the magnetosphere, and particles from the Sun and elsewhere can reach it almost unimpeded. Increasing the thickness of the walls of the spacecraft can protect it from the effects of most incident particles, although technology remains to be developed to shield it from high-energy cosmic rays. Eventually the use of electromagnetic shields may become necessary to enable stays of many years duration. The impingement of cosmic rays on the retina is thought to have been the cause of vivid light flashes observed in the darkness by certain Soviet and American crewmen.

Artificial Gravity

Homo sapiens, like all other terrestrial species, has evolved under the influence of gravity. Man depends on gravity for stationkeeping, for locomotion, for orientation, and for an infinite number of activities that are performed on the surface of the Earth. Although a variety of movements on Earth can change the direction of the gravity vector (lying down, standing on one's head, etc.), very few circumstances can reduce its size. When a man falls or starts to run down a hill the vector is reduced for a very brief period. Although parabolic flight in high-performance aircraft has recently exposed humans to periods of weightlessness lasting several minutes, it is only with the advent of orbital flight that man began to be exposed to protracted periods of weightlessness.

Weightlessness has many effects on the human body, some of which must be prevented if long stays in space are to occur. Gravity can of course be imposed artificially on the occupants of a spacecraft by subjecting them to constant linear or angular acceleration. Artificial gravity has been used experimentally in the flight of the Soviet Cosmos 936 spacecraft in which rats were housed in a rotating centrifuge developing 1 g at the periphery. Ways can also be found to counteract the effects of weightlessness on a system-by-system basis. It is the latter approach that is being pursued for present-day spacecraft and for those planned in the immediate future.

Alternatives to Artificial Gravity

There is no single alternative to artificial gravity but rather a series of measures that can be used to stave off the deteriorative effects on human physiology of exposure to weightlessness. None of these measures are completely effective, and none are ideal solutions that can be adopted unequivocally by the occupants of space stations and colonies. Rather these measures point the way to what might be done eventually to enable human beings to live and work indefinitely in space. In order to assess the adequacy of today's countermeasures and evaluate the improvements that have yet to be made, it is necessary to review briefly the changes that take place or can be expected to take place in human physiology in weightlessness.

A. Blood and the Circulatory System

One of the most obvious clinical signs of the weightless condition is a puffy face and bulging eyeballs. This sign is accompanied by a feeling of congestion and nasal stuffiness that frequently persists throughout a mission. The cause of these signs and symptoms is a headward shift of fluids from the lower extremities, which occurs following insertion into weightless flight. The result of this shift in fluids toward the head appears to be a stimulation of pressure receptors in the upper part of the body giving rise to a cascade of hormonal events that lead to a loss of water and electrolytes by the kidneys. The volume of the circulating blood is adjusted downward, and with this reduction an inhibition to red-cell synthesis also occurs. This change in the circulating volume of blood seems to be of no consequence as long as the astronauts remain aloft but has potentially dangerous effects during reentry and in the immediate post-flight period. As the g forces begin to build up during deceleration through the atmosphere, the reduced blood volume tends to shift back toward the legs and pelvis and away from the head where it is most needed. Some light-headedness or even fainting could occur at this most critical flight phase were not the crews protected in some way. G-suits, which prevent the accumulation of blood in the lower part of the body, are routinely worn by Soviet and American crewmen. Prior to reentry an attempt is also made to temporarily restore the missing blood volume by the administration of salt solutions with the same osmotic pressure as the blood. From an operational standpoint these procedures seem to work. Cardiovascular changes, based on a reduction of plasma volume, seem not to threaten the longevity of the individual living in space.

Other more serious cardiovascular alterations remain a possibility and must be looked into in more detail before humans can be allowed to remain indefinitely in a space station or colony. Changes in the neuroendocrine control of cardiovascular dynamics may occur and may be accompanied by pathological alterations in the heart muscle itself. Evidence for this has been noted in animal studies and in the examination at autopsy of the hearts of the Soviet Salyut 1 cosmonauts who perished during the accidental decompression of their return module.

B.   Bones and Muscles

When bones and muscles do not receive the stimuli associated with normal activity, they deteriorate. This happens to the patient temporarily immobilized in a plaster cast or to the permanently immobilized person following a severe spinal injury. Any chronic illness that confines a person to bed for weeks at a time also results in the atrophy of muscles and the rarefaction of bone. So too in space, where the lower limbs hang as useless ap-

pendages and there is a loss in bone and muscle substance. These losses begin almost immediately following
the onset of weightlessness and tend to accelerate for at
least the first three months. Such telltale chemical signs
as an elevated content of calcium appear in the blood,
urine, and feces. Some danger exists that such elements
might be deposited in soft tissue, for instance, as stones
in the kidney where they might have very painful consequences. In time the bones might lose sufficient strength
that they could fracture when subjected to an unusual
load in space, or what is more likely, during and following reentry. Several steps might be taken, short of artificial gravity, to prevent these changes. Some of these
measures used on all long-term flights to date may have
prevented much more serious losses from occurring.
Certainly if bone and muscle substance is being lost in
urine and feces, it should be replenished continuously by
sustained, high-quality nutrient intake. On both Soviet
and American long-term flights, the astronauts' diets
have been closely monitored and regulated so that energy, protein, and minerals were consumed in the required amounts. Since the basis of the bone and muscle
loss is thought to be the removal of the normal stimuli
of earthbound activity, the artificial reimposition of such
stimuli is likely to be of benefit. Both astronauts and
cosmonauts exercise extensively. On Salyut this sometimes amounts to as much as 2.5 hours a day. Both tread-
mills and ergometers are used, as well as rowing devices
and muscle electrostimulation. The mainstay of Soviet
countermeasure equipment is a compressional suit,
known as the "Penguin" suit, which is worn throughout
the waking hours and which applies approximate body
weight across the longitudinal axis of the body. Devices
of this kind as well as osteogenic and myotropic drugs

must be improved before any individual can be permitted to live indefinitely in a weightless environment.

C. The Brain and Special Senses

Most animals, including man, are equipped with special sensors to detect the force and direction of gravity relative to their own bodies. In the inner ear, tiny calcium-containing crystals normally rest upon sensitive nerve endings. When these crystals are moved slightly by tilting motions of the head or by linear acceleration, an appropriate signal is sent to the brain. Because both types of motion produce similar displacement of the calcite crystals, the brain must rely on information from other sensors, such as the eyes and pressure receptors in the skin, to confirm what type of motion is actually taking place. In weightlessness, pitching or yawing movements of the head have no effect on the position of the calcite crystals relative to the nerve endings. Only linear acceleration can displace these crystals. In weightlessness, therefore, actual pitching motions of the head confirmed by visually perceived movements of the surroundings and by the stretching and contraction of muscles in the neck are not accompanied by the usual signal from the middle ear. A type of sensory confusion ensues that is often accompanied by various signs and symptoms of space motion sickness.

For two or three days following the start of a space mission there is a loss of appetite, nausea, vomiting, and headache. Occasionally there are visual illusions in which the surroundings are displaced at unusual attitudes. Following two or three days all these signs and symptoms disappear as the brain learns to accommodate and adapt to the unusual mix of sensory stimuli. Once again, as with changes in cardiovascular and musculoskeletal systems, changes in the neurovestibular system are not thought to present a hazard to spacecraft occupants as long as they remain aloft. Following reentry, however, the brain must once again learn to reinterpret stimuli from the inner ear, and once again this process is accompanied by central and peripheral disturbances. Evidence for these disturbances seems to persist long after reimposition of the 1-g field and raises the question as to the possibility of long-term or permanent alterations. At the present time space motion sickness is treated with drugs. Other more efficient drugs and special adaptation training procedures are on the horizon. Fundamental studies to determine what permanent effect the removal of gravity might have on the brain, inner ear, or other special senses must also be undertaken before unqualified approval for prolonged sojourns in space is given. Investigations conducted recently on the Shuttle have not shown any significant change developing in vision, taste, or proprioception.

D. Reproduction, Growth, and Development

As an adult individual the astronaut may be able to spend months and even years in weightlessness provided that he is protected by some form of physical or pharmacological countermeasure. A similar projection cannot be made for the growing embryo or developing child. To date there have been very few studies that shed light upon this question. Female rats impregnated prior to flight and then placed on board Soviet biosatellites have yielded normal offspring postflight. However quail eggs hatched inflight on board the Salyut 6 space station have shown some abnormalities. There is no theoretical reason to believe that the mammalian embryo will not develop normally in space, although for other species, such as the frog, some dependence on gravity for normal development is possible. There are density inhomogeneities in different parts of the developing frog embryo that cause it to orient itself in a particular manner in a 1-g field. This type of orientation may be necessary for continued normal development of the embryo. Experiments to demonstrate the validity of this hypothesis are planned for later Spacelab missions on board the Shuttle. Many such experiments with species of animals much closer to man than the frog will have to be undertaken before there is any assurance that the human organism can successfully sustain itself for an indefinite period of time in the absence of gravity.

Psychological Support

The space environment can be expected to affect not only the physiological health of the individual but psychological health as well. The absence of gravity, danger, monotony, and isolation from friends and family on Earth may exact a toll, not only on the mental well-being of the individual but also on the effective function of an entire crew. No overt psychological problem has been documented to date during any Soviet or American mission, perhaps because of the considerable attention that is given to psychological factors in the selection of cosmonauts and astronauts and to the intensive measures that have been adopted by Soviet medical personnel to provide psychological support to long-term Salyut crewmembers. Nevertheless space planners are acutely aware not only of the potential danger posed by psychological disorder but also of the great gains in productivity that can be realized by paying proper attention to the psychological needs of humans in space. Experiments are underway to better predict the makeup of successful crews, to develop more effective command and control procedures, and to decide which tasks should best be automated and which should be performed by the human operator. With proper attention to the interior design of the spacecraft, to the food, to the waste-management systems, and to the recreational facilities placed aboard, there is no reason to believe that mental well-being cannot be sustained indefinitely in space.

Conclusion

The human species is expanding into the most barren environment ever confronted by life. Despite the constant influence of gravity throughout the course of its evolution, the human organism seems to have developed not much more than a simple mechanical dependence on gravity and appears able to live without it with relative impunity. The individual living cell seems to function with equal ease in the presence or absence of a 1-g field. This is perhaps not surprising in view of the much larger forces that govern the interaction of molecules in the cell or that are necessary to disrupt the integrity of subcellular structures. From a physiological standpoint, life on a space station as presently envisioned is certainly feasible. There is also no theoretical reason to believe that much longer trips and even permanent settlement in space are not possible. Such a prospect underscores the need to examine the many formidable ethical issues that this technology is unfolding.

Consent to
Risk in Space

NORMAN DANIELS

---

1. Earthbound Consent to Risk

*L*et me begin with a disclaimer. Unlike most readers and my eight-year-old son Noah, I have never thought seriously about space travel. Nor am I a "space buff" —I have deep reservations about investing resources in space travel and about the militarization of space. When I was asked to write about the medical-ethical issues raised by space travel and colonization, I thought this would mean taking fantasy much too seriously, even for a philosopher who is all too happy to retreat from the real world into hypothetical examples. For better or worse, however, reality imitates fantasy. Paul Rambaut has argued persuasively that long exposures to space travel and zero gravity may well be within the realm of biological possibility, even though it involves some risks and important compromises, for example, developmental problems for children that might mean not returning to Earth.

My first reaction was to think, "The issues in medical ethics that bear most on the topic have to do with consent to risk, but what interesting issues can be raised about people who are so willing to take risks that they will sit on top of a tube of explosives and hurtle themselves into a radioactive vacuum?" The risk I faced in consenting to deal with this subject was that there might not be any distinctive issues here at all. But further thought, and some discussion with Paul Rambaut, has persuaded me that there are some deep questions about consent to risk that do emerge as a result of special features of space travel. In fact, these issues push us beyond mere questions of medical ethics into some issues of political philosophy, but I am getting ahead of my argument.

I shall start with some general remarks about medical ethics in earthbound contexts in order to justify my focus on the problem of consent to the health risks of space travel. Medical interventions have the potential to deliver both good and harm. The good results—the preservation or restoration of normal functioning—are of fundamental importance to individuals. Indeed, considerations of justice bear on the distribution of this good.[1] But with the potential for benefits there is also the risk of harms. Treatment decisions always involve decisions about risk, and consent to treatment involves consent to risk—the risks of improper diagnosis, of side effects, and of complications.

A fundamental fact about the medical context is the imbalance of knowledge that exists between the physician and the patient. This imbalance works in two directions. Medical expertise is necessary to determine the course of treatment with the best ratios of benefits to risks. Thus the patient can determine the risk/benefit ratios of alternative treatments only by consulting the physician. But the physician cannot determine the worth to the patient of pursuing a particular course of action, even if he is able to give a good estimate of the risk/ benefit ratios. Only the patient can make that judgment, since individuals will differ in their assessments of the value to them of facing certain risks in order to procure certain benefits.

To accommodate concerns about patient autonomy and this fundamental fact about the two-way imbalance of knowledge in the doctor-patient relationship, a new model of that relationship has evolved, as much under pressure from tort law as from the prodding of ethicists. In it, the physician acts as an agent of the patient only with the patient's *informed, competent, voluntary consent.* This formula means that (1) a patient will have to be given adequate or reasonable and comprehensible information about the benefits and risks associated with a treatment and its alternatives; (2) the patient must be mentally competent to make the decision—that is, rational and of age; (3) the patient must do so without coercion; and (4) the consent is agreement to receive a specific set of well-defined treatments. The medical ethics literature is rife with elaborations and qualifications of what I have sketched here, but the fine details of informed consent will not be at issue in what follows.

The appeal to informed, competent, voluntary consent (informed consent, for short) acts as a mechanism for distributing the benefits and burdens of risk taking in other contexts as well. In nontherapeutic medical experimentation, for example, the benefits of risk taking may primarily be to individuals other than the risk bearer. Despite this difference from the medical context, informed consent remains the key moral constraint (other constraints also apply) on acceptable experimentation.

In some hazardous workplace contexts, a model of informed consent also plays an important role in the distribution of risks and benefits. The moral acceptability of bargaining for hazard pay rests on several presuppositions: (1) the requirement that workers be informed of the risks they will face; (2) the requirement that they bargain about a relatively determinate set of risks; (3) the requirement that they bargain without coercion; (4) the assumption that they are competent to assess the risks they face; and (5) the assumption that bargains they make do not impose externalized costs on nonconsenting third parties. Notice that the crucial issue here is not how risky the work context is; workers accept great risk of accidents when they are stunt drivers, test pilots, tunnel diggers, and so on. As long as there is good reason to think the presuppositions are met, hazard pay may be thought a morally acceptable way to distribute the benefits and burdens of risk taking. Though health protection is generally a good valued by individuals, hazard pay allows an individual to trade other goods, such as increased income, for willingness or daring to face risks. It permits an individual to value his well-being in his own way, according to his own conception of a good life. At the same time, it allows society to benefit from the willingness of individuals to take risks. Hazard pay thus seems to preserve individual autonomy and ought to be preserved if other moral considerations do not intervene, which they often do.

Consider a case where the exception proves the rule, namely, the stringent OSHA standard that requires employers to reduce exposures to health hazards to the extent it is technologically feasible to do so. Such stringent regulation, where it is enforced—I am not talking about our current paper tiger OSHA—actually eliminates the possibility of negotiation for hazard pay, apparently undercutting autonomy for a broad group of workers. I have elsewhere argued that this extra protection OSHA requires for many regulated workers may be justified if consent to risk in these settings is not strictly voluntary, for example, because the range of options open to typical regulated workers may be unfairly or unjustly restricted.[2] Such extra protection would not be justified by this argument for special groups of workers, say stunt drivers or test pilots, whose special choices of career and special expertise make it clear that their choices are truly voluntary and are made against a background of a reasonable set of alternatives. Astronauts fit this category as well, even if they do not bargain for hazard pay, and even if other factors, such as the publicity that attends space activities, puts a premium on reducing risks to the degree it is technologically feasible to do so. Still, their consent to risk is an issue I will return to shortly.

Before leaving earthbound contexts of risk taking, I want to highlight two very general features of the decisions about risk taking I have been discussing. First, we are for the most part talking about decisions to take quantifiable risks. Most issues in medical or health protection contexts do not involve true uncertainty, where we can assign no probabilities to risks, though we may often mistakenly believe we can. This distinction between decision making under *risk* and decision making under *uncertainty* is important, though little discussed. For example, rules of rational choice differ for the two kinds of decision making. In addition, it becomes much less clear what informed consent is when consent is not consent to face quantifiable risks.

Second, in earthbound contexts, we are generally

concerned with relatively short-term exposures to risks, or at least we are concerned with cases in which exposure to risks can be reassessed within relatively short periods of time and consent withdrawn or revised—as in decisions to work with hazardous materials. Long-term space exploration and space colonization lack this crucial feature, which permits the reassessment of risk and consent to it. The effect of duration of exposure to risk may convert what appear to be decisions under risk into decisions made under uncertainty. For example, we may be able to assign probabilities to short-term risks but not to long-term ones. Similarly, long-term missions may undercut the sense in which the original consent was consent to a specifiable set of risks. Moreover, where duration is short, new consent will be required when new risks are encountered. Thus short-term consent allows an individual to reevaluate what facing the risks is worth to him. Where duration of expeditions is long, the original consent would have to involve consent to a further procedure for determining acceptable risks and procuring consent to them. In what follows, I examine more carefully the implications of the special problems for consent to risk raised by these special features of long-term space travel and colonization.

2. *Consent to Risk in Current Missions*

Before turning to the issues raised by long missions, it is worth noting some of the features of the consent to risk now given by astronauts to current missions. I noted earlier my initial, naive belief that someone willing to be launched into space must be so nonrisk averse that little interesting could be said about consent. This belief is not only naive but false. Collectively the astronauts have consistently supervised almost all aspects of equipment and mission design with a view toward risk reduction. They have wanted to know just where compromises in safety have to be made, and they want a say in what they will be. They behave in this regard much like associations or unions of Hollywood stunt drivers who retain veto power over what stunts will have to be performed. The astronauts' participation in planning, and their involvement in decisions about acceptable risk, is clearly a way of assuring that their own consent to risk is informed and voluntary.

A quite striking feature of the assessment of risks by astronauts concerns their reluctance to participate in medical and physiological experiments. All medical experiments require standard "human subjects" review, in which astronauts sit on the review boards. Paul Rambaut has told me that there is considerable reluctance on the part of astronauts to participate in experiments, especially if the experiments involve either an extra risk to the astronaut or the kinds of monitoring that might detect a disqualifying medical condition. No astronaut who has succeeded in going on a mission, and who wants further assignments, wants to risk mission authorities spotting a disqualifying condition as a result of intensive or invasive medical surveillance that is part of an optional experiment. For the astronaut, this represents extra, avoidable risk. Of course this aversion to the risks of experimentation can increase the avoidable risks for later astronauts. The tension between career interests of current astronauts and the health and safety of later ones is a classic distributive problem about the benefits and burdens of risk taking.

One route around the control astronauts have exercised over consent to experimentation is through the use of mission and payload specialists. These nonpilot astronauts may sign on to be the subjects of experiments along with their other duties on particular missions. This use of mission specialists raises the following problem about consent to risk: If consent to certain extra risks, say those imposed by experimentation or some special activities of the mission, is a condition of being allowed to play the role of mission specialist—if the consent comes with the job—then there is a great pressure on individuals very anxious to participate in missions to undertake these risks. Whether or not this pressure constitutes undue pressure, or something like coercion, I am reluctant to say, given how little I know about manpower for these missions. But this is a question worth some discussion.

One last point about current missions is worth making. The astronauts are drawn from the ranks of test pilots, and they bring with them a certain ideology about the competency of such pilots to operate under the stresses imposed by space and zero gravity. For such pilots, individual control over risk assessment in the course of missions is a crucial element of consent to risk. Astronauts have not wanted to be "monkeys in a capsule" for whom all risks are assessed and controlled by mission control. The tension, perhaps struggle, between astronauts and mission control over the determination of acceptable risk suggests how important it is to astronauts to be in a position to revise and reassess their own consent to risk as missions proceed. But if this is an important issue on short missions, it becomes even more important on long ones. So I return to my concerns about consent to risk on long missions.

3. *Consent to Risk on Long Missions*

I have suggested that in a variety of contexts the morally acceptable method for distributing the benefits and burdens of risk taking is voluntary, informed consent. Where we refuse to allow consent to risk taking, for example, in some workplace contexts, and instead we impose stringent risk-reduction measures, we do so for two reasons. We fear either that consent to risk would not be fully voluntary or that it would not be fully informed. I have assumed that voluntary informed consent should be the method of determining acceptable risk for space travel as well. Surely we could accept nothing *weaker* as a constraint, such as a method which allowed not obtaining voluntary, informed consent. And it is difficult to see that protection more stringent or paternalistic than voluntary informed consent is appropriate for such specialized contexts of risk taking.[3]

This assumption is also in accord with actual practice, judging from the behavior of the astronaut corps. Astronauts, despite their general willingness to take risks, are very much concerned with the reduction of avoidable risks and rely on voluntary, informed consent as a mechanism for the controlling exposure to such risks. Their concern about consent to risk shows up in their participation in mission and equipment planning, their desire for control over mission decisions, especially those that involve risk assessment, and their attitude toward taking extra risks, such as those involved with medical experimentation.

Even on short missions, the consent to risk given explicitly and implicitly by astronauts has some features not usually encountered in risk taking in other situations. We know, for example, that calcium is lost from bones under zero gravity conditions, but we have little way of assigning probabilities to the increased chance of fractures faced by astronauts who have experienced this bone loss. So some risk taking by astronauts involves conditions of true uncertainty and not mere risk. Similar uncertainties are involved when we consider radiation risks outside the protection of the Earth's magnetic field. (A point I will not discuss here concerns the special problems involved in consent to risk for children who might take part in long missions or colonies. For example, there may be special risks to cardiovascular and bone structures as a result of developing in a zero-gravity environment, and animal experiments may not answer all questions we have about human physiology in these settings.)

Though real uncertainties may affect some decision making even about short missions, I want to suggest that long missions are qualitatively different. First, as I suggested earlier, some risks to which we can now assign probabilities will deteriorate to real uncertainties over long missions. Consent to risk under these conditions has a qualitatively different character.

In decision making about risks with assignable probabilities, we can imagine someone saying, "I can estimate the following benefits and harms that may come from this mission, and I can assign probabilities to them, and I can say that those ratios of risks to benefits or that expected payoff is one that is worth it for me to gamble on." Built into this remark is the person's own degree of risk aversion and the preferences or conception of a good life that make it worth it to him or her to take those risks. But on long missions, if many probabilities cannot be assigned, and instead we have true uncertainties, then we must imagine a person who is consenting to risk saying, "Although I cannot even assign an expected payoff to the sum of benefits and risks I face, it is worth it to me to face the uncertainty of those risks to achieve those benefits." It is far from clear what "it is worth it to me" means here, once we cannot calculate expected payoff. It is also not clear that we can reconstruct the person's deliberation about what is worth doing in a way that we would recognize as conforming to plausible rules of rational choice. (Of course, no such set of rules is available to give us necessary and sufficient conditions for a choice counting as rational, but plausible reconstructions of choices with reference to such rules are part of an effort to explain what rational choice is.)

Perhaps we can carry out such a reconstruction, but doing so would be a challenging philosophical and scientific task. For my purposes, it is enough to see how different this kind of risk taking is from the contexts in which we ordinarily rely on informed consent. In therapeutic experimentation, for example, even where we allow an experimental treatment whose likelihood of success is a true uncertainty, we will do so only because the patient who consents to it faces much worse alternatives—continued progress of the disease with certain death or severe disability. Here we may think that the individual who consents under conditions of uncertainty may in fact merely be trying to reduce the chances of his worst outcome taking place—an outcome to which he can assign a high probability. The person has nothing to lose. But that is not true of astronauts facing uncertainties on missions. The problem remains, What does it mean when they say "it is worth it to me to face those uncertainties in order to accomplish the goals of the mission"? Remember, the ability to accomplish the goals of the mission may now also be a true uncertainty. (I am not suggesting that we do not in fact make everyday choices involving uncertainties. We do. Rather, the problem of understanding when such choices are rational and what informed consent to them means is more general than I have suggested so far.)

There is a second way in which consent to the risks of long missions may be qualitatively different from consent to short ones. Judgments of acceptable risk will turn crucially on the individual's preferences or conception of what is good in life—his values, if you will. We saw, for example, how astronauts were unwilling to face even small extra risks that might accompany medical experimentation, because the threat of those avoidable risks to further mission assignments was not worth the cost, as judged by the astronaut. We may ignore such changes in preferences and values in the course of short missions, but long missions make it reasonable to think participants will undergo some important changes. In general, individual preferences or values change over time. Moreover, on long missions, some new information about risks will be available only to participants on the missions, and new information affects not only risk assessment itself but the underlying preferences against which background judgments about the worth of taking risks are made.

Individuals who are concerned to protect their autonomy will want to be able to reassess and revise their consent to risk taking on long missions. They will be unhappy with an original consent, thought of as a blanket consent to everything that happens on the long mission or in the space colony. This suggests that consent to risk for long missions or colonies must be consent to abide by a *fair procedure* for assessing and reassessing risks and obtaining renewed consent. Specifically, it must be a procedure that involves continued respect for the autonomy of all parties.

This is not a minor point. It is hard, for example, to

think of strictly hierarchical command structures, say on a military model, which are compatible with respecting individual autonomy over time. Such structures will centralize decisions about acceptable risk—from the point of view of the mission commander and his understanding of the collective goals of the mission or colony. But these evaluations may not, over time, coincide with the judgments other members of the mission will make, even if all individuals initially had complete confidence in the commander to make such decisions—as they would on a short mission. But if hierarchical command structures cannot adequately respect individual autonomy over time, then individuals will end up facing risks to which they no longer give informed, voluntary consent.

I began these remarks well within the framework of my charge, namely, to consider a central medical issue facing long space missions and colonies. But consent to risk seems to jump out of its medical-ethical skin when it encounters the special features of long missions. It really becomes a problem in political philosophy and political science. Can we design a morally acceptable political structure for long missions, that is, one embodying a procedure of risk determination that respects individual autonomy over time? Moreover, that procedure must be one to which it is reasonable to expect people to give consent when the mission is formed. This is not a question I can answer here—it is the ancient privilege of philosophers to raise questions they cannot answer.

Even if I cannot answer the question, however, I would like to comment briefly on its implications. The question assumes that we are not interested in sending personnel out on missions to face risks to which they have not consented. But the problem is to make that consent real, given the length of the kinds of missions we are discussing. If the consent is to be real, it must be consent to a procedure that continues to respect autonomy. But such procedures may involve granting degrees of control over risk taking to members of missions and colonies that are not normally granted to hierarchically commanded space or military missions. Those who finance and launch such missions or colonies will have certain goals in mind. Procedures that grant autonomy to individuals may permit revisions in the goals of missions or colonies, and such revisions might be incompatible with the intention behind financing and launching them. Thus, our problem of consent to risk raises a question with a hoary tradition: Will mother countries be willing to let their offspring go?

Notes

1. Norman Daniels, *Just Health Care* (Cambridge, England: Cambridge University Press, 1985).
2. Ibid., chap. 7.
3. Enormous sums are spent to reduce risks below what astronauts might consent to were budgets lower, but this may merely internalize the great externalized cost a disaster in space would impose.

Theology and Space

JOHN B. COBB, JR.

---

*M*y discussion has four parts. First, I reflect on our planet in relation to the whole. Second, I consider two themes that affect our attitudes toward the exploration of space: the celebration of human progress and the suspicion of human power that emerge from this reflection. Third, I address the question of how a contemporary Christian can reconcile these two themes. Fourth, I draw some implications of this reconciliation for an evaluation of one argument for the urgency of enlarging our space program.

I. Our Planet

We all have in our imaginations some picture of our planet in the scheme of things. For most Westerners, especially for most Jews, Christians, and Muslims, this picture is deeply affected by the Biblical story. In order to appreciate this more fully, it will be well to contrast briefly the myths of India with those of Israel.

The Indian myths stress the vastness of time and space. Nothing of importance ever began and nothing of importance ever ends. The general implication is that this planet has been forever circling this sun, just as millions of other planets forever circle other suns. Of course there are ups and downs; things are destroyed and begin again. But what comes into being after the destruction is very similar to what occurred before, or it repeats very similar cycles.

If one lives into this myth, one can soon sense how Indian religious thought has moved away from historical concern. This does not mean that Indians have not sought to alleviate human suffering. Buddhists, especially, have emphasized compassion and even opposed social institutions that created unnecessary suffering. But the idea that one should leave the world a better place than one found it has little power in this context. The vision trivializes any such goal or purpose of life. More important is to find the transhistorical reality, the timeless mode of being, and to help others to find it.

The Biblical myth works in a quite opposite direction. Interest centers on this planet. The other heavenly bodies show the greatness of the creator, but they do not function to trivialize the importance of what occurs here. The vision is thoroughly geocentric. In this myth the time span is foreshortened drastically. It has been calculated that according to the Biblical story the world was created just six thousand years ago. That six-thousand-year period has seen a number of crucial, irreversible changes, beginning with the expulsion from the Garden of Eden. Seeing things this way generates the sense that the condition of human beings could be quite different from what it is. Hope for some kind of future fulfillment of history has characterized those whose sense of reality has been shaped by the Biblical myth, even those, such as Marxists, secular humanists, and technocrats, who are not consciously part of the Jewish, Christian, and Muslim movements.

Today the evidence is that both myths are in error. The steady-state theory of creation, reflective of a basically Indian vision, has been largely abandoned, although its basic spirit is renewed in the view of infinitely repeated cycles of expansion and contraction. The consensus now emphasizes a more historical view of the universe. Our universe, at least, did have a beginning in measurable time, and the indication is that in one way or another it will have an end. Certainly this is true of this planet and this solar system.

On the other hand, the time and space scales of modern science differ drastically from those of the Bible. To view our planet as one of intermediate size circling a minor star in one among many galaxies is a far cry from the geocentric vision of the Bible. And to locate ourselves in a time span of, say, forty billion years is utterly different from the six-thousand-year history that a reading of the Bible alone suggests.

What are the existential implications of shifting from both Indian and Biblical views to the scientific one? I suggest that there are three main options. One option is to conclude from the vastness of the universe and the triviality of what happens on this planet in relation to the whole that the Indians were existentially correct. It seems inappropriate to attribute much significance to what happens here. It may be argued that if human beings are to set themselves goals of any importance, these will need to be transhistorical. From this point of view, relative improvement in the human condition over a generation or two is too tiny an aberration in the whole to be worthy of particular effort.

A second, quite opposite, option is to contrast this planet as the one locus of knowledge about the whole with the vast silence and apparent emptiness of the rest. Of course, we do not know that there are no other planets on which intelligent life exists or even that there are no beings further developed than we. But we are clearly alone in this solar system, and of the remainder we are quite ignorant. So far as we know, we alone have the knowledge and ability to explore and conquer space. We may draw the implication that this exploration and conquest are our fulfillment and our destiny.

A third possibility is to be struck not so much by the uniqueness of human knowledge and technological prowess as by the uniqueness of this planet as the locus of a rich biosphere. Instead of viewing the Earth as one heavenly body among billions, one can conclude that it may be unique with respect to what is alone of significant value: the ability to nurture and sustain complex forms of living things. This vision intensifies the sense of responsibility to preserve this precious heritage. Human activity destructive of this heritage is deplored, and the extension of similar activity to outer space is viewed with deep suspicion.

II. The Celebration of Human Progress and the Suspicion of Human Power

Although the first option, in the form of Eastern mysticism or Western nihilism, is a possible response to the modern scientific vision of the universe, I will not pursue it, for the second and third options are the only real possibilities for the most part. We are existentially geocentric despite the minor place of the planet in the vastness of space-time. And the tension between these options continues a tension that can be found both in the Bible and in modern European thought generally.

The tension expresses itself today in the scientific myths of evolution and ecology. The former emphasizes human progress in mastery of nature; the latter stresses the importance of respecting existing natural processes. The evolutionist focuses attention on the emergence of new species in biology and, as the myth is extended to human affairs, on the emergence of new technologies, new social structures, and new modes of consciousness. To fail to push forward the frontiers of knowledge and power is, in terms of this myth, to fail to align ourselves with the fundamental movement of life itself.

The ecological myth, on the other hand, emphasizes the interdependence of all things. Attention focuses not on individual species but on the ecosystem as a whole. The well-being of the individual species depends on patterns of relations so subtle and complex that even contemporary scientific knowledge is aware of only a few of them. Hence tampering with the whole by introducing new species or new products of human technology is always dangerous and often disastrous. Scientific research should be devoted more to understanding and preserving our biological heritage than to developing new threats to its survival.

The evolutionary myth dominates the work of Teilhard de Chardin, who reinterprets Christianity in its terms. By means of it he seeks to reorient Christianity from its tendency to cling to past forms toward an enthusiastic acceptance of scientific and technological achievements as part of the means through which God's purpose for the planet will be realized. As with evolutionists generally, the focus of attention is upon the leader of evolutionary development, with those others, who fall behind, no longer of real interest. Thus with the emergence of the human species, other animal species no longer have independent importance in his vision.

The connection between Christianity and this kind of thinking can be found earlier in Hegel. Although the scientific myth of evolution was not available to Hegel, he already read human history in much the same way. *Geist,* the divine-human Spirit, realized itself successively in different cultural forms. As it moved on to a new form, the old ones lost their importance, surviving, really, only as fossils.

The ecological myth gives rise to a very different reading. For this myth the human species is one among others. As long as human beings find their appropriate niches within the ecosystem all is well. Paul Shepard, perhaps the most brilliant contemporary exponent of the ecological myth, sees hunting and gathering peoples as fulfilling this norm. But ten thousand years ago our ancestors broke out of their niche by domesticating plants and animals. From that time on the biosphere has been progressively degraded and human beings have become psychologically maladjusted to both nature and society.

The resonance of the ecological myth can be seen in the existence of an influential literature that supports its implications apart from the influence of biology. Norman Brown's *Life Against Death* will serve as an example. For Brown, like Shepard, civilization is a disease. The resurrection of the body for which he calls is a return to a naturalness like that of wild animals.

It is significant that whereas the proponents of evolution I have mentioned stand within the Christian movement, the advocates of the ecological myth are far more critical. Although Shepard's work can be read by the Christian as a powerful, and almost literal, account of the fall, and although Brown uses Christian symbols extensively, both see Christianity as having been involved with the history they reject. In this they are quite correct.

Yet, when one rereads the Christian story with these questions in mind, one finds the ecological theme interwoven with the evolutionary one. It was only in the nineteenth century that the ecological note was submerged. Hegel himself was profoundly influential in this regard. Among the Neo-Kantians, especially Ritschl, the contrast of history and nature was thematically developed as the way of contrasting Biblical religion with all others. In this context, to be a Christian was to think and live historically in triumph over nature. Biblical scholars used this thematization to distinguish the true Israelite-Jewish-Christian tradition from the pagan influences in the scriptures.

Much in our Christian story supports this nineteenth-century emphasis on human progress. (I have built upon it in claiming that theology is the effort to think faithfully as part of a particular historical movement in a new historical situation.) The distinction of human beings from other creatures is much stronger in the Jewish scriptures than in those of India, and it is further accentuated in the New Testament. There is no question but that according to the Bible human beings are unlike all other creatures in being created in the image of God, and that this is closely associated with their rightful dominion over both plants and animals. Further, the prophetic principle, accented in Christianity, is always a criticism of what *is* in light of what *can* and *should be.* Although this is often associated with the idea of returning to an earlier, purer condition, the dominant understanding is that the future will not be the repetition of the past but rather the attainment of a state that resembles the past in the desired respect without negating the intervening history. In Christian rhetoric, even the fall of Adam can be called blessed, since God's answer was to send a redeemer who makes possible a new condition superior to what was lost in the fall. The New Jerusalem is pictured as different from the Garden of Eden.

Despite these and many other arguments for Christians to support the forward movement of history rather than to idealize earlier and simpler times, an open reading of our story shows that it includes another side as well—one neglected in recent times under the influence of modern philosophy. Before placing Christianity fully on the side of the evolutionary myth, it will be well to note these other themes in our story.

First, the attitude of the Bible on the relation of other species to human beings is mixed. It is important to note that in the first creation story God sees that what is created is good quite apart from human beings. There is no indication that this goodness depends on usefulness to the human species. It is inherent in the creation. The paeans of praise to the Creator because of the marvels of creation—found scattered through the Jewish scriptures—are not to be understood as pagan interruptions. They are consistent with the fundamental Biblical vision. Indeed, in the Jewish view animals have some rights over and against human exploitation. Furthermore, if the granting of dominion to human beings is understood in the general Jewish sense, then it cannot be exercised without regard to the welfare of those who are ruled. When Jesus wants to assure human beings of God's great care for them, he does so by arguing that God cares for all creatures and that among them all human beings are of special importance. Jesus does not thereby deny the importance to God of other creatures. Even for Paul in whose thought the natural world plays little role, the eschatological vision includes the salvation of the whole of creation, not of human beings only.

Although Christianity has been a major supporter of science, within the Christian heritage there are also cautionary images. The first is that the tree from which Adam and Eve were not to eat was the tree of knowledge. Of course, the knowledge in question was not what we associate with science. It was knowledge of good and evil. Yet it is significant that the myth associates the fall with knowledge.

The second myth that bears on our topic relates more clearly to technology and social organization. This is the myth of the Tower of Babel. Here human pride in human capacities is seen as a threat to God, and the realization of human ambitions is thwarted by social disruption.

Third, there are many passages in the prophets in which human pride and ambition associated with wealth and empire are decried. The perspective of the herdsman often comes through in the denunciation of urban society. This tradition appears in a different guise in Paul's contrast of the foolishness of Christ and the wisdom of this world. As so often in scripture, God affirms and uses what the world regards with contempt.

Apart from the association of the fall with knowledge of good and evil, these Biblical themes do not oppose knowledge but rather oppose human pride, which can often be associated with knowledge. True wisdom is often contrasted with mere human knowledge. Knowledge needs to serve God through serving the creatures rather than becoming an end in itself. This is commonplace Christian teaching.

In the modern period, because of reverence for science, this commonplace Christian teaching fell into abeyance. Scientific knowledge came to be accepted as good in itself, and technological progress came to be regarded as a mark of true human progress. Such opposition to progress as was to be found within Christianity seemed to come not from thoughtful leadership but from unthinking bigotry.

It has been only recently that the close association of science and technology with human pride in power has been vigorously reasserted by Christian leaders. I recall vividly a dramatic moment at the 1978 World Council of Churches meeting at MIT on Faith, Science, and the Future. A Third World caucus, including Third World scientists, under the leadership of the Brazilian Rubem Alves, demanded time for a special statement. The members assembled on the platform and read a manifesto that began, "We denounce science and technology!" The audience was stunned. In subsequent revision for publication the statement was softened. But the first unqualified statement has left an impression.

The point being made had nothing to do with the threat of science to traditional Christian beliefs. It had to do instead with the fact that, sociologically speaking, science and technology are possessions of the First and Second Worlds, and their global function is to establish and increase the hegemony of these worlds over the Third and to strengthen each against the other. One could point out that the proper object of such denunciation is not "science-as-such" or "technology-as-such." The problem is with a global power structure that uses science and technology in these ways. But the point of the denunciation is that in fact these are the science and the technology that actually exist and function in our world. That another science and another technology are theoretically possible only intensifies the condemnation of science and technology as they actually exist and function. As a part of the shocked audience I felt that I was hearing a voice in line with the Hebrew prophets.

To say that the voice was in the tradition of the Hebrew prophets is both a statement of appreciation and a criticism. With courage and without qualification the caucus named an evil and denounced it. Its contribution to describing a course of action that would purge science and technology or replace them with some improved form of knowledge and action was very limited. In today's parlance, the caucus was much stronger at consciousness raising than at guidance of positive action.

Overall in this section I have wanted to indicate a duality of emphases within a common Western consensus. The consensus has to do with the specialness of this planet and the importance of what happens on its surface. The duality has to do with the two themes of advancing domination of nature, on the one hand, and suspicion of human pretensions and human power on the other. My assumption is that our present attitudes toward the conquest of space express these two themes. Some call for such conquest as the further realization of human potentiality, and others decry it as an expression of the same destructive attitude that has already done so much harm to this planet.

III. A Christian Reconciliation

By showing how both of these attitudes are rooted in the Christian heritage, I have indicated that we should expect to find Christians on both sides in this debate. Yet, just because both themes are present in our story, we should expect to find most Christians torn between them and reluctant to endorse either side without qualification. For the most part this serves to make Christian comments largely irrelevant to the discussion. But it could lead to the development of a responsible Christian vision that would have policy implications. This paper is an attempt to take a step in that direction. I shall begin by formulating a few generalizations acceptable to many Christians.

First, all creativity is divine. That means not only that it is a gift of God but that it expresses the working of God as Holy Spirit. Apart from the Spirit of God there is no life at all. (In John the same point is made in terms of the Word of God.) This life that is of God is particularly manifest in human thought and activity. Human insight, human originality, and human freedom are all to be affirmed emphatically.

Second, human creativity should be in the service of God. This does not mean that it is directed away from the human sphere to a divine one. That dualistic misunderstanding has been present all too frequently in Christian history, but its sources are not Biblical. From the Biblical point of view, to love God is to love God's creatures, and the only way to serve God is through the service of the creation. Among these creatures human beings are of primary, but not exclusive, importance. The love and service of God is at once the love and service of the biosphere.

Third, whatever functions to discourage and oppose creativity is against God. This opposition is often in the name of religious traditions, including Christian ones. Some past form of life or organization of thought is sacralized and opposed to the life-giving power of the Holy Spirit. To cling to the products of past creativity against the present working of creativity is idolatry. Of such idolatry all of us are guilty. But awareness of that constant temptation should serve to help Christians repeatedly to free themselves from its clutches.

Fourth, even more dangerous than idolatry is the demonic. The demonic is the distortion of creativity by its subordination to ends other than the service of God through God's creatures. The demonic does not, like idolatry, simply resist the working of God. On the contrary, it participates in that working, availing itself of the divine power of creativity. It uses human freedom against the creatures and thus against the Creator. We all participate in the demonic as well as in idolatry. Again, Christians should be sensitized to the need constantly to repent of this involvement, that is, to turn away from it.

So pervasive are both idolatry and demonism, that we can describe many public debates as between the advocates of these two forms of sin. The idolaters see the dangers into which we are being led by the demonic exercise of creativity and seek to impose restrictions on creativity itself. The opponents rightly oppose every restriction on creativity, but in the process they often defend uses of creativity that are demonic.

In this light let us consider the Biblical theme of suspicion of human knowledge and power. In its contemporary form it leads to resistance to change and to the exaltation of natural harmony. In doing so it is in danger of opposing human creativity in general. Those who live by the ecological myth rightly recognize that human creativity since the fall has been corrupted by demonism. It has in fact degraded the biosphere, enslaved masses of human beings, destroyed community, alienated human beings from their own bodies, subordinated women to men, and brought the human race to the verge of suicide. In their horror at what demonic creativity has done, the ecologically oriented often appeal for a restriction of creativity to safer channels.

Those who live by the evolutionary myth see that this restriction on human creativity is contrary to what makes human beings fully human. Indeed, it is idolatrous. It was necessary to eat of the fruit of the tree of the knowledge of good and evil despite the cost, and it is necessary to free human beings to be creative even though they often go awry. It can only be by further creativity that human beings can deal with the problems that their misdirected past creativity has brought upon them.

Because Christians agree that all creativity is of God, we must follow the evolutionary myth to this point. But from our point of view it is not creativity as such but creativity in the service of God and creatures that alone can save us from the consequences of the demonic distortions of creativity—the powers and principalities of this evil age—that have brought us where we are. Every discovery of new facts, every advance in capacity for action, is in itself, as an expression of creativity, good. But as long as it functions in a context in which the direction of inquiry and technological development are controlled by goals other than the service of God and creatures, it remains demonic. Demonism is a greater threat to all of us than is idolatry. In a world in which the most powerful institutions are clearly demonic, Christians may need to ally themselves practically with idolaters in efforts to halt the mad rush to destruction. But the practical alliance does not imply fundamental agreement.

IV. Implications for the Conquest of Space

In this context let us consider the specific topic for this discussion. What, as a theologian, do I have to say about space exploration, colonization, and exploitation?

First, from a Christian point of view there is nothing morally wrong with any of these activities. On the contrary, they are marvelous expressions of human creativity, and it is right to be in awe of what has been accomplished.

Second, such activities can be proposed in the service of God and creatures. Some have argued for the conquest of outer space as an activity that could draw human beings together into a sense of our shared humanity transcending national rivalries. Also, by mining other heavenly bodies, we could reduce our despoliation of our own planet. Space colonies could provide restless spirits with opportunities for experimentation in new forms of society. Indeed, through freeing the human race from confinement to a finite planet that can only support human life for a limited time, the conquest of space can extend the period of human survival in the universe.

There is no reason to doubt the sincerity of those who seek to advance this program for the sake of God and creatures. There is reason, however, to raise two serious questions. One, of the various priorities for the expenditure of human resources and energies today, Should those who are concerned primarily with the service of God and creatures place the conquest of space high on their list? Two, Can we expect that the vast scientific knowledge and technological development involved in the conquest of space will in fact be used for the benefit of living creatures in general?

At a superficial level, the first question obviously requires a negative answer. When hundreds of millions of people are actually starving or threatened by severe food shortages, and when our current methods of food production continue to destroy the land from which future generations must live, research into sustainable agriculture, especially in tropical climates, has obvious priority from a Christian point of view over the conquest of space. Problems of habitation are hardly less urgent. The suffering engendered by the breaking up of traditional communities and the vast concentrations of population in decaying urban areas requires fresh study and response. To stem the spreading of deserts and the increase of flooding, vast programs of reforestation are needed. The list can go on and on. It hardly needs reciting.

Since this is so obvious, we should press beyond this level of the argument. What reason can be given now, in the context of love of God and creatures, for diverting research and action from direct response to such matters as these to the conquest of space? While acknowledging that there are other arguments to be considered, I shall consider only the economic argument as the one most directly relevant to the concerns I have just raised. I am aware of two aspects of this argument.

First, it can be argued that the ability to deal with problems of poverty and maldistribution of resources depends on a vigorous economy. Such an economy requires rapid technological advance. Only governments are capable of the expenditures needed for such advance. The space program is ideally suited to promote the appropriate experimentation and development of new techniques. Once developed, these can be used in commercial ways. This has in fact already happened and has been an important stimulus to the economy.

Second, it can be argued that we are rapidly approaching the exhaustion of many important resources on this planet. Their unavailability will lead to the end of the type of economy that makes possible prosperity for many and can one day include all in its sphere. The collapse of this economy can be avoided only by exploiting extraterrestrial resources. But to initiate such exploitation will itself require enormous resources. If we wait until these are rare on Earth, we will not be able to pay the requisite costs. If we act now, we can avoid a crisis of scarcity and prepare for a long future of prosperity.

These arguments should be taken seriously. Whether the scenario proposed is technologically possible, I do not know, but I shall leave that question to others. If it is, then, given the correctness of certain other assumptions, the arguments are strong. It is these other assumptions that I find doubtful. The chief assumption, underlying both of these arguments, has to do with the economic order now dominant on this planet. Since the assumption in question is very widely shared, I will give some indication of my reasons for questioning it.

Both arguments assume that the only economy that is capable of meeting human (and other creaturely) needs is the one now dominant in the First World. This is an economy that aims at increasing production and consumption and counts on the enlarging of the product to benefit people at all economic levels. This requires industrialization as its major means. Technological advance is needed by this economy in three ways. First, it increases the productivity of workers. Second, it makes possible the exploitation of new resources as old ones are exhausted. Third, it stimulates the economy by introducing new products that evoke new wants.

To support this approach to dealing with human needs requires the further assumption that there is a general correlation between the growth of the economy and the economic welfare of the people. I am skeptical of this assumption. There are many ways in which the national product increases that do not benefit its citizens, even economically. Nordhaus and Tobin, two Yale economists, responded to this skepticism some years ago in an essay entitled "Is Growth Obsolete?" They concluded that the growth of the Gross National Product was accompanied by increase of economic welfare and that, therefore, growth is the appropriate goal of economic policy. However, their findings can be used to make a different argument. From 1947 to 1965, according to their figures, the Gross National Product in the United States per capita grew around 47 percent. During those years economic welfare increased only about 6 percent. These figures force one at least to ask whether increase of production is the most efficient way to improve economic welfare.[1]

Further, there are a number of important issues that Nordhaus and Tobin do not consider that environmentalists see as having long-term economic importance. They do not calculate reduction of mineral resources or deterioration of soil and forests as negative factors in determining economic welfare. Much less do they consider the effects of industrial production on weather and on the ozone layer. If these and other factors are considered in estimating economic well-being, the 6-percent gain would disappear despite the large growth of the economy. Furthermore, in terms of a number of social indices, it seems that rapid growth of GNP has been accompanied by decline in the quality of life.

If human welfare is not necessarily advanced by increasing the Gross National Product, then the second form of the economic argument for high priority for exploiting extraterrestrial resources also is weakened. It can be reformulated, however. It can be argued that without these resources masses of people on this planet will be condemned to lack of the physical goods they truly need.

This would unquestionably be correct if general economic growth were the only way of meeting human needs. I have suggested that in fact such growth is an extremely inefficient way of meeting needs and at certain stages of development actually worsens the human condition. But there remains the question of the alternative. What sort of economy is sustainable based on Earth's resources alone? Can such an economy allow for a satisfying life for all the world's people?

I believe that if we devoted half the effort to studying and implementing sustainable patterns of human life that we now devote to the space program, the answer would be positive. It is true that, if I am wrong, if after twenty or thirty years we find that the answer is that the only society this planet can sustain is one of widespread misery, it may be too late for the massive expenditures required to exploit space on a large scale. But the argument cuts the other way as well. If we use up many of our remaining resources in such a crash program, it may be too late to develop a satisfactory economy here! My vote is to give our major energies now to moving toward a healthy, sustainable order on this planet, one that establishes itself within a regenerated biosphere.

My argument has dealt with the question of priorities, not with the legitimacy or illegitimacy of continuing the space program at some level. Other programs more directly related to achieving a satisfactory sustainable economy should have higher priority. But some features of the space program can contribute to that goal as well as to other worthy ends. The creativity the space program elicits and the excitement associated with it deserve consideration in themselves. I am not opposing all adventures in space.

The second question addressed to enthusiasts for the conquest of space is, Can we expect that the vast scientific knowledge and technological development involved in the conquest of space will in fact be used for the benefit of creatures in general? My answer to this, too, is negative. I am suspicious of the human use of power. The role of rivalry with the Soviet Union in our expenditures to date is too obvious to require comment. President Reagan's advocacy of a Star Wars military strategy makes it clear that the exploration of space has military as well as economic goals. That security on this planet will be long enhanced by the militarization of space seems to me exceedingly improbable. Only the most resolute commitment and careful watchfulness will keep this demonic distortion in check.

In conclusion, let me emphasize that I am not proposing the total abandonment of the space program nor declaring space conquest immoral. We have dominion over other creatures, and that includes our neighboring bodies in space. To the Christian all things are permitted. There are no taboos that set limits to our exploration and use of space. But just because these questions are not settled by taboos, it becomes especially important that they be settled by thinking that is in the service of God and all creatures. Thinking that is in the service only of national power and national economic interests is demonic. In Paul's language, all things are permitted, but not all things are helpful. Diverting attention from the pressing problems of a sick and suffering biosphere to the conquest of space is not helpful.

Thinking that is in the service of God and creatures is not less creative than that which serves special interests. To propose that the creative energy now demonically directed to the extension of national power and wealth be employed instead for human welfare generally is not to ask for less rigorous and vigorous thought and action. It is not to propose that we return to the Dark

Ages or to the hunting and gathering society, although neither of these was as bad as is suggested by the images they conjure up in many minds. It is to propose that human creativity be directed to the solution of the most serious and urgent of human and biospheric problems. These are far more difficult and challenging than the technical questions on which so much expertise has been developed. To expend energy upon them will make us all more human.

Notes

1. William D. Nordhaus and James Tobin, "Is Growth Obsolete?" in Milton Moss, ed., The Measurement of Economic and Social Performance (New York: National Bureau of Economic Research, 1973), pp. 509–31.

The Political
Dimension

Star Wars:
The Nuclear/Military
Uses of Space

DEAN RUSK

---

*L*et me say at the very beginning that I myself believe that moral and ethical values do and should play a major part in policy decisions by those who carry out public responsibilities on our behalf. I do not agree with my friends, the late Hans Morgenthau, George Kennan, and others, who try to downgrade the role of such values in public policy formation. You don't hear too much about these values because the men and women with public policy responsibilities do not wear them on their sleeves or shout them from the housetops. Nevertheless, although you will not find much said about them in the official documentation of the government, moral values do infuse the discussions that contribute to those documents and they are a necessary part of the formulation of policy in our kind of society.

I want to offer a certain contrast between the 1960s and the 1980s as far as outer space is concerned. I was present for the beginning of the space age. Very shortly after I joined The Rockefeller Foundation in 1952, we went to friends in four or five of our most distinguished universities and asked them if it would be a good idea to provide someone with some time to begin thinking about the law and politics of man's entry into outer space. I could summarize the reaction as *colossal indifference.* Indeed, one distinguished professor of international reputation told us at that time that the future is not the business of the university, even though the laboratories of his own university were hurling us into the future at a breathtaking pace.

Then came Sputnik in 1957, and there was a scramble for funds to give some attention to these issues. Some of us can remember with considerable embarrassment the consternation that swept over the United States when Sputnik went up. Sputnik was about as big as a basketball, and it could only issue an occasional bleep as it orbited the Earth, but it threw panic into our society in so many different ways. It was not until 1958 that we put up Explorer I, but as soon as that happened, particularly when the Soviets launched their first manned spacecraft, this matter was given immediate attention by the United Nations. The General Assembly established a committee on the peaceful uses of outer space. Eventually, a far-reaching resolution was adopted unanimously by the United Nations General Assembly about man's relation to outer space. That in turn was transformed into the extraordinarily important Outer Space Treaty of 1967. Under that treaty, outer space was to be an arena of scientific research and exploration, an arena of international cooperation. The orbiting of nuclear weapons in outer space was prohibited. Astronauts were declared to be the envoys of all mankind and were entitled to assistance from anyone who was in a position to give them any help, and so forth.* If you look over the treaty, you might understand why we sensed a real uplift of spirit—that somehow the human race had addressed itself to this question and had come out with what seemed to be reasonable, hopeful, intelligent, civilized approaches to the problems of space.

It was not very long before we ran into some environmental issues involving space. For example, we exploded a device in space, which spread millions of little metallic needles over a considerable area of outer space. It was a part of what we were told at the time was a communications experiment. The outcry against it was so strong and so general that that kind of thing was discontinued. On another occasion, before the Test Ban Treaty, President Kennedy received a request from the military for permission to explode a nuclear weapon far out in space on the inner edge of the Van Allen Belt. Some of us wondered whether or not this explosion would have any effect upon the Van Allen Belt. President Kennedy, therefore, asked his science advisors to come in the next day and give him some advice on that point. They came back with a report that began, "The following is a negotiated, scientific conclusion to the question you posed to us"—which in itself was a flag that something was wrong. Since, in effect, the report said that we could disregard the possibility that the explosion would affect the Van Allen Belt, the President authorized the shot. Two days after the test, however, the same advisors came back and said,

---

*That was not just an empty phrase, by the way. On one occasion, there seemed to be an interruption in the communications between Houston and our astronauts in space. When we checked our assigned frequencies, we decided that the problem was a spillover from one of the assigned Russian frequencies. A telephone call to the U.S.S.R. embassy in Washington, D.C., and a telephone call by them to Moscow followed. The interference stopped literally within a matter of minutes.

"Sorry, we were in error by a factor of two thousand." It did indeed have a slight effect on the Van Allen Belt: It created a little Van Allen Belt of its own.

We began to discover rather quickly that there were some environmental issues about space to which there would be sharp reaction. Some of you may remember the silly idea that somebody came up with that we station giant reflectors in space and eliminate night, providing ourselves with perpetual daylight. The reaction was general, negative, and derisive, and I hope that idea has been buried forever. In the early 1970s we tried prematurely, I believe, to get the United Nations General Assembly to endorse the idea that we had a right to broadcast programs from satellites directly into television receivers on the ground—it was strongly rejected by the United Nations General Assembly. The same thing happened when we asked the United Nations for blanket approval of our right to engage in remote sensing. These kinds of things tend to be sensitive, and when you come up with outrageous suggestions about them, they are sometimes promptly turned down.

We now are facing the prospect of an arms race in outer space, which I would suggest is the most outrageous proposal to date, for I can think of no other way to more massively increase the pollution of outer space than to allow the arms race to move out there. Unfortunately, in my judgment, we have prematurely raised an artificial complication for the arms-reduction talks in Geneva. I call it premature and artificial because it will be at least ten years before we know whether or not these anti-ballistic space missile weapons are possible from a scientific and technical point of view. President Kennedy used to tell us that if you have a fight, have a fight about something. Don't have a fight about nothing. We won't even know for another ten years or so whether there's anything to quarrel about. Yet, this issue, by being raised so dramatically by President Reagan, has literally put the brakes on any prospect of success in the arms talks in Geneva.

If I seem critical of President Reagan on certain points, it is with some pain that I am. Although Mr. Reagan was not my candidate, he is my President, and I wish him well in foreign policy. We are all in the same canoe together, and we are going to have to come through these turbulent waters together or go down together. Yet, although I do not wish to throw rocks gratuitously at those who are wielding the paddle, there are considerations that simply cannot be avoided in any discussion of these matters. First, we know that any program to deploy space weapons of any kind—laser beams, x-ray lasers, particle beams, cannisters filled with this and that—will cost hundreds upon hundreds of billions of dollars. The Pentagon has already told the Congress that this effort would be at least ten times the effort required by the Manhattan Project to develop the atom bomb in the first place. It's a very expensive undertaking.

Second, we have to assume that whatever we can do in these areas the Soviets can also do. The idea that we might get some kind of an advantage over the Soviet Union in this field is ridiculous. We greatly underestimated their ability to make an atomic bomb, and then a hydrogen bomb, or to put an object in space, and then a man in space. They have very intelligent people working for them, just as we do. If they commit their resources and brainpower to a particular project, they can match whatever we do. If they lack a little of the required technology, they can get it from us by looking at our congressional testimony and our technical journals— with a dash of espionage thrown in. Any idea that we can somehow get an advantage over them is illusory. Indeed,

Mr. Reagan has indicated that he would be in favor of giving this technology to the Soviet Union when we ourselves develop it—something which for political reasons is probably not likely to happen.

My third point takes us back to the inner rationale of the Anti-Ballistic Missile Treaty, negotiations which were started in my time and were completed in the early years of the Nixon administration. We went through an extensive period of analysis, a period of at least a year, of the anti-ballistic problem and came to the conclusion that if we or the Soviet Union began to deploy anti-ballistic missiles (ABMs), the inevitable result would be that each side would simply multiply its offensive missiles in order to be able to penetrate or overwhelm the ABMs before the main strike was delivered. The ABMs themselves, therefore, would have had a very stimulating effect on the arms race. When President Johnson met with Premier Kosygin in Glassboro, he had his homework in his pocket, and he pressed Mr. Kosygin very hard to sit down and begin talks on eliminating anti-ballistic missiles. Mr. Kosygin, however, obviously had no instructions from Moscow and could not go down that trail. Even though Lyndon Baines Johnson gave him the full LBJ treatment, he could not respond in any way. He did make the remark, "Well, of course, one can't object to defensive weapons," which I would call the naïveté of the first look. Nevertheless, when the Russians went home and did their own homework, they came to the same conclusion that we had reached. We then put our heads together and came up with the ABM treaty, which limited ABM sites to two in each country. The Soviets had wanted one around Moscow; we wanted one around our missile sites in the West. Since we couldn't agree on which to protect, we decided to have two on each side. Later the number was reduced back to one each: theirs around Moscow, ours around some missile sites in the West, both of which now are largely in mothballs for all practical purposes.

If we or the Soviet Union begin to show any real progress in developing space weapons that can shoot down missiles, then we will be asked for additional hundreds of billions of dollars to devise offensive missiles that can penetrate or evade these space defenses. To me that is just as certain as the rising of the Sun. Thus, these space defenses will simply be a stimulus for another arms race in offensive weapons. It is important that everyone come to realize that the science and technology of developing offensive weapons that can evade such space defenses are really much easier and cheaper than the science and technology needed to provide the defenses in the first place. It is my understanding that the Pentagon has already assured the Congress that we will be able to develop offensive weapons that can evade or penetrate Soviet space defenses if they develop them in the same way we are planning to do. If this is true, then surely the Soviets can also develop missiles that will penetrate our defenses. If we were to give the question, How do you evade such space defenses? to the high-school students who participate each year in the Westinghouse Science Fair, they could come up with some very simple and relatively inexpensive answers. Indeed, some of these answers are so simple that I am reluctant to mention them, for fear that they might provide someone with an idea that might otherwise be overlooked accidentally. In any event, we can expect massive changes, and very expensive changes, in the delivery of offensive weapons in the face of such space defenses.

We have to anticipate, I believe, that such space defenses will require the pre-positioning of orders to fire in computers and other forms of technology. I am in principle utterly opposed to doing this because I do not have much confidence in technology of any kind. We lost ten astronauts to the most expensive and well-tested technology we have ever had. Another manned Shuttle flight aborted four seconds before it was to lift off the pad. We have put satellites up there that would not work. Some just got lost. All of us in our daily lives live with a gap between the promise and the performance of technology. The cycling mechanism on the washing machine or the dishwasher fails. The television set goes blank and someone says, "Please stand by. We are experiencing technical difficulties." Only once in sixty years have I had a clock in an automobile that would keep time. I, for one, therefore, do not believe that we should turn over such important decisions as when to fire to *any* kind of technology.

If we did put the three hundred satellites supposedly needed for such a space defensive system into place in orbit, those satellites themselves would immediately become vulnerable. Any country that can put up a maneuverable space object already has an anti-satellite weapon. It is not unlikely that we will soon have some ground-based anti-satellite weapons that can knock down these satellites or at least break them up. They will be vulnerable, and they will be tempting targets. If the Soviet Union were trying to get ready either for a first strike or for a defensive second strike, as they might judge it, one of the first things they would do would be to go after these satellites. They would probably also position large numbers of Soviet submarines off our coast that could fire short-range, low-altitude, high-velocity missiles that could almost certainly not be intercepted by these space devices. Under these circumstances, any premature action by anyone might cause the other side to believe a nuclear war is imminent and make the fingers on the nuclear triggers pretty itchy.

There is a final question that needs to be considered, which also has something to do with plans for such things as space colonies. Just how do we want to use our resources? They are not infinite, and there are many national human needs. When I was Secretary of State and a member of the Space Council, I helped to veto a $200-billion, two-year, round-trip, manned flight to Mars, because I felt that our society could use $200 billion worth of our resources more effectively in other ways. It was one issue at least that I could leave to another generation. Now, however, we are talking about at least $1 trillion, if not more, for this space-defense program. I would imagine that almost any fourth-grade school child asked to evaluate this project would say, "For heaven's sake, why should we do it, if we can possibly find some way to avoid it?"

I think that our present problem is to find some way to postpone this issue in Geneva until such time as we know whether or not there is something to quarrel about. Since we raised the issue, it seems to me that it is up to us to try to find some way to postpone it. I myself would go ahead with research, ground-based research, in such things as lasers and particle beams and things of that sort, partly as a hedge against a breakthrough in the state of the art by someone else, but also because I see no way to verify an agreement to ban research and I don't think we can enter into agreements that cannot be reasonably verified. After all, a man with a fine brain and a slide rule might be the person who achieves the essential breakthrough in some of these key scientific problems.

I think the Soviets today are overreacting or over-reaching when they claim that research on such things is a violation of the anti-ballistic missiles treaty. That treaty does not try to deal with research: It simply prohibits the testing, development, and deployment of anti-missile devices in outer space. I would say that we should go ahead with research—recognizing that there will be considerable wastage in such a research program, because it is in the nature of such research that a good many ideas will be tried that simply don't pan out in the end.

Although these activities are prohibited in outer space by the ABM treaty, the ABM treaty itself has a withdrawal clause that allows either party to withdraw after giving six months' notice. We might be able to work out an arrangement with the Russians that prohibits the testing, development, or deployment of these things in outer space for a flat period of, say, ten years, postponing the debate over this issue until we know what there is to quarrel about. This flat period of ten years would not be subject to a withdrawal clause, leaving as the only basis for withdrawal the traditional grounds in accordance with international law that any major violation by one side releases the other side from its obligations under that particular treaty. If we did this, we might then be able to get down to some serious talk about limiting intercontinental and intermediate-medium-range missiles and begin at last to get hold of an arms race that is now becoming almost literally insane.

To me the very aesthetics of moving the arms race into outer space is repulsive. I have on many occasions in the past expressed the hope that my grandchildren will be able to look up into the vast universe and recall with the Psalmist that the heavens declare the glory of God and not the folly of man. We have a very big question in front of us that will be decided by the society around us—not by the experts, not by the scientists with their various opinions pro and con, but by the society as a whole reflected in our Congress.

Let me say that I do not approach these issues or the issue of nuclear war in the spirit of gloom and despair.

It is important to remember that it has been forty years since a nuclear weapon has been fired in anger, despite a number of serious and even dangerous crises. During this forty-year period, we have learned, I think, that the fingers on the nuclear triggers are not itchy; they are not just waiting for a pretext to launch these dreadful weapons. If you have any doubt about this as far as the United States is concerned, just recall that this country has taken something like six hundred thousand casualties in dead and wounded since the end of World War II without firing a single nuclear weapon. I think we have also learned in these forty years that Russian leaders have no more interest in destroying Mother Russia than our own leaders have in destroying our beloved America.

These forty years, nevertheless, are no sure guarantee for the future, so, of course, we still have to be careful. For example, we and the Soviet Union should not play games of chicken with each other just to see how far one can go without crossing that lethal line. Down that trail there is always the possibility of a miscalculation or a mistake that could have terrible consequences. We especially ought to watch the level of rhetoric between the two capitals. When that rhetoric becomes too vitriolic over too long a period of time, there is always the possibility that one side or the other will begin to believe its own rhetoric. If this happened, then we could have some serious problems.

Our young people in particular are being battered with a lot of doomsday talk these days. It comes from a variety of directions: from those supporting dramatic increases in our defense budget, from those who are trying to organize various peace movements over on the other side of the spectrum, from some in the news media who want to produce shock effects to increase viewers and ratings, from think tanks, and from some professors. These people can string all sorts of words together and present the most horrifying scenarios. Although I myself cannot put my finger on a real situation in the real world that is pointing toward nuclear war, I am concerned that we may have managed to take away from our young people the elements of hope and confidence that are just as important to their lives as the food they eat and the water they drink.

We have a lot of thinking to do as a society about the problems posed by space. I can remember a time during the 1960s when we thought that outer space would be a great arena of international cooperation. The last thing that we had in mind in those days was that it would become an arena for battle. We recognized, of course, that there were certain things about outer space that could be used with military benefit. For example, satellite photography, a passive use of outer space, proved to be very valuable to us in monitoring certain arms-control agreements. We took a major step in that direction with SALT I, in which we and the Soviets agreed that satellite photography was an appropriate way to verify compliance with that agreement. We also now use space satellites for military communications. When we began, however, we did not think that we would ever be putting weapons of any kind into space. We thought it would be a place of peace, more or less like Antarctica. In much the same way that we prohibited the stationing of nuclear weapons on the deep ocean seabed, we believed that we had permanently prohibited the orbiting of them in space. But it appears that we may have been wrong. In the next ten years we as a society will have to decide whether we must now go down the trail that moves our arms race into outer space with potentially disastrous consequences or whether we and the Russians can somehow put our heads together and find a way to make that journey unnecessary.

Bibliographical Note

Although there is an enormous literature on space exploration, there is virtually none specifically on environmental ethics and space exploration. Thus, for readers interested in going beyond this volume, one option is simply to launch into general space literature, perhaps starting with the extensive number of NASA publications available in most libraries. For those with less time, the following remarks might be helpful.

With regard to philosophy and ethics specifically, the reader should attempt to become familiar with the general debates of the last decade over the limits of moral considerability. There are several book-length discussions of environmental ethics that might be helpful. John Passmore's *Man's Responsibility for Nature* (New York: Charles Scribner's Sons, 1974) is a good starting point, even though it is an attempt to denounce environmental ethics, since so much of the later literature is a response to it. Other books include Robin Attfield's *The Ethics of Environmental Concern* (New York: Columbia University Press, 1983); Robert Elliott and Arran Gare, eds., *Environmental Philosophy* (University Park: Pennsylvania State University Press, 1983); and Donald Scherer and Thomas Attig, eds., *Ethics and the Environment* (Englewood Cliffs, N.J.: Prentice-Hall, 1983). For the problem of future generations, see *Responsibilities to Future Generations,* edited by Ernest Partridge (Buffalo, N.Y.: Prometheus Books, 1981), which contains nearly all the important papers.

The key issue regarding the Solar System is probably the moral status of nonliving entities. Much of this debate can be found in my journal *Environmental Ethics.* Donald Scherer's "Anthropocentrism, Atomism, and Environmental Ethics,"

Environmental Ethics 4 (1982): 115–23, is the only philosophy paper to deal specifically with extraterrestrial bodies and is interesting in this regard, although the discussion is intended as a device to criticize positions that make no reference to the subject of space exploration. Three other especially important papers from the viewpoint of this volume are J. Baird Callicott's "Animal Liberation: A Triangular Affair," *Environmental Ethics* 2 (1980): 311–38, and two papers by Holmes Rolston, III, "Values in Nature," *Environmental Ethics* 3 (1981): 113–28 and "Are Values in Nature Subjective or Objective?" *Environmental Ethics* 4 (1982): 125–51.

With regard to the military uses of space, I recommend Thomas H. Karas' *The High Ground* (New York: Simon and Schuster, 1983). Concerning the social aspects of space exploration, one might read Ben Bova's *The High Road* (New York: Houghton Mifflin, 1981). I have found Philip José Farmer's afterword to "Riders of the Purple Wage" especially helpful (in Harlin Ellison's *Dangerous Visions,* available in many different editions), although Farmer has since mellowed his criticism.

One especially useful book to read is *Life in the Universe: The Ultimate Limits to Growth,* edited by William A. Gale, AAAS Selected Symposium 31 (Boulder, Col.: Westview Press, 1979), which examines the prospect of an extraterrestrial settlement (see especially Leonard W. David's "Space Exploration: Prospects and Problems for Today and the Future," pp. 47–69). Two more recent books by James E. Oberg are useful in assessing the likelihood of such colonies and their impact on other planetary bodies: *Mission to Mars: Plans and Concepts for the First Manned Landing* (Harrisburg, Pa.: Stackpole Books, 1982) and *New Earths: Restructuring Earth and Other Planets* (New York: New American Library, 1983).

Since the environmental movement itself is historically associated with an aesthetic appreciation of nature, books of photographs and paintings are also worth looking at. One of the earliest is James D. Dean's *Eyewitness to Space* (New York: Harry N. Abrams, 1971), which contains paintings by many mainstream artists involved in NASA's art project. Also of special importance are *The Grand Tour: A Traveler's Guide to the Solar System* (New York: Workman, 1981) by Ron Miller and William K. Hartmann, and *Out of the Cradle: Exploring the Frontiers Beyond Earth* (New York: Workman, 1984) by William K. Hartmann, Ron Miller, and Pamela Lee. In these two books one can find views of a wide assortment of extraterrestrial environments depicted in a nearly photographic manner, actually bordering on the nineteenth-century luminist style that had great impact on the creation of our aesthetic attitudes toward nature in the first place. Finally, for a discussion of the history of the space art movement and characteristic works by a large number of space artists, see *Space Art* by Ron Miller (New York: Starlog Press, 1978).

For a critical look at life on a space station, I recommend C. J. Cherryh's award-winning science-fiction novel *Downbelow Station* (New York: Daws Books, 1981) and for a look at a planetary colony involving the presence of extraterrestrial life her more recent book, *Forty Thousand in Gehenna* (New York: Daws Books, 1984). All in all, science-fiction film has been somewhat more successful in depicting possible near futures in the Space Age. Of special note are *Silent Running,* about the U.S. Forest Service in space; *Blade Runner,* which depicts a badly polluted Earth in a period of high space technology; *Alien,* which presents a very believable and not very pleasant look at life on a mining ship; and *Outland,* which deals with the sordid details of life in a mining colony on one of the moons of Jupiter.

For the official plans of NASA as they currently stand, the best source is *Planetary Exploration through Year 2000: A Core Program* (Washington, D.C.: NASA, 1983). The discussion in the present volume by Geoffrey Briggs is essentially an explanation and update of that core program. For the most recent proposals concerning the future of our space program, see *Pioneering the Space Frontier: The Report of the National Commission on Space* (Toronto, New York, London, Sydney, Aukland: Bantam Books, 1986). The work on the commission's report and

Beyond Spaceship Earth took place simultaneously, so that neither was able to take into consideration the other. Since the report is intended as a formulation of "a bold agenda to carry America's civilian space enterprise into the 21st century," it does not address environmental and ethical issues critically or in any detail. It may, nevertheless, prove to be a good indication of the direction space exploration will take in the decades to come, since it is likely to be the basis for any bold program that Congress may someday approve.

List of Contributors

Authors

Eugene C. Hargrove is editor of *Environmental Ethics.*

David Brin is a consultant to the California Space Institute at the University of California, San Diego, and an award-winning science-fiction novelist.

T. Stephen Cheston is vice-president of Geostar Corporation and the president of the Institute for the Social Science Study of Space.

Donald J. Kessler is head of Orbital Debris Studies at Johnson Space Center.

Radford Byerly, Jr. is staff director of the Subcommittee on Space Science and Applications of the U.S. House of Representatives.

Geoffrey A. Briggs is director of the Solar System Exploration Division of the National Aeronautics and Space Administration.

William K. Hartmann is an astronomer, artist, and writer living in Tucson, Arizona. He is a senior scientist at the Planetary Science Institute.

Holmes Rolston, III is a professor of philosophy at Colorado State University.

Paul F. Uhlir is a senior staff officer of the Space Science Board of the National Academy of Sciences.

William P. Bishop is acting assistant administrator of the National Satellite, Data, and Information Service of the National Oceanic and Atmospheric Administration.

Frank B. Golley is director of the Institute of Ecology at the University of Georgia.

J. Baird Callicott is a professor of philosophy at the University of Wisconsin, Stevens Point.

Paul C. Rambaut is currently deputy director of the Division of Extramural Activities at the National Cancer Institute of the National Institutes of Health. Previously he was manager of Biomedical Research in the Life Sciences Division of the National Aeronautics and Space Administration.

Norman Daniels is a professor of philosophy at Tufts University.

John B. Cobb, Jr. is a professor of theology at the School of Theology at Claremont.

Dean Rusk is Sibley Professor of International Law at the University of Georgia. He was Secretary of State under Presidents Kennedy and Johnson.

Artists

Chesley Bonestell, 1888–1986, the Dean of Astronomical Artists, was an architect and Hollywood special-effects artist who is best known for his oil paintings.

Michael Carroll is staff production artist at the Reuben H. Fleet Space Theater in San Diego, California.

Kazuaki Iwasaki is Japan's best-known astronomical artist. Iwasaki, who works as an industrial designer, is a native of Osaka.

Roger Rampley is an artist and photographer who specializes in graphic arts and illustration for the Department of Defense.

Index